UNDERSTANDING DUNBLANE
AND OTHER MASSACRES

UNDERSTANDING DUNBLANE AND OTHER MASSACRES

Forensic Studies of Homicide, Paedophilia, and Anorexia

Peter Aylward

(with collaboration from Gerald Wooster)

Routledge
Taylor & Francis Group

LONDON AND NEW YORK

First published 2012 by
Karnac Books Ltd.

Published 2018 by Routledge
2 Park Square, Milton Park, Abingdon, Oxon OX14 4RN
711 Third Avenue, New York, NY 10017, USA

Routledge is an imprint of the Taylor & Francis Group, an informa business

British Library Cataloguing in Publication Data

A C.I.P. for this book is available from the British Library

ISBN-13: 9781780490946 (pbk)

Typeset by V Publishing Solutions Pvt Ltd., Chennai, India

This book is dedicated to all victims, including those whose voice can only be heard through their crimes

CONTENTS

ACKNOWLEDGEMENTS

I want to start by thanking Lord Alderdice for very generously giving his time in providing a supportive and insightful foreword. He emphasises that while there is substantial resistance to in-depth reflection on violent criminal acts there could be significant benefits for society if such informed understanding could be embraced, leading to the development of specific interventions to prevent similar incidents in the future.

I also want to thank Gabrielle Brown for her timely support and skills in not only editing the manuscript but also quite ironically drawing my attention to the need to triangulate better with the reader and avoid confusion, given that most of the chapters had hitherto been created for a conference presentation. This necessitated replacing "we" where Gerald and I had presented, with "I" as author of the text for the reader.

A big thank you to Jennie Harrison for her patience, commitment, and dedication in the invaluable administrative task she undertook in her spare time in making this publication possible.

I am also indebted to the many patients, patients' families, and colleagues who have given their consent for me to publish their stories, all of whom have expressed the hope that future crimes might be prevented as a result. In addition my thanks also go to my "siblings" in the psychotherapy department at Broadmoor Hospital for their support and understanding over the many challenging years of working in such a complex environment.

While I refer the reader to my preface I want to repeat here my gratitude to Gerald Wooster for his wisdom and guidance over the years.

I thank Karnac for providing me with this opportunity to give voice to a wider audience and to Brett Kahr for his facilitation.

Finally this book could not have been produced without the unwavering support and love from my wife and children where there has been a mirroring of significant events linking our personal and professional lives.

ABOUT THE AUTHOR

Peter Aylward undertook his psychoanalytic training after exemplary service for fifteen years in the Metropolitan Police Service as a Special Branch officer (1977–1992). Following graduation at the Foundation for Psychotherapy and Counselling (FPC) he married the two together to specialise in forensic psychotherapy at Broadmoor Hospital where he has worked as a member of the psychotherapy department since 1996. He also consults and supervises with clinical teams in a wide variety of other National Health Service (NHS) settings, primarily at the Maudsley and Bethlem Royal Hospitals, and including the National Eating Disorder Service, the National Specialist Day Service for Complex Personality Disorder, the National Self Harm Unit, the National Child Care Assessment (expert witness) Service, the Bill Yule Adolescent Medium Secure Unit, and the National Psychosis Unit. He also runs a private practice offering further individual treatments and supervisions.

Peter Aylward has primarily focused his clinical work on understanding murder. This has been achieved by taking particular account of the perpetrator's trans-generational family history, and he has pursued a breakthrough of the knowledge in this area. This has been achieved in his time in supervision with Dr Gerald Wooster, FRC Psych, who received his psychoanalytic training at the British Psychoanalytical

Society. Moreover, Dr Wooster's experience as a consultant in the NHS in London (in supervision and group practice), together with his avid interests in history and Shakespeare, all helped inform Aylward's work. In the high secure setting of Broadmoor Hospital, Aylward has assessed and treated a wide range of patients (including the most notorious) whose severe, complex, and enduring psychopathologies are inextricably linked to their offences of (serial) homicide and sex crimes. Also at Broadmoor he supervises the two homicide groups for men who have killed, which is a unique psychotherapeutic group programme not available anywhere else in the UK.

Given the prevalence of mass killings worldwide, exemplified by the atrocity in Norway last year, he has more recently sought to apply his understanding to mass killings and chose to research the Dunblane Massacre of 1996 culminating in its presentation at both the International Association of Forensic Psychotherapy (IAFP) Conference and the Group Analytic Society (GAS) Symposium last year (2011). It is his fervent belief emanating from his extensive experience that all such mass killings can be understood if the perpetrator's history is examined in depth.

FOREWORD

by Lord Alderdice

Individuals and communities react with rage and profound anxiety when confronted by violent criminal acts that they do not understand, especially multiple killings involving children, such as at Dunblane. While one can appreciate that this is a natural response, it does tend to make thoughtful reflection difficult and even render it suspect. The person who tries to explore why such events arise is often criticised as either being more sympathetic to the criminal than the victims, or at least as being naïve about the evil nature of those involved. This is unfortunate and counter-productive, not only because some of the community-anxiety could be ameliorated if such events were no longer regarded as frighteningly incomprehensible, but in addition understanding them better may raise the possibility of preventing some terrible events in the future.

Peter Aylward brings an unusual contribution to this important field because of his substantial and relevant experience in the police service and his subsequent training and psychoanalytically informed work in forensic settings. The first helps inoculate him against charges of naïveté about violent criminals and the second has provided him with tools to explore this extremely difficult area of work, both theoretically and in proposing effective interventions.

The public demand for "something to be done" after atrocious crimes encourages inquiries, professional, judicial, and otherwise, to focus on what procedures or public institutions were at fault in failing to stop the commission of the crime, and how better regulation or legislation might prevent such crimes in the future. However, this societal approach largely fails to address in-depth the questions of why this person committed this particular crime, at this time, and in this way. The value of Peter Aylward's chapters is that in probing the background of the individuals concerned the author gives us good reason to believe that a detailed and in-depth examination of the personal and family histories of those who commit very violent crimes may go much further than merely suggesting in a general sort of way that those who have difficult childhoods are more likely to be troubled adults. He demonstrates in a number of cases that the timing, style, and context of these violent crimes may be very precisely understood. This suggests that if the individuals concerned—who have often been identified as vulnerable beforehand—could be properly assessed, it may be possible to develop specific interventions for them that could actually prevent the occurrence of the violent criminal offence, even if they remain very disturbed, unhappy people.

One might imagine that with the potential benefits being so significant these insights would be eagerly seized upon by the public and by the authorities and that substantial further research would promptly ensue. However, the experience of the relatively few forensic workers who have undertaken such an approach is that the resistances to public understanding are substantial. The value of these chapters is that they put into the public and professional domain sufficient material evidence that it may be hoped that other workers with courage and insight will be encouraged to build upon them by following similar lines of enquiry.

Individuals who have not been able to explore how their personal and family experience has left them captive by dangerous passions may be doomed to act on them. Since all societies contain such people it is in the interests of communities to act through informed understanding rather than react after injury and suffering. This series of chapters points in the right direction. For this the author is to be commended and I very much hope that his lead is followed.

John, Lord Alderdice FRCPsych
House of Lords, London, SW1A 0PW

PREFACE

This book is a collection of chapters, largely written during my time with Dr Gerald Wooster, where they passed through his reflective prism and were almost all jointly presented at consecutive IAFP (International Association of Forensic Psychotherapy) conferences, from 2002 to 2011. They individually and collectively emphasise the crucial importance of taking into account two key factors when attempting to understand the serious offender and the crime. The two factors are diagrammatically represented in the shape of a cross. The vertical (hierarchical) axis relates to the individual's trans-generational family history and the horizontal (peer) axis relates to sibling relationships. It is postulated that it is the complex combination of conflicts in both these areas from birth onwards that can lead to the sort of catastrophic events described in these pages.

These factors are too often ignored in history taking, leading to incorrect formulations from the start and the consequent lack of a more holistic treatment plan that includes the perpetrator within his or her family context. Such neglect, paralleled in the media and wider society, displaces understanding of the family context and life trajectory of the perpetrator and the crime, which all too often leads to non-reflective repetition compulsions and recidivism.

Most notably, my recent research into the Dunblane Massacre in Scotland (1996) illuminates this thinking, which I believe has general characteristics relevant to understanding all mass killings worldwide. It is all too common that explanations for such events are either inconclusive or, in my view, superficial, in focusing upon the political and/or religious beliefs alongside apparent grievances of the perpetrator and the need to review gun laws. While punishment for the crime is a vitally important part of the process, both for society as well as the offender (in mediating guilt), it is crucial that alongside the thinking that addresses "What have you done?" there is also sophisticated and truly reflective thinking focusing on "What has happened to you?"

This enables a full understanding of such events by embracing history, again, both for society (particularly the victims) and for the offender. Moreover, when distilled down, it is suggested that the essence of all conflict can be seen to be rooted in the origins of marginalisation and exclusion where the consequent feelings become uncontainable and erupt cataclysmically into violence.

I trust that this book will demonstrate that as individuals, families, and communities (the arena of "governance") we need to move from the destructive domain of narrowed-down dyadic functioning, and embrace the opening out into triadic functioning. The former is exemplified in relating to the world as if there is only you and me, that there is only right or wrong, and that you are either for us or against us—creating scapegoats and the excluded and marginalised. The latter, more mature functioning, embracing the third standpoint, and intrinsic to inclusion, represents a universal requirement and the best and possibly only long-term and effective prophylactic to the acting-out scenarios described in the clinical cases in this book.

It would perhaps be remiss if I failed to include a little of my own history in relation to this book. In essence it represents the culmination of a period of immersion into the forensic arena from two very different yet linked perspectives. Prior to my psychoanalytic training I served for fifteen years in the Metropolitan Police Service, primarily in anti-terrorism. A highlight of the latter was the surveillance and arrest of Patrick Magee—the Brighton bomber. He received eight life sentences, although was released after fourteen years as part of the Northern Ireland peace process. Around twenty years later, on 19 May 2005, while waiting outside Dublin airport en route to attend the IAFP Conference (to present Chapter Four of this book "Crossing the divide"), I saw

Patrick Magee for the second time as we stood alongside each other waiting for a bus. While I chose not to speak to him regarding our shared experience, it served to highlight the two contrasting yet connected journeys we had undertaken since 1985 in reflecting upon forensic events. Moreover, given such links with Northern Ireland, I was delighted when Lord Alderdice agreed to contribute a foreword, particularly given that he embodies the very essence of addressing sectarianism and healing splits as an Alliance politician in Northern Ireland.

I have often been asked what had led me from policing (and in particular the specific type of policing I undertook) into the psychoanalytic world. My first response was to say that it always felt insufficient to just apprehend the perpetrator in that I was so curious to understand why he/she was driven to do what he/she did. I had therefore become as preoccupied with what had led him to do what he did as I had with what he did. Moreover, my time in undercover work could be described in such a way as to mirror working psychotherapeutically in the transference. That is, one's task is to enter into the subject's environment/world in such a way whereby trust develops and information is consequently shared, resulting in the prevention of future acting-out/crimes. Crucial to both processes is the importance of not going native and acting into the countertransference (being pulled into the internal world of the subject) by keeping one foot outside the door and holding on to the capacity to reflect and think one's own thoughts.

Pivotal to my own psychotherapeutic development was Sylvia Millier who helped me reconcile areas of my own history and unconscious and enabled me to negotiate the turbulent waters of training, graduation, and life after. When I was seeking a clinical supervisor for my work, Sylvia suggested Gerald Wooster. I have benefited considerably from Gerald's experience and his expansive approach to psychotherapy (which utilises his extensive knowledge and interest in Shakespeare) and how psychodynamic thinking can help us make sense of the political world. I continue to be impressed by his unwavering commitment to including the unconscious content in all conscious functioning. This was enhanced when he introduced me to the work of the Chilean psychoanalyst Ignacio Matte Blanco, which increased my capacity to think about emotions, using the concepts of "symmetry" and "asymmetry", which you will come across in the following chapters. The foregoing is all indicative of the crucial role of triangulating in all that we do (see Chapter Two "Perverse triangulation") and I know that Gerald's meticulous attention in this area has had an influence in all of my work. My association with Gerald over the last fifteen years has been most valuable in developing my own thinking and work culminating in this collection of chapters, for which I am deeply grateful.

Given my police background and my psychoanalytic training I was fortunate in being able to marry the two to develop a specialism in forensic psychotherapy through my employment at Broadmoor. When I started working there in 1996 I received gold standard mentoring by Murray Cox whom I shadowed for six months, before he sadly died while undergoing heart surgery. With the exception of Chapters Seven and Nine, this book has been generated from my clinical work at Broadmoor and, apart from Chapters Seven and Eight, have all been presented at IAFP conferences. In all clinical cases informed written consent has been obtained, counter-signed by the patient's treating consultant.

The chapters follow in chronological order in relation to when they were written and presented. The perceptive reader will also notice that they represent an unfolding picture of my own psychotherapeutic development towards finding my own voice. This process started in 2002 in Stuttgart with detecting the re-enactment of original trauma by the acting-out through murder (Chapter One). In 2003 in Arnhem, the perversion of the triangulating process through serial sex offending was highlighted, through the killing off of the third (developmentally represented by the father) as a defence against psychic pain, associated with sibling arrival (see Chapter Two). Then, in 2004 in Edinburgh, the case of a patient who had been in treatment for murder (and has now been successfully rehabilitated) was discussed, and the exposition related to his internal conflict in feeling persecuted by jealousy originating from the very early experience of containing toxic projective processes from a traumatised mother whose husband had suddenly died, just before his birth (see Chapter Three). In 2005 in Dublin the presentation was of a clinical case of the murderous outcome following the inability to cross the divide from unconscious enactment to conscious reflection (see Chapter Four). The presentation in Oxford in 2006 considered the revenge inherent within psychiatry by suggesting "untreatability". I suggest that this stance is an extension of an inability to contain and process anxiety, which prevents movement towards a healthy triangulation in understanding (see Chapter Five). Chapter Six explores the dynamics of paedophilia from the viewpoint that the paedophile, through his offending, seeks to eliminate anxiety emanating from the dreaded emotional experience of exclusion, isolation, emptiness, and non-existence. It is postulated that the paedophilic solution is rooted in his hatred of reality and of the natural order. In Venice in 2008 the fatal case of an anorexic patient was presented, illuminating the definitive position established in all previous presentations: the need for meaningful engagement with the past. Without such engagement the capacity to understand the terrors involved and thereby safely understand and contain them is irreparably disabled. Moreover, huge potential is then created for those terrors to become manifest (displaced) in a different way, thereby perpetuating the original conflict in another form (Chapter Seven). In London in 2010 (at a Bi-logic meeting where members discuss papers based upon the ideas of Ignacio Matte Blanco) the clinical case of a man convicted of the homicide of a woman and her two young children was presented to demonstrate the defences and identification processes which enabled him to protect himself from an awareness of his murderous feelings in relation to original family members and who they represented (Chapter Eight). Finally, last year in Edinburgh in 2011, the Dunblane chapter was presented which portrays the powerful picture of a man destined to act out the unresolved conflicts of his family history at a critical time, given the absence of a meaningful intervention into the historically perverse and enmeshed dyadic relationship with his mother. This absence of another dimension (ordinarily the father) to mediate between the two, ensured that through repetition compulsion he went on to relate to his environment as a re-enactment of his personal history—resulting in the massacre of innocence of infancy that was originally his own (Chapter Nine).

All nine chapters are necessarily detailed in describing family backgrounds and relationships (which I am very aware can challenge the reader to maintain triangulation) and contain within them a common thread of the importance of taking a meaningful account of history, which can become the forgotten past and is indicative of the psychological process of pushing away (repressing) into the unconscious. This emphasises the importance of taking particular note of the family order from one generation to the next. The parent whose child shares the same birth order (e.g., is like the parent in being the youngest child) can provide a greater intensity of (self) projective identification. This sometimes gives more of a boost, sometimes more of a burden, and may overlap or not with the idea of the favoured child or the wrong child in the next generation. It has been learnt—since the introduction of the point by the Australian psychotherapist Averil Earnshaw—that crucial events often occur on those dates, sometimes destructive ones, like death or the onset of a serious illness, but sometimes ones of great creative change.

By triangulating the patient and his offence with his history, I hope it is demonstrated in the following chapters that real understanding and meaning can be achieved. For the victims and those affected by the crimes committed, such understanding can help the very difficult mourning processes. In the foregoing summary of chapters, I have also drawn attention to the importance of triangulating, for you the reader, that is, in needing to hold in mind the image of the chapter being presented at conference (engagement as listener) alongside the different experience as reader. Moreover, is it not that the former is a sharing of the intra-psychic with the inter-psychic and the interpersonal, while the latter lacks the interpersonal?

The triangulation process in stereotypically developmental terms represents the vital role of the father in his difference to the mother/child dyad, particularly the father's mediating role where there are enmeshment and perverse possibilities which Estela Welldon has brilliantly illuminated (1988, 2011). Moreover, I would like to think that this book in some small way contributes to her important body of work in drawing attention to the contribution to subsequent acting-out scenarios/crimes by the child in such a relationship, given the absence or or equally malevolent presence of the perverse father. The potential for the healthy difference that the father could represent is excluded and exacerbates the perversity of the mother/child dyad.

In my view, it is the excluded and the excluding (of difference) that is the greatest stimulus to acting-out and criminality, and I particularly refer the reader to my concluding comments in Chapter Nine on Dunblane. This third, represented developmentally by the father, is also symbolic of all thirds. It lies, as we know, at the core of the psychodynamic discipline where thinking and reflection and taking account of unconscious process is intrinsic to the patient/therapist dyad. As such, the third is ubiquitously susceptible to exclusion or, under powerful dynamic forces, to being excluded in ourselves, emphasising the important role that supervision has in our profession in triangulating the potential for any unhealthy dyadic processes that inevitably occur.

CHAPTER ONE

Palindrome spotting within the calendar of the mind: detecting the re-enactment of original trauma in the crime*

"The fathers have eaten sour grapes and the children's teeth have been set on edge."

—Jeremiah 31:29

This chapter describes an understanding of a patient unconsciously re-enacting, through homicide, an original trauma, at a critical time in her life, by suddenly "giving birth" to a crime that at once symmetrically matched the unexpected presentation of a sibling, by her mother. The offence, standing for the baby, albeit in a psychotic and delusional form, was the perpetrator's way of playing back to her mother what had been played out to her at a much earlier time. This draws attention to the crucial importance of the lateral sibling relationships in families, in relation to subsequent acting-out scenarios of homicide, which the psychoanalytic world has been remiss in not sufficiently triangulating with the significance of the vertical relationships with parents.

---

*This chapter was first read at a meeting of the International Association of Forensic Psychotherapy (IAFP) Conference on 6 April 2002 in Stuttgart, Germany.

1

I allude in my title, and hope to present, the notion that a crime can be understood as representing an earlier trauma and that the trauma is being played back in the same form at an emotional level at a particular time. This reinforces the characteristic of the timelessness of the unconscious by suggesting that there is a calendar of the mind that may dictate the pertinence of both the timing and type of offence. "Palindrome" comes from the Greek *palindromos* meaning "running back again", and is a word to describe something that is the same backwards as forwards. The sentence "Able was I ere I saw Elba" is the same when read forwards as when read backwards, and is therefore a palindrome. The traumatic experience I will focus upon will be the arrival of a sibling which, because of its ubiquity and ordinariness, is not always seen with its full psychotic and forensic possibilities. Juliet Mitchell in her publication on sibling relations and hysteria—*Mad Men and Medusas* (2000)—suggests that when a child is faced with the arrival of a sibling there is a protest against this by trying to become the only baby or favourite offspring: "By which time he is utterly dependent and helpless. The dread of the death-like experience of trauma, which is the equivalent of an absence of subject or ego, is warded off by a mimetic identification with another person" (Mitchell, 2000 p. 41).

The patient I will present demonstrates this mimetic (in mimicry) identification with her mother by giving birth to an offence (of murder) which symmetrically represents her mother giving birth to a sibling. The offence occurred at a time that matched a traumatic event experienced at the same point of time in her mother's life. I shall refer to this as a "critical date".

To give an example of critical dates:

> Adolph Hitler, Dictator of Nazi Germany, was born on April 20th 1889. His father Alois was born in 1837 and was fifty-one when Adolph, his fourth child, was born. The next child, Edmund, was born in March 1894 when father was fifty-six. Alois had fathered three children, Gustav, Ida, and Otto before Adolph was born, when he was aged forty-eight, forty-nine and fifty, and they had all died in infancy. Adolph reached fifty-one in 1940, and having dealt with Czechoslovakia, Austria, Poland, France, Denmark and Norway he embarked on plans to subjugate the rest of the world … Adolph reached 56 in April 1945 and is said to have shot himself in a bunker ten days after his fifty-sixth birthday. As noted above fifty-six was

his father's age when the next baby Edmund was born. Adolph's reign was over, as indeed in 1894 his reign as the only child had been when baby Edmund was born.

(Earnshaw, 1995, p. 108)

While I appreciate that there are considerable socio-political factors surrounding the story of Hitler, I want to draw attention to a time-linked factor of a killing off and displacement/replacement that represented a crime revisited.

I am here considering that something, in this case a trauma, is repeating itself, and that there is a "compulsion to repeat", a phrase coined by Freud to describe what he believed to be an innate tendency to revert to earlier conditions (Freud 1920, pp. 18–22). Through the repetition compulsion, the unconscious tries to master earlier traumatic experience, repeating or re-enacting it, without actually bringing it into conscious awareness in the form of a recollection (Freud, 1914). This is particularly relevant to the opportunity for repeat enactments in the transference, which may then be consciously understood and worked through in the clinical setting (Freud, 1914). Moreover, I wish to explore the observation that there is a correspondence between the dating of events which constitute repetitions and the dating of an original traumatic event. I shall illustrate this theory by using some clinical material in which the crime of murder was used by a patient to play back to her mother in a palindromic form what she felt was played out to her at an earlier time and that this occurred at a critical time in her own mind. I shall show that the dating of the two correspond to each other. The clinical tools that I shall use will include Klein's (1946) projective identification, Segal's (1978) symbolic equation, and Freud's (1900) ideas on the characteristics of the unconscious. Furthermore I shall make use of the important theories of the Chilean psychoanalyst Ignacio Matte Blanco (1975). For those unacquainted with his work I intend to offer a rudimentary introduction to the man and his thinking as I believe it will help in providing some clarity to what appears to be the illogical mind of the unconscious, and more exceptionally, the psychotic. For those more familiar with Matte Blanco's work the following will offer a little revision.

Before doing so, I want to briefly comment upon the recent completion of the genome project/the DNA (deoxyribonucleic) profile. Originally it held out the fantasy that it would provide an understanding of how humans function. It is now a much more complex picture involving the production of proteins and their propensity to be affected by, amongst other things, intense emotional states. This raises the question about the capacity to inherit "time-tagged" DNA/protein, an issue to which I will return in the final chapter of this book. It was proposed that trans-generational factors are as relevant to the unfolding of trauma as they are to the present internal calendars that dictate when our teeth might erupt from our gums or whether and when our hair begins to go grey.

I will now lean extensively on the efforts of Eric Rayner, whose book *Unconscious Logic* (1995) provides a good introduction to Matte Blanco's ideas. Matte Blanco's thinking is a blend of classical psychoanalysis with mathematical logic, which at first sight appears esoteric and forbidding. While Matte Blanco is quite clear that psychoanalysis could not be practised based on bi-logic alone, once his ideas have been grasped, they add a new dimension to our thinking. In short, borderline/psychotic levels of thought are rendered more comprehensible. Of particular importance has been Matte Blanco's new theoretical vision about "emotionality" and how strong affect acts as a bridge between psychoanalytic forms of theory and those of other disciplines.

A brief biographical picture might help to place Matte Blanco in context. He was born in 1908 in Chile and graduated in medicine at the University of Chile in Santiago. His interests soon turned towards psychiatry, particularly psychoanalysis, concentrations which led him to London in the mid-1930s. He undertook his first analysis with Walter Schmideberg, a classical Freudian psychoanalyst and son-in-law of Melanie Klein. He went on to study under many of the best-known analysts at the time, including Klein, Anna Freud, and Ernest Jones, the founder of the British Psychoanalytic Society and one of the first and most faithful disciples of Freud himself. In 1940 he moved to America, where he was employed as an analyst and pursued his mathematical interest by attending weekly seminars with the esteemed mathematician Richard Courant. In 1948 he returned to Chile as chair of psychiatry at the University of Santiago in Chile. His work with psychotic patients was particularly notable at the time. "Psychosis", being a term that encompasses many of the most severe and disturbed forms of mental illness, had been found to have been almost inaccessible by conventional psychoanalytic techniques and Matte Blanco's interest focused on its phenomena. A desire to pursue his own theories led to another move in

1966 when he arrived in Rome as chairman of psychiatry at the Catholic University of Rome, and in 1975 he published the first of his two major works, entitled *The Unconscious as Infinite Sets*. In 1988 a sequel was published called *Thinking, Feeling and Being*. In 1990 an accident caused him severe brain damage and his health declined rapidly until his death in 1995.

In short, Matte Blanco found the germ of his theory of the logic of the unconscious when dealing with psychotic patients. He discovered that the apparent irrationality of these patients was not a wholly arbitrary chaos, but one that exhibited certain patterns. The basis of the pattern was what he termed "symmetry", using that word in its mathematical sense.

It was the application of this mathematical interest to which I now want to turn. The pattern is at odds with common-sense logic, which was first codified by Aristotle (384–322 BC) and involves the clear distinction between true and false. This common-sense logic underlies most of the ordinary transactions of life and also underlies most of humanity's scientific descriptions.

However, Freud's (1900) brilliance in uncovering the characteristics of the unconscious was to indicate that the unconscious does not conform to these known logical rules and that it has its own system of rules, its own mode of thinking. So that while the conscious logical thinking usually works within a framework of distinguishing things, the unconscious that Freud investigated tends to unite and fuse everything. The former is regarded as rational at a precise and impersonal level, whereas the latter is in every respect its reverse.

Matte Blanco's (1975) genius was in bringing the two together creatively. He argued that the unconscious must obey some rules. As we go about our business the human mind continuously classifies, whereby constant acts of recognition are made all the time so that an experience, when repeated, is not treated as new. This classifying involves the registration of sameness or identity.

Relating to the world also entails discriminating the relationships between things. Again, without such discrimination it would be impossible to negotiate the environment. Matte Blanco coined the registration of sameness as "symmetry" and difference as "asymmetry". "A is to the left of B" has the converse "B is to the right of A". Here the converse is not identical to the original; this is asymmetrical. However, "A is near B" has the converse "B is near A"; it is reversible and thereby symmetrical. Matte Blanco proposes that ordinary logical thought, which is primarily scientific logic about the physical world, must entertain asymmetrical relations. The mind must be able to conceive of relations whose converses are not identical to them. In such asymmetrical thought, since recognition is essential, symmetry (sameness) must be registered, but only in strict accordance with the discrimination of difference. The functioning of this logic is dominant within secondary process, that is, in thinking which is governed by conscious reality. In primary process, however, we often find the converse of a relation treated as identical; for example, regardless of external evidence, a baby may think "I need my mother" and therefore "my mother needs me".[1] This is not a deduction that ordinary common-sense/asymmetrical logic would necessarily make, but such descriptions of unconscious symmetrical logic are the keystones to Matte Blanco's work. He called this "illogical" pattern of thought "symmetrised logic" and this often entails the simultaneous use of symmetry and asymmetry (Matte Blanco, 1975, p. 11).

The apparently inappropriate mixing or insertion of symmetrical thought into asymmetrical relations is called "symmetrisation". Matte Blanco gives an example of symmetrisation: "Prison windows have bars. The windows of my room have bars and my pyjamas have stripes like bars of the windows. Hence, I am in prison" (1975, pp. 162–163). At first this may be perceived as mad and Matte Blanco himself, studying schizophrenic thought, was aware of this impression. However, he took pains to show that such madness uses symmetrised logic when asymmetrical logic is appropriate to the conscious sane mind. Let me here cite a more immediate example. Allow me for a moment to be arrogant and suggest that in writing this chapter I am giving something good to you. In ordinary logic, I could conclude that you are being given something good by me. But if this then becomes suffused by unconscious process and we slip in to what Matte Blanco would call symmetrisation, I might say that I am giving something good to you, so you are giving something good to me. Ordinarily this is not a very logical conclusion, but affectively this is in fact the experience. Here subjects and objects would become less differentiated so that there is more of a diffuse feeling, akin to "goodness is happening". So, in this example, subjects and objects tend to be fused, merged, or reversible. The same can be applied to a time relation. In ordinary logic we might say "Event B follows Event A so A precedes B". If symmetrisation intervenes, then we might say "B follows A so A follows B", and there then becomes no awareness of time sequence, so time as we know it disappears.

In this way, Matte Blanco begins to provide a handle on the momentousness of the idea of timelessness in the unconscious that Freud established (Freud, 1915). Moreover, Freud was more than aware that he himself had made little progress in this area when he wrote a few years before his death:

> Again and again we have had the impression that we have made too little theoretical use of this fact established beyond any doubt of the unalterability by time of the repressed. This seems to offer an approach to the most profound discoveries. Nor unfortunately, have we made any progress here.

> (Freud, 1933, p. 74)

Moving on, let us next take the notion of an object and its parts. We are all familiar in our clinical work with a part equating to a whole and vice versa. This symmetrisation can become exaggerated into classes of things. This is an area to which prejudice is germane. For instance: "[I]t must be a man that lives here—it's in such a mess." Here the classes of "men" and "messiness" are equated. Symmetrisation has changed any asymmetrical perception that some men are tidy. Rayner and Wooster state:

> We think it would be right to say that Matte-Blanco considers his most fundamental contribution to be the demonstration that Freud's main characteristics of the unconscious can be understood in terms of symmetrisation of ordinary logical thought.

> (Rayner & Wooster, 1990, p. 428)

A further point to add regarding the part equalling the whole, is in the application of the question in mathematics: "[W]hen is a part of a set (of numbers) equivalent to the whole set?" The answer, mathematically, is when the set is infinite. Take the set of all whole numbers—1, 2, 3, 4, etc.; this is an infinite set. Now take a part of this set, for example, the sub-set all even numbers—2, 4, 6, etc.; this sub-set is also infinite, so for every whole number there corresponds one and only one even number: 1 corresponds to 2, 2 corresponds to 4, 3 corresponds to 6, and so on ad infinitum. This whole–part equivalence is a paradox that characterises infinite sets, but not finite ones.

Matte Blanco went on to introduce the notion of infinity in emotional experience. We are all familiar with a patient's sense of omniscience, omnipotence, and idealisation. There is infinity contained in all; for example, in omniscience we can know everything that it is possible to know. This is always recognisable in feeling states, easily seen in feelings of being in love. Extreme emotional states therefore display a quality of irradiation and maximalisation. If the assumption is then made that extreme emotions are contained as nuclei in any feeling, then Matte Blanco concluded that all affects contain elements of infinite experience, which involves symmetrisation. Both affects and unconscious processes thus involve infinities.

Both Rayner and Wooster suggest that this conclusion is new (1990). In thinking about psychotic processes, the psychotic sees symmetry where the normal person does not and emotion may be accompanied, therefore, by inflation to an infinite degree. The stronger the emotion the greater the door is opened to such symmetric deductions.

Turning now to the clinical material, a murder was committed in the vicinity of my patient Cherie's home when she was fourteen. It remained an unsolved crime. When Cherie was sixteen she was convicted of an offence of grievous bodily harm (GBH) and received a minimum detention of two years. While detained for this offence (at the age of eighteen) she began to disclose details about the murder that took place two years prior to the GBH offence (when fourteen). Cherie was subsequently charged and convicted of the murder and received a life sentence. She was dealt with under the Mental Health Act (1983) and diagnosed with mental illness and psychopathic disorder alongside borderline personality disorder and sexual paraphilia (approximating to a morbid craving or attraction for sex). I have been meeting with her for the past two years.

Her family circumstances at the time of her birth were that she was the fourth born to her mother, who had conceived her first three children with two separate men. Cherie's conception was with a third man. Her mother and father (both French) apparently stayed together for the first year of Cherie's life before her father left. By the time Cherie was two, her mother had met and married another man, called Draiveur. Cherie and her elder brother were fostered out to a relative in France, while her mother and new husband moved to England (a work posting). During that same year, in England, Cherie's next youngest sibling was born and when Cherie reached four years of age her mother returned to France (almost exactly two years following her departure) and introduced Cherie to her new stepfather and new half-brother. It was this early experience, as well as trans-generational factors, that I believe created the template for Cherie's subsequent behaviour. Not only did there appear to be an insecure and dysfunctional attachment to her mother, but this was exacerbated by her mother's abandonment of her at two, as well as her mother's subsequent return two years later when Cherie was unexpectedly faced with a new stepfather and half-brother. We might reasonably speculate that feelings of envy were rekindled and were inflamed by jealousy, provoked by the experience of being displaced by the new sibling. Cherie's mother had one further child, later in that same year, which was to become her sixth.

Cherie's mother had fluctuating periods of mental illness which often necessitated hospitalisation. Care orders were implemented for the children. Cherie often became the mother figure for her younger siblings, taking responsibility during her mother's absence through illness and/or working and socialising. However, as Cherie approached puberty, self-harming, sniffing solvents, drug-taking, and promiscuity became features. By the age of ten or eleven, having been monitored for several years by social services, Cherie was showing signs of disturbance at school. At the same time Cherie's mother had met another man whom she was to subsequently marry. He brought with him two daughters from a previous relationship. The imposition of stepsisters was to adversely influence Cherie in the following years. As the stepfamily moved into Cherie's home, Cherie was put in the care of a friend, apparently to prevent her being badly influenced by her new stepsisters. Again, Cherie was displaced (mirroring the events when she was two) at fourteen years of age and this was the year the murder took place. A picture emerges of Cherie's deteriorating behaviour and involvement with the police.

I will now turn to the GBH that Cherie committed aged sixteen. The background to this offence is that Cherie had become powerfully attracted to one of her female teachers in school, to the point of idolatry. Cherie was then moved to a different class. Cherie believed the move to have been prompted by her teacher, as a response to the intensity of Cherie's feelings, and this gave her the need to respond to her feelings of humiliation by acting on the murderous impulses that were provoked. Two weeks prior to the GBH, Cherie prevented the teacher from leaving a classroom, demanding to be told why she had been moved. At the time, she had a knife concealed on her and intended to use it, but had been interrupted by another teacher. On the day before the GBH, Cherie was arrested on suspicion of arson. Apparently, while with a boyfriend from school, a fire had started in a disused area and, upon being seen leaving, both were arrested. Cherie states categorically that she did not cause the fire. To her shock she learnt that while in custody, her boyfriend had pointed the finger at her. The next day she attended school, again with a concealed knife, in order to attack him. During that morning Cherie bumped into a fellow pupil in the toilets and apparently saw in her eyes the same look that the teacher had when Cherie was rejected; she stabbed the fellow pupil. This GBH offence took place exactly two years *to the day* after the unresolved offence of murder, equating in time with the absence of her mother from the age of two to four.

The conviction for GBH was incontestable. The subsequent murder conviction raised question marks. While Cherie was convicted for the murder on her own testimony, it was clear that she could not have committed the offence alone, alongside the feeling of some ambiguity about her direct involvement at all. The concerns were that at the time of the murder offence Cherie was fourteen years old and the victim an eighteen-year-old young woman.

I want now to think about her offending in the light of Matte Blanco's ideas. I will start with the time that I awoke one weekend morning, approximately twelve months into the work, to a question in my mind. Clearly, in my unconscious sleeping state something had been at work in relation to Cherie's story and the question that I awoke with was: What was happening to Cherie's mother at the same point in time (i.e., the same age) that Cherie chose to talk about the murder? It later occurred to me that I was also sleeping in a spare room, having been displaced from my usual bed by a sick child.

As a result of my growing familiarity with trans-generational factors, I was not surprised to establish that Cherie was eighteen when she began to talk about the murder and that Cherie's mother was eighteen when she was raped and fell pregnant. Cherie knew that her mother had been raped at eighteen. Matte Blanco's thinking around symmetrisation helps to make the circumstances of Cherie's disclosure of the murder explicable. For if Cherie's disclosure, aged eighteen, is more than just coincidence, it is "inviting" an over-intrusiveness (unconsciously analogous to rape) that results in the conception of murder.

In working with Cherie a persistent undercurrent of confusion arises when making reference to the first or the second offence: her first offence, she claims, is the GBH, and while convicted of the murder (which she refutes), this represents the second offence, being the conviction that followed that for GBH. However, the murder was committed prior to the GBH and naturally one is drawn to referring to that as the first offence. I feel that this confusion is significant, and has resonance with A before B and B before A in relation to timelessness and unconscious functioning. My associations, however, are drawn to try to empathise with her early experience, in that I am focusing on two significant periods in her life, that is, at the age of two and at the age of four, and to wonder whether the abandonment by her mother at age two into the care of a relative (her second mother) was two years later changed by the re-emergence of her (biological) mother who then took her back. In my thinking and in parallel symmetry, I might think that mother one (biological) became mother two (relative) and subsequent mother two became mother one. This could equally apply to her paternal line, in that up until the age of approximately ten Draiveur had been her father, until she learnt that her biological father was still alive in France. Here also father one (biological) became father two and father two (stepfather Draiveur) had been father one.

Let me now look at the GBH offence in the light of symmetrisation. The background to the offence was of feeling abandoned by the boyfriend regarding the arson, in such a way that she was expected to take responsibility for her partner's fire. Here I might think of her unconsciously equating this with having to deal with the "fire" of passion between her mother and her stepfather that produced her younger sibling. I suggest that conscious asymmetrical thinking, differentiating her boyfriend from her mother, had been overwhelmed by unconscious symmetrisation, whereby her boyfriend belonged to the same class as her mother (that of important people who betray and abandon her) and so were symmetrised, that is, felt to be the same. Cherie's anger prompted her attendance at school concealing a knife. Cherie stabbed a fellow pupil in the back in the school toilets. All Cherie can recall is that the look in the girl's eyes was the same as the look in the teacher's eyes when she had rejected her. Again, asymmetrical thinking would have separated the girl from the teacher, by recognising difference as well as similarity in the eyes, but this then became overwhelmed by symmetrical thinking, when Cherie was fully under the control of her unconscious. I might add that the girl in the toilets became the abandoning teacher who in turn became the abandoning mother. That is, they were all classified within the same set and were subsequently symmetrised. Here the part-equals-whole equation also applies, in that the girl's eyes equated with the whole class of abandoning figures.

This is an area that links with Hanna Segal's thinking on symbolic equation (1986). Psychotic symbolic equations involve gross symmetrisations that distort the extent of the self in relation to internal and external reality. Moreover, without symmetry there is no metaphor, and without metaphor there is no make-believe "as if" play. Play breaks down into delusion when the self has no containing framework of awareness of asymmetrical relations. Segal discusses the mental processes involved in dealing with the absence of an ideal object, for Cherie we might say boyfriend/teacher/mother. Segal suggests that initially the concept of "absence" hardly exists, such that the infant's ego becomes assailed by the bad object/objects, and it is here that the mind creates, in a hallucinatory way, something representing what has been lost. This is the beginnings of the process of symbol formation. These early symbols, however, are not felt by the ego to be symbols or substitutes, but to *be* the original object itself, and she terms the process "symbolic equation":

> Parts of the ego and internal objects are projected into an object and identified with it. The differentiation between the self and the object is obscured. Then, since a part of the ego is confused with the object, the symbol—which is a creation and a function of the ego—becomes, in turn, confused with the object which is symbolized.

> (Segal, 1986, p. 53)

Here Segal is describing the early mental processes involved in counteracting the experience of absence and for Cherie her boyfriend was symbolically equated with teacher, such that they became the original object, mother. Moreover, I will show that this is further exemplified in her murder offence.

Now turning to the murder offence itself, at around the time of the offence, when Cherie was fourteen (not unlike what happened at the age of four), Cherie's mother became involved with another man who had children from a previous relationship. The new family moved in with Cherie's mother, while at the same time her mother placed Cherie in the care of a friend of hers, so Cherie was displaced. It is a memory that still fills her with rage and jealousy, when she recalls telephoning her mother and one of her stepsisters picking up the phone and calling, "*Mum*, it's Cherie". Here again, while conscious asymmetrical thinking would differentiate between her stepsisters and her half-brother (at four), when symmetrised, they both became part of the same class—as a sibling who displaces her position. It was not surprising that Cherie began to exhibit severe behavioural problems at this time and she began to come to the notice of the police. However, it was later, while Cherie was detained for the GBH aged eighteen, that her mother and her two younger siblings decided to return to France and to meet again with the extended family. Because Cherie was detained, she was unable to go with them and felt angry and jealous as well as abandoned.

She claims that in an attention-seeking ploy she began to talk about the murder. She had developed an affectionate and idealised relationship with a female staff member (transferential?) and began to confide in her details of the crime. This staff member called the police and Cherie felt honour bound to the staff member to talk to the police. Cherie was subsequently charged. There was sufficient evidence in her six statements of admission and one of denial to suggest that she had been intimately involved or apprised of the details of the offence. At the time of writing this, Cherie's mother appeared to be nearing the birth of Cherie's seventh sibling.

In working with her, I always have to hold in mind the proposition that she did commit the offence (with others) of which she has been convicted. However, I also have to hold in mind her protestations of innocence in addition to the repeated experience, in the sessions, of her abandonment of me. Therefore, I must allow for the consideration that we are dealing with a deeply repressed unconscious attempt to ward off the trauma of loss and displacement. Here the asymmetrical relation that M is the mother to Cherie is symmetrised so that Cherie is the mother of M. I referred earlier to the notion of a critical date and the question that was on my mind upon waking from a dream in the spare room of my house. Cherie's mother was eighteen when she was raped and subsequently fell pregnant. When Cherie was eighteen, while away from home (in detention for her GBH offence) and at a time when she was feeling angry, jealous, and abandoned by her mother for visiting the family home in France with Cherie's two younger siblings, Cherie chose to begin to talk about the unsolved murder. This naturally received the attention of the police who, after lengthy questioning, charged her with the previously unsolved murder. Cherie's mother was informed of the murder charge upon her return from France; Cherie said that her mother was furious and traumatised.

At the point when Cherie's mother learnt of her daughter's murder conviction, she had had two years to come to terms with the offence that Cherie had been detained for originally (the GBH). She was then to be shocked by the sudden arrival of another far more traumatising offence, after having been away; replicating Cherie's experience at two and four. Moreover, while Cherie invited the interest of the police, she herself became concerned about how things got out of control (like rape) and that her consequent engagement with the police resulted in the charge of murder (like conceiving a pregnancy). In applying Matte Blanco's symmetrisation, the first factor surrounds the trans-generational transference of the trauma that occurred to Cherie's mother at the age of eighteen (as a result of being raped and falling pregnant) so that here Cherie at eighteen could justifiably claim the same, following the unwelcome intrusion of the police, resulting in a charge of murder (standing for pregnancy, discussed below). In addition, I am wanting to highlight the trauma that was Cherie's, both at the age of two, but more importantly at the age of four, so that there were for her two traumatic experiences: the first one of abandonment by her mother; the second, the return of her abandoning mother, two years later, who was not only accompanied by the man responsible for taking her away (the GBH offence), but also inextricably linked to the creation of a sibling, resulting in anger, jealousy, and displacement. So at the age of four Cherie was faced with having to accommodate these two factors in her relationship with her mother—that is, her stepfather and half-sibling—in the same way that her mother, upon returning from France, had to accommodate two different factors—the GBH and the murder. In symmetrical terms, the offence of murder that was conceived by Cherie symmetrically represents the sibling that was conceived by her mother during an absence. In the world of symmetrisation, a sibling is an offence as an offence is a sibling, in that it represents something that is created by inviting the interests of another party, which bears fruit.

There might be a number of ways of understanding the process whereby, when the murder offence had been conceived, Cherie "became" her mother, to defend herself against the pain of anger, jealousy, and displacement. First of all, I want to consider that this was a massive form of projective identification with her mother. Klein comments that an "aspect of projective processes ... concerns the forceful entry into the object and control of the object by parts of the self" (Klein, 1946, p. 11). A part of Cherie that she herself found intolerable/unbearable she projected into her mother, in the hope of providing immediate relief, and perhaps with the aim of acquiring an intimidating control of her mother. This corresponds exactly to my countertransference experience of Cherie. This type of projective identification also corresponds to Bion's concept of "abnormal projective identification" (1959). Rosenfeld (1987) comments that this is projective identification used for defensive purposes, and has a number of phantasies attached, which include that of an omnipotent intrusion, leading to fusion or confusion with the object (mother).

Such omnipotent intrusion is part of an expulsion of tension by someone who has been traumatised as a child by violent intrusions. Moreover, Rosenfeld adds there is a concrete phantasy of passively living inside the object—a form of parasitism. This excessive use of projective identification erases the boundaries between the self and the object (Rosenfeld, 1987). The confusion of mutual fusion is compounded by the reversal of subject and object, all adding up to an inability to keep hold of a space between the self and the object in its absence. I return here also to the foregoing reference to symbolic equation, in which confusion exists between the inner world and the external object.

Jordan (1990), in a compendium of articles celebrating Matte Blanco's eightieth birthday, explores this phenomenon of intrusive projective identification from a bi-logic point of view. Klein describes this intrusiveness as "forceful entry into the object and control of the object by parts of the self" (1946, p. 11). Jordan discusses the relationship between the mother's body, an infant's body, and the infant's own mental space, so that the statement "I am contained within my mother", when expressed as an asymmetrical relation (Aristotelian logic), would read "My mother is the container of myself". However, when applying the principle of symmetry, the proposition "I am contained within my mother" is equivalent to "My mother is contained within myself". So that in relation to Cherie, her own body, mental space, thoughts, and actual space, become equivalents of a phantasy of the interior of the maternal space, where she feels she is contained and, simultaneously, she contains. Jordan states: "An internal space different from the maternal container is not established; thus, the interior of [*Cherie's*] body and the interior of [*her*] mind are confused with the phantasy of the interior of [*her*] mother's body" (1990, p. 433; my emphasis). Linking this to Cherie's story, I can see that the interior of her mother's body produced a hated sibling that had to be accommodated, whereas for Cherie's mother, what was equally true was that she had to accommodate and accept her already convicted daughter with her more major offence.

Jordan goes on to say that the analytic process, based on the interpretative function, allows for the sequential unfolding of the symmetrical undifferentiated experience in the relationship with the maternal object. For Cherie, this will dictate her capacity to let go of (give up) the baby / offence and separate from the safety of a symbiotic relationship with mother. Matte Blanco might say that she needs to gain sufficient internalisation of the asymmetry, involving differentiation through time and between objects.

I now want to turn to the offence that represents the sibling, in that Cherie's "holding on" to this offence reminds us of the creation by the infant of a transitional object. Transitional object phenomena were explored extensively by Winnicott (1951) and, in health, the infant's development is aided by the creation of a transitional object to help bridge the gap left by the absent object. In order to do so, the infant must first have a memory trace of a friendly, nurturing mother (object), which helps the infant to exist without panic when the mother is absent. The infant needs to find a way to hang on to this kind of lively internal object and to be able to create and recreate it internally. Through the use of the transitional object the infant is dealing with the absence of a mother's presence. However, in thinking about Cherie I want to draw upon a work by Elisha Davar (2001) where he explores the distinction between the creation of a transitional object to overcome absence, as opposed to an object that is used (and here I am thinking of Cherie's offence) to gain a feeling of a presence.

Davar refers to the objects created to provide a sense of presence as "pre-transitional phenomena". In circumstances where profound maternal deprivation was experienced, an object serves to create a feeling of mother's presence, as opposed to bridging her loss. Davar refers to these pre-transitional phenomena as "existential objects". Davar writes about patients he has seen who have needed to make use of existential objects, all of whom have had traumatic experiences around early bonding. A consequence of this is that a fracture develops in the patient's sense of self and the use of this existential object thus prevents further fragmentation. He says that the existential object functions as a symbolic equation rather than a true symbol (Davar, 2001, p. 25), an argument that again reinforces earlier comments in this chapter.

The absence of presence (transitional use) is not the same as the presence of absence (existential use), and Davar suggests that the presence in absence is an aspect of an enduring psychic structure for a particular group of patients. If the mother was an absent object for the infant, as in Cherie's case, the internal object is likely to be a vacuous presence, which leads to the development of a blank area of experience in his connection with others and this becomes a core experience (Davar, 2001, p. 16). So the internal object, which is part of that core sense, will have a primary quality of absence. This means that the transitional area of experience is not available to that baby. Instead, an "existential object" will need to be used in order to give life to the internal object, to fill the vacuum. Davar says: "When we look at the use of an object in this existential way it seems to me that what the baby is trying to do is to create an illusionary responsive mother figure by any means it can in order to revive a living feeling" (2001, p. 16).

Davar's idea of an existential object comes about from the use of an object for the purposes of making a live mother, as opposed to the transitional object that gradually comes to replace mother through being able to absorb the anxiety of her non-presence in totality. Unlike the transitional object, the existential object is used to gain a sense of aliveness and existence of the self (Davar, 2001, p. 24).

I feel that Cherie's creation of the murder corresponds with the pre-transitional phenomena of an existential object and came about for the purpose of creating an alive mother. This was a way to revive a living feeling in herself so that there was an existence of an experience of herself. Perhaps, not unlike the victim of the murder whose life had been so powerfully erased, this demonstrates identification with the victim, symmetrising with her early experience of feeling both alive and dead. It is along these lines that I have often interpreted. Being dead and alive is an appropriate place to come back to.

To summarise, Matte Blanco helps us to formulate that, to defend against the painful feelings of an asymmetrical relation between Cherie and her mother, symmetrisation took place. Any difference in space and time was obliterated for Cherie so that, in symmetrical terms, Cherie became her mother as her mother became Cherie. The original trauma was one of abandonment, at two, so there was a trauma of loss and enduring absence, only for this trauma to be exacerbated two years later, aged four, by the return of her mother simultaneously displacing Cherie by the arrival of a new sibling. The two offences that Cherie has been convicted of exactly two years apart symmetrically match the foregoing traumas. Symmetrisation has been discussed relating to the circumstances of the GBH, but more importantly to the murder offence. The murder represented what I refer to as a palindrome. That is a symmetrical playing back to her mother in exactly the same form, affectively, in which trauma was played out, at a much earlier stage, to Cherie. Moreover, I have discussed the significance of this occurring at a critical time in her mother's life (at eighteen) and that this was inevitably played out in Cherie's life when she was exactly the same age.

At the beginning of the chapter I referred to the example of Hitler and the psychopathic replaying of an earlier trauma, that was also Cherie's. I will close the chapter on an example of a more creative playing out by referring to critical dates in Sigmund Freud's life. Before doing so, I want finally to comment upon the issue of siblings and return again to Juliet Mitchell. She writes, in her recent book, *Mad Men and Medusa* (2000), about the culturally universal condition of hysteria, which she claims is still as much with us today, but under other names. From a feminist perspective she unearths the male hysteric and argues that the discovery by Freud of the Oedipus complex blocked the understanding of hysteria. She says:

> I do not for one moment want to contest the importance of either the Oedipus or the castration complex. What I want to propose is a different ordering which implicates siblings. I propose to invert accepted psychoanalytic ordering which leads from the Oedipus complex onto the siblings and suggest instead that it is the initial awareness of the presence of the siblings which produces a catastrophic psychosocial situation of displacement. This triggers in turn a regression to the earlier parental relationships which were without their psychic implications until this moment. Cast back on to babyhood and defence against displacement the relationship to the parents becomes fully Oedipal … In Freud's account love and hate derive from the parental relationship and are subsequently transferred to siblings. We read these events the other way round;

faced with a sibling the child regresses to its [*sic*] wishes for infantile unity with the mother, it is then that it finds the father in the way.

(Mitchell, 2000, p. 23)

Mitchell sees the onset of hysteria as the catastrophic moment of the subject's displacement and that this was Cherie's fate is undoubted. The emotions that lie under the hysteria are jealousy, confusion, and revenge. The subject seeks to create (or stir up) these emotions in the person responsible for creating them in the first place. The emotions that lay under hysteria, that of jealousy, confusion, and revenge are then sought to be created in the person responsible for the original feelings. Projective identification is used to put these feelings into another, that is, to stir him up. This is classically demonstrated in Shakespeare's play *Othello* in which Othello (General and hero of the Venetian army) becomes possessed with Iago's murderous jealousy having been displaced by his preferred new brother Cassio. Here is the expelling form of projective identification, where, in the face of jealousy, there is a retreat to being at one with the object that caused it (Klein, 1946). Thus Cherie wanted to become her mother giving birth as she did, as well as being her mother's baby. Mitchell comments that the catastrophic displacement by a sibling produces a range of responses in hysterical form from a temporary Oedipal picture to a delusional psychosis, which would explain the madness of taking full responsibility for an offence, such as murder.

The arrival of a sibling has occurred clinically in the work with Cherie. After seeing Cherie for approximately nine months, I started working with another female patient on another ward. I was to learn that this new patient was a close friend of Cherie's. The week following my first session with this new patient a range of powerful feelings emerged from Cherie, principally stemming from jealousy. At the time I was more conscious of the approach of the anniversary of the date of the murder and GBH offences and less conscious of the rivalry dynamic with the other patient.

After arriving on the ward one morning I was engaged in conversation with one of the nurses primarily responsible for Cherie's care. While talking with her, Cherie emerged, somewhat aggressively, from another part of the ward and jealously remarked, "Are you talking about me?" Upon arrival in the therapy room she emptied her pockets, something she had not done before. Moreover, her mouth was now contorted every time she spoke and I understood this to be a somatising hysterical reaction to a traumatic event. She began the session by expressing her murderousness towards the evil place in which she was detained. She went on to talk about knives and the time she used to carry them around, and I was becoming very conscious of a feeling of dangerousness.

She began to describe a scenario a few days prior to being arrested for the GBH, in which she and others had been approached by police on the streets and, as they approached, she had managed to conceal a knife in her sock. She explained that because neither of the police officers was female she could not be searched and so managed to get away with possession of the offensive weapon. She said that a few days later, after being arrested for the GBH, the same policeman who had stopped her was in the police station. The thought that occurred to her was that if he had been able to search her then he would have found the knife, and so she said to him that if he'd done his job properly he'd have been able to have stopped the GBH.

Cherie was telling me a story about the days prior to the GBH (and for GBH we can read murder; that is, both offences occurring on the same date of the calendar are symmetrised), and recounting this to me a few days prior to the anniversary of the offences. This alerted me to the importance of ensuring that I became aware of the dangerousness in her at that time, both during and after the session. She was unconsciously alerting me to her concealed murderousness.

While my attention was drawn to the approach of the anniversary, I missed what had been the arrival of a sibling in Cherie's current life (my other patient). Her jealousy and anger were palpable in this session and my concern was such that, unusually, I asked to speak with her consultant as well as the nurse I had been speaking to at the beginning of the session. I also felt it important to meet them away from the ward, to prevent inflaming feelings further, and to alert the clinical team to the perceived dangers that were around. I believe that this act of making conscious any unconscious feelings prevented any acting-out. Following on from our understanding of the hysterical reaction to being displaced (by both the nurse as well as the other patient), it was perhaps not surprising that in the following session she attempted to make me (the offending parent responsible for her jealousy) feel all the jealousy and hatred that she herself had felt. She informed me that there had only ever been one special person with whom she had shared the complete details of the offence surrounding the murder and this had been a fellow inpatient while in detention elsewhere. At that moment Cherie had become the offender parent who had produced the pre-ferred sibling as well as also being the baby. This was clearly re-enacted in this session when she arrived with a photo album and sat at my feet showing me photographs of her family and friends.

It was a few months later that a re-enactment occurred in a session (of abandonment and return) with a symmetrising of subject and object with time. Cherie began the session sleepily saying that she was too tired to do therapy and it was clear that she was struggling to stay awake. The not unusual responses around the destruction of conscious-ness were pointless. She left the session knowing that I would remain there for the duration, commenting that she might be back. (After a patient leaves like this they rarely, if ever, return.)

During her absence I found myself being drawn to take from my briefcase an assessment I had penned on another patient whereby ques-tions had been raised by that patient's treating consultant. In my mind I sat very much involved in a triadic relationship (consultant, assessed patient, and myself) in the absence of Cherie. After some twenty min-utes or so, I was surprised by the return of Cherie and rather messily replaced the chapters in my briefcase. She said she'd had a drink and a walk and had woken up.

Her return gave the opportunity of exploring the notion of leaving and returning and its familiarity. She linked this to her experience of a mother who gave her up to someone else, like a parcel, at the same time as feeling replaced by other siblings, and enabled me to interpret along palindromic lines relating to the index offence. Her response was: "When my mother came back and heard about the murder charge she was very angry and shocked … She was really angry with me." She closed the session by rather dreamily commenting that it's "all begin-ning to make some sense".

More recently she has been able to comment about her hatred ("with a vengeance") of her next sibling and about her desire to make her mother feel guilty, in that she created something for her mother to be jealous about, and has recently referred to this as "payback time".

I have referred to the trans-generational transference of trauma and its identification through the critical date that exists in the calendar of the mind. This trans-generational factor is referred to by the late Murray

Cox in his book *Mutative Metaphors in Psychotherapy*, when he talks about life sentences investing a patient with an emotional legacy from a previous generation: "Unexpressed affective loadings may be handed on to their successors by those who were unable to tolerate experience which was rightly theirs" (Cox, 1987, p. 45). This then is no new phenomenon, and Cox goes on to suggest that people are not free to live their own lives because of the secret lives of their parents.

I now want to end the chapter by referring to a more creative reaction to the arrival of a sibling that was Sigmund Freud's. Freud's father, Jacob, was forty-one and a half when Sigmund's younger brother, Julius, was born. When Sigmund Freud was forty-one years of age he gave birth to his own (metaphorical) baby in the summer of 1897, namely psychoanalysis. Moreover, it was in the summer of that year, aged forty-one, that Freud dreamt his own incest dream and in subsequent letters of that year that he established, through his own self-analysis, that he had discovered in himself his passion for his mother and his jealousy of his father (Earnshaw, 1995, pp. 100–102). Might this suggest that, in the face of his displacement, as Juliet Mitchell (2000) writes, he was thrown back to the Oedipal arena and to those responsible for his sibling's arrival? It is surely more than coincidence that the Oedipus complex within psychoanalysis was born at that point. Murderous phantasies by Sigmund towards Julius might have been expected. The fact that Julius died after eight months may have explained the reparative work that became psychoanalysis and it is perhaps no less ironic that the story of Oedipus begins with attempted infanticide that is never mentioned by Freud. In the Sophocles play, on which Freud based his account, a shepherd recounts that at Oedipus' birth his mother had instructed that her son be left on a hillside to die (Sophocles, 2008). I am more and more struck by the way the sibling link and death theme, at the birth of psychoanalysis, has got buried until much more recently by the concentration on the Oedipal triangle, as if Sigmund was the only one who counted with his parents.

Note

1. Primary process describes the logic found in dreams rather than conscious thought and is not governed by the ego's reality principle. Primary process thinking does not conform to a sense of space or time and produces symbols by condensation or displacement of significant attributes. See Freud (1911a).

CHAPTER TWO

Perverse triangulation*

This chapter explores the thinking around the psychodynamics of power and its effects upon treatment. The subject area will be to look at the necessity of triangulating treatment (through the application of dynamic thinking) by specifically focusing upon the way in which this process is not being appropriately undertaken. An assessment on a serial sex offender is presented and the subsequent formulation is shown to have aspects of a generalising value that helps in looking at what such patients need institutionally in order to address conflict and to counter perverse defence formations. Moreover, consideration is given to the significance of institutional mirroring in the way that it meets such patients' perverse defensive needs, rather than facilitating their true needs.

Mathematically, when one corner of a triangle collapses it reverts to becoming a straight line. As a result of such a collapse, this straight line would indicate a preceding perverse triangle.

---

*This chapter was first read at the International Association of Forensic Psychotherapy (IAFP) Conference on 25 April 2003 in Arnhem, Holland, and was first published in *Forensische Psychiatrie und Psychotherapie* (2004).

Developmentally, perverse triangulation could be presented as occurring when the absence of recognition and inclusion of the father into the mother/child dyad takes place.

Politically, perverse triangulation occurs when, in problem solving, a particular type of reflective thinking collapses or is eliminated in the pressure of seeking solutions. This results in the perpetuation of original problems in a different form, so that one of the three factors involved is lost to view.

Thus in all of these three situations, the potential of three becomes an actuality of two, or one.

This triangulation of perspectives, namely the mathematical, developmental, and political, allows us to focus on a clinical example whereby a patient, Richard, compulsively re-enacts his need to pervert triangulation. When we broaden our gaze, we see problems of perverse triangulation occurring and mirrored within his institutional structure. My patient Richard eliminated another's perspective (representing the father developmentally) which caused the collapse of the triangle into the straight alternative "tram lines" of mathematically serving his time (his sentence) to satisfy the institutional/political perspective. In this way the third reflective factor can have a tendency to get left out of the treatment programme.

My formulation of Richard's psychopathology centres on the trauma experienced around the birth of his next sibling, when he was three years of age, and develops the thinking from the previous chapter. The arrival of the sibling generated acute anxiety in his understanding of his relation to his mother, with the consequence that he then had to encounter the triangulating inclusion of father's penis into mother— their union. This union presented the exacerbating corollary that he was now displaced/replaced in his position with mother in reality, by the arrival of the sibling. To defend against this annihilatory experience (whereby he felt potentially eliminated in the triangle with mother and father, as well as mother and sibling), he in his turn eliminates his father, and thus creates the illusion that he is the father to the hated sibling. This I experienced at first hand when interviewing Richard for an assessment, in that he would dismantle any comment that I made and put it back together again in his own way. This response of his had a compulsive quality.

At this point it is important to mention Abelin, who coins the term "triangulation" (referring to the father) in his contribution to the book

Rapprochement (1980). Abelin presents as a core concept the important role of the father in early development in conveying the contrast in gender identity, and, in so doing, the presence of father's penis demonstrates the first powerful landmark of bodily difference in early development. Moreover, it has been my understanding in two recent assessments on child sex offenders that the roots of their psychopathology lay in the traumatic experience of the "elimination of the penis". In particular, this has been linked with the arrival of a sibling, and that a distinctive feature of this new arrival (sister) was of its "hermetically sealed" nature, that is, an un-negotiable idealisation of the sibling's gender. Richard, as the less ideal boy, experienced feelings of elimination, displacement, and jealous rage.

The positive role of father in healthy triangulation is perhaps emphasised by the following:

1. Richard gave his permission to be thought about outside of the clinical setting.
2. His treating consultant was present when this chapter was first presented at the International Association of Forensic Psychotherapy (IAFP) conference in Arnhem.
3. The bringing of this thinking in the UK to Arnhem, as a third dimension, for international discussion and its subsequent publication, represents the trans-cultural dimension.

Triangulation has had particular resonance on the international stage recently, where it has been difficult to achieve in the political sphere, affecting the United Nations (UN) in the US/Iraq conflict with unresolved disagreement over issues of war and peace.

Closer to our home in the UK politically, in 1998 the government drew attention to what was presumably experienced as a perverse situation in relation to the case of a man called Michael Stone. The perversity was highlighted by the state feeling *"powerless* to intervene in a case where someone has yet to commit a criminal offence and whom the medical profession consider to be untreatable, even if that person poses a very real danger to society" (Home Affairs Committee, 1999–2000, paragraph 3; emphasis in original).

In 1998 Stone received three life sentences for murder. He was a drug addict with a history of violence and criminal convictions and was diagnosed with a severe personality disorder, but was not classified as mentally ill. He apparently sought medical support before the crime, but had been refused (because he didn't meet the criteria), having previously been treated by local agencies over a long period, but not detained. The government became concerned to express "the reconciliation of two powerful forces—the need to protect the civil liberties of those who had not committed an offence; and the need to protect society from the offence that they commit" (Home Affairs Committee, 1999–2000, paragraph 2).

The result was to propose mental health legislation introducing a generic and inclusive definition of mental disorder, which meant that in future people with all forms of personality disorder could be subject to compulsion, and that Primary Care Trusts (PCTs) could no longer easily dodge provision of services for personality disorder on the grounds of "untreatability". Under the existing legislation, individuals deemed untreatable could be excluded from compulsion, and for a long time people with personality disorder have been excluded from services because of ambivalence about treating them.

The political process was triggered through the experience of feeling powerless within the dyad of patient and carer, when faced with that such as Stone and his doctor. The position of the doctor in his triad (of himself, patient, and presenting symptoms) was one of also feeling powerless, given the lack of legislation available to treat personality disorder. Moreover, the patient also felt powerless to face or reflect on parts of his mind most relevant to his behaviour. This powerlessness within the triangle, whereby somebody who has something to contribute is left out, can be perpetuated. We might say a perversity can be recreated if the powerless third intervenes without being able to hold the other two in tension, rather than merely eliminating one from the dyad and consequently from the triad.

In forensic settings, both doctors and the therapeutic process can be pushed to the sidelines when security is stressed above therapy. This reminds me of the beneficial potential of the father's initiation of flexibility in a triangle involving mother and child, and the necessity of the father to have worked through his initial three-person jealousy about the newcomer breaking up the husband/wife duo. Wooster has argued that the "father's initiation of flexibility in a triangle may be the later counterpart of mother's flexibility in the dyad" (Wooster, 1983, p. 38). This is perhaps best reflected in the Perseus myth, where Perseus' mirror creates a triangle that resolves his dilemma in being able to slay the

Gorgon without himself dying in the process were he to look straight at it. With the absence of the reflective mirror (father), the twosome can get caught up in a form of malignant mirroring, from which often only one survives.

Nonetheless, there can be huge resistance to accommodating this reflective other and many of the problems of the triangle surface in families, therapeutic groups, and institutions. I am suggesting that all these difficulties have in common their tendency, under such pressures, to collapse in overt or covert ways into unrepresented one- or two- dimensional thinking. When this chapter was initially presented as a paper I sought to keep our chair Louisa Brunori in the triangulation of presentation by quoting from her article "Siblings", where she says: "The newcomer will be put in a position within the continuum messiah—demon expected to be either the exponent or destroyer of the status quo" (1998, p. 312).

For the developing child, the recognition and inclusion of the father in the dyad with mother is essential to the maturation process. I am particularly drawing attention to the situation that arises when confirmation of the presence of father occurs at the moment of birth of another sibling, which demands a stretching of the numbers involved from two to three or more. I would like you to consider in similar terms to the arrival of a new family member, a new unit in a hospital, because it is at this point in time that I am identifying as crucial the development of natural or, alternatively, perverse accommodations to such an event.

One of the four sites chosen in the UK known as the "Dangerous and Severe Personality Disorder Unit" (DSPD) was in Broadmoor, opening in 2005.[1] It constituted an early pilot centre with an infrastructure dedicated for assessment and management of dangerous male patients with a severe personality disorder. It was this "special new arrival" in the institution that required additional reflective thinking and consideration, in the way that it corresponded to the new arrival of a sibling, regarding the effects both on the institution as a whole, and on how the new arrival was to be treated. The new DSPD Unit was a standalone unit, its residents hermetically sealed off from the rest of the Broadmoor population, creating the potential for the feelings generated by this arrival to be exacerbated, if it was not conceptualised and thought about. The potential that a perverse solution could result was very possible. That which the father represents, that is, reflective thinking (particularly thinking that links the past with the present—

the father of the past who created the child of the present) could be eliminated and replaced by a form of delusional thinking of paternity, which eliminates any significance given to the past. This, in a forensic setting, is tantamount to a denial of an offender's history with significant ramifications in relation to treatment and care plans. This perverse solution to the circumstances parallels the clinical example I am about to present of Richard. It also serves to emphasise the importance and appropriateness of "other" thinking, represented by the father. This is a core feature of psychodynamic work, where the relationship between the patient and therapist (transference) provides a way of understanding how the internal world (past relationships) affects current relationships.

In the annihilatory anxieties generated politically by the Michael Stone case, it was important for the government to become involved in the dyad, represented by the health service and patient, in such a way that both health service and patient felt included in finding a creative way forward and enabling all corners of the triangle to be firmly in place. The perverse solution results if insufficient sensitivity and thought is given when working both with the existing patients in Broadmoor and with the new DSPD patients. I am highlighting as a critical feature, the simultaneous birth of three-person jealousy, when a new unit arrives in the institution, and this is a part of what Michael Jacobs describes as the eternal triangle, "linking two points of the triangle out there and in here … and using the third point back there—the past" (1999, p. 10). The "out there" is the information that a patient brings to any therapeutic context. The "in here" is the transferential relationship as it links with the "out there" and "the past".

To highlight how triangulation can be perverted, a recent extended assessment on a patient called Richard will now be presented.

Richard was referred by his consultant for a psychodynamic assessment to consider his suitability for psychotherapy. My formulation regarding Richard's psychopathology is that he repeatedly and compulsively separates out any meaningful understanding of cause and effect in relation to his early life and his offending history and creates his own understanding of it. This forms a defence against feelings associated with two-person and three-person jealousy, which were traumatically experienced in his early life and became re-enacted in his offending, and there has not been any drawing out of his capacity to reflect.

The pattern of his offences took the form, on repeated occasions, of Richard hijacking a courting couple in a car and tying up the male, either placing him in the boot or on the back seat of the car. He then sexually assaulted/raped the female in the front. He would then put them back again in their original location, before departing the scene.

In our exchanges, he denied there being any significance in a man being present while he assaulted the woman. Once challenged, however, he acknowledged the importance he had attributed to this generating impotent rage in the male. Hitherto, his understanding of his offending focused solely on needing to take control over women. He would not tolerate any link being made with the original woman in his life, that is, his mother, even though she had been a pivotal figure regarding major events.

This splitting up of the couple was to feature as a significant dynamic between the two of us in that, as I have stated, he would dismantle any potential meaningful comment that I might offer and put it back together again in his own way. For example, he was able to talk about a dream he had had between our sessions that featured his inability to play (control) the keys on a piano, until that is the piano split into two. He then found that he was able to begin playing really well as the piano reformed into a whole again. When I suggested that this was indicative of my experience in his dismantling of any comment I might make before putting it back together again in his own words, he somewhat predictably said that he disagreed! He also furnished a number of examples regarding the breaking up of a couple. An important memory he related serves, I think, as a striking example in its representation of this splitting up of the parental couple dynamics.

He was working as a mechanic in a coach firm, as a young man, where coaches used to fill up from the fuel line in the mornings before they did their runs. One morning he chose to close the valve down on the injector pump that controlled the fuel, which consequently prevented the coaches from receiving any diesel. When the problem came to light and he was informed, he obviously knew how to resolve the problem and after setting it right he received the due applause and admiration for his cure. This is indicative of him delusionally triumphing over the male (penis/fuel line) in dismantling the potency of its interaction with the female (coach) and how this is linked to his early history and trauma. It is noteworthy that the index offence was committed when he was the same age as his father had been when

Richard's younger sister was born (Richard had been three years old). I believe this represents a fixed point of trauma in his mind that he has attempted to defend against re-experiencing since. His sister's birth was followed by idealisation of her by both parents ("hermetically sealed") and by the subsequent denigration and abuse of Richard, particularly at the hands of his father. Enuresis developed (the leaking of anger) and behavioural problems, resulting in the end with his expulsion from the home.

There is, in addition, the significance of his being sexually abused as a child (aged about six) by a door-to-door salesman who had become a regular visitor to Richard's family home, taking Richard on occasions for a ride in his car. Richard subsequently felt power over his abuser when bumping into him on an occasion of being out shopping with his mother—who was apparently unaware of the abuse. Richard recalled the unease in the face of his abuser and further recalled the feeling of control he felt he had over the man, as if keeping him tied up. He remembered the look in the man's eyes as the same as a look he recalled in his younger sister's eyes when she was a baby in her cot and he'd fed her with Smarties through the cot bars, causing her to choke. This look was one of anxiety and fear and Richard felt a degree of control, not only over his abuser in the shop, but also over his sister. This control of the male abuser, while with the female (mother), I feel links with the formulation and perhaps presents an understanding of the significance of the car in his crimes.

More crucially, in linking the abuse to the arrival/birth of his sister together with my experience of him in the sessions, I wondered whether he needs to split up any meaningful contact, that is, between mother and father or mother and mother's friend, the visiting salesman, or, as he subsequently did with me, any meaningful links made in our interview. My thinking is that he does this because he finds the possibility and consequences of meaningful contact too traumatic to bear, that is, the arrival of a sister, who removes him from his position and subsequently receives his abuse. Following his splitting up of the meaningful contact, that is, through his envy and jealousy of their connection, he then puts them back together again in his own way. It is as if he now carries the illusion that the couple is of his own making and, rather like mending the valve on the injector pump at the coach garage, he can now bathe in the fantasy of being responsible for bringing the couple together again.

We might say that he defends against the trauma of the birth of his "hermetically sealed", impenetrably protected, sibling, by deluding himself that he was responsible for creating her. Moreover, he compulsively and repeatedly separates out any meaningful understanding of cause and effect external to him, which is effectively an abuse of all the psychological input that he has received to date, since it would appear to be free of any direct transferential understanding. Therefore this has enabled him to create his own omnipotent understanding of cause and effect.

Richard has had seventeen different types of therapeutic group experience (where any psychodynaimc input was rare) and two brief supportive individual therapeutic experiences. This dismantling of cause and effect provides some understanding behind the fact that he changed his name at the time of his index offence, indicating a break with any link with the past, such that he has recreated himself.

This separating out of the potentially creative couple, whom he then controls, enables him to act out the delusion of becoming the partner to the mother while unconsciously projecting into the father, who is tied up, his own feelings of being replaced, left both powerless and full of jealous rage. This results in him remaining free from re-experiencing those feelings, while he can continue to projectively identify them into his victims. All of the offences contained a figure in his external life/relationships of whom he was jealous. This clinical example I feel serves to highlight both the intra-psychic and interpersonal struggle that Richard has in being able to accommodate somebody else into a dyadic relationship—that is, father into the dyad of mother and himself.

So, not unlike the government in its consequent reaction to the problem posed by Michael Stone, for Richard there was a similar feeling of powerlessness in the face of potential annihilation/elimination. Richard, as I have described, resorted to a perverse solution. Might it therefore not be that father's/the government's renewed involvement with Broadmoor has mirrored this dynamic by producing this new, hermetically sealed, sibling? Sufficient reflective thinking must therefore be entertained to prevent a similar perverse solution being repeated. I have wondered whether this is in part mirrored by the institution's removal/elimination of the female patients from Broadmoor, representing the idealised daughter.

I have already commented on the importance of reflective thinking about the impact upon the existing siblings in Broadmoor in relation to the new arrival of the DSPD unit and want to extend it further in relation to one aspect of the planned thinking about the new unit itself, namely the lock-up policy at night. Before doing so, I want to draw attention to the article by Joyce McDougall (1972) entitled "Primal Scene and Sexual Perversion". In her article she writes about the scene I have been describing, that in which a defensive compromise was reached by Richard to deal with his rage at displacement from his position with mother. Joyce McDougall, in exploring the sexual perversions, comments that perversion is "an answer to incestuous wishes and the frustrated rage which greets their non fulfilment, [sic] little is explained since these disappointments form a universal trauma, an integral part of the human predicament" (1972, p. 371). She goes on to question why those children who adopt a perverse solution are specially marked for this illusion. She suggests that an outcome to this is that a new sexuality is created and the primal scene reinvented, which contains the wish to annihilate the original primal scene and the complimentary wish to recreate the child as the sole object, with the mother. Her clinical experience indicates that precipitating factors which in many cases have the force of screen memories (like those of Richard with his sister in the cot, the abusive man in the shop, and the petrol fuel line) are often family events "such as the birth of a sibling [interpreted as] ... incontrovertible proof of the mother's infidelity" (McDougall, 1972, p. 375). More centrally, Joyce McDougall writes about the all-important negation of the genital relation between the parents in perversion. She writes:

> "[T]he father's penis thus has no role in the mother's sexual life ... in his attempt to know nothing of the relation between his parents ... the pervert is facing a losing battle with reality. Like trying to repair a crumbling wall with Scotch tape—it has to be redone every day."

> (McDougall, 1972, pp. 377–378)

Behind these anxieties and the narcissistic wounds of the primal scene lie deeper terrors concerning separation and individual identity, namely terrors of annihilation.

With such patients, the father, although possibly present, is re-presented as an absence. This lack in the internal world threatens the pervert's identity, and it is only the perverse, or reconstituted, primal scene, as in Richard's case, putting the couple back together again in his own way, that permits some sort of illusory recovery of the father (penis). This perverse solution affords some protection against the overwhelming dependence on the mother and the equally dangerous desire to merge with her. Richard's case follows McDougall's clinical experience, where she says that "many cases of addiction or delinquency of severe acting out character pathology show similar mental mechanisms" (1972, p. 371). McDougall ends her article saying that the reinvented primal scene is a privileged form of manic defence, which is preferable to madness. These points are also taken up by Dorothy Lloyd-Owen (from the Portman Clinic) in her 2003 article on perverse females where she discusses the valuable insight offered by Mervyn Glasser regarding core complex phenomena. "Core complex" describes the individual's terror of annihilation through being abandoned or equally engulfed by the object, which results in painfully conflicting impulses to both merge with and flee from the object (Glasser, 1979, pp. 278–279). Most strikingly Lloyd-Owen concludes:

> I cannot over emphasise the importance of thought over action in the face of the pressure for action that such patients exert on both individuals and institutions. For the therapist, the struggle to maintain a thinking space and a capacity to think is critical in the face of activity as defence.
>
> (Lloyd-Owen, 2003, p. 295)

She emphasises the importance of supervision as a reflective space to facilitate triangulation, when such patients have rarely experienced a good containing couple and have consequent difficulties around Oedipal resolution.

In concurrence with Joyce McDougall, my own understanding of the original traumatic roots of Richard's psychopathology lie in the incontrovertible proof of mother's infidelity to Richard—the primal scene that produced a sibling who displaced and effectively eliminated Richard. His inability to accommodate the triangulation inherent in his family structure caused his manic defence and the addictive quality of his compulsive behaviour in the shape of perverse triangulation. This involved the elimination of the father and the illusion of a reconstituted primal scene where Richard becomes the partner to mother while projecting into the father, that is, splitting off his own traumatic experience of powerlessness, castration, and rage. The modus operandi of his offending acted out and encapsulated this perverse triangulation. It provides both a projective identification of his infantile boy self and a product of the fused punishment both of his own penis and that of his father, in a retaliatory, and vengeful, way which we might also describe as "talionic".

In summary, therefore, I am drawing attention to the situation that arises when confirmation of the presence of father occurs at the moment of birth (of another sibling) that demands a stretching of the mind. Perhaps, of all the places in the world, Arnhem, where this chapter was first presented, has given us the metaphor of "a bridge too far". This relates to the story of the failure of Operation Market Garden during World War II with the allied attempt to break through German lines and seize several bridges in the occupied Netherlands including one at Arnhem, with the main objective of outflanking German defences. The comment is attributed to General Frederick Browning, deputy commander of the First Allied Airborne Army, who told Field Marshall Bernard Montgomery, the operations architect, before the operation: "I think we may be going a bridge too far." The operation to take the bridge at Arnhem failed. This makes me realise how careful we need to be in stretching the mind to create a bridge that represents the father, given that if a perverse alternative is adopted, the consequences may be in terms of greater nightmarish proportions.

The defensive mechanism of splitting draws attention to not only the splitting endemic in separating out the male and female, but all forms of splitting. Klein comments: "[T]he infant splits the object and the self, but the effect of this phantasy is a very real one, because it leads to feelings and relations (and later on thought-processes) being in fact cut off from one another" (1946, p. 6). For instance, it alerts me to the consequences that may emanate from the night and day lock-up policy in the new DSPD unit. In the policy there was as many hours locked up alone with a television as there was therapeutically engaged on the ward. This reminds me of a paper presented by Dr Sarkar at the IAFP Conference in Stuttgart entitled "The other 23 hours" (2005), and I feel I extend some of his thinking here. While there appeared to be very sound pragmatic reasons for this lock-up policy, which I understood had been imposed by the Home Office, it nonetheless appeared that the joint plans of the Department of Health and the Home Office indicated that the latter have not been reflective enough in their thinking. This all had the potential of the balance in the triangle (care-security-patient) potentially becoming disturbed. I wondered whether the elimination of the patient might represent an equivalent to the elimination in the mind of the healthy triangulating primal scene, as a perpetuation of the perverse triangulation. The creative solution would have been to allow for the existence of the split-off night-time, in the form of some shared activities, to become an inclusive part of the ward milieu. It is easy to allow reflective thinking about what happens at night to slip, effectively eliminating this aspect of reality. One wonders what happens when you replace primal scene time by an omnipresent television. Finally, I want to stress that, when all eyes are on the new arrival, what can get left out are the father and/or existing sibling or, in the way that I am looking at it, the forgotten night-time, when feelings of two-person envy and three-person jealousy can be exacerbated.

Note

1. Since writing this paper the government has decided to decommission the DSPD service in Broadmoor; see postscript at the end of Chapter Five.

CHAPTER THREE

Murder: persecuted by jealousy*

"Full fathoms five thy father lies;
of his bones are coral made:
Those are pearls that were his eyes
Nothing of him doth fade,
But doth suffer a seachange
Into something rich and strange
Sea-Nymphs hourly ring his knell:
Ding-Dong
Hark! Now I hear them,—ding-dong, bell."

—Shakespeare, The Tempest, Act 1, Scene 2

This chapter develops the thinking of Chapter Two on perverse triangulation. Its focus is on exploring the dynamics surrounding the offence of murder, in that murder I believe represents the "solution" to experiencing persecution (rendered impotent as a

---

*This chapter was first read at a meeting of the International Association of Forensic Psychotherapy (IAFP) Conference on 2 April 2004 in Edinburgh and subsequently published in *Murder: A Psychotherapeutic Investigation* (2008). This is the amended version.

result of feeling harassed, tormented, and pursued) by a threesome experience, that is, in three-person jealousy, in the delusional belief that the resulting twosome will eliminate any further feelings of persecution. The persecution is an intrinsic part of an internal configuration so that any external act of murder only represents a momentary, perverse, and ultimately ineffective solution. It is my view that three-person jealousy is a critical feature in all murder in that it represents, externally, the internal experience of being killed off in a relationship that the perpetrator had with another by the arrival of the third. By extension, the persistent persecution at having to accommodate the third into a two-person relationship, particularly when the subject has not yet digested the dynamics involved in the two-person relationship, creates the environment for murderousness to be triggered when external circumstances mirror or approximate to such an internal configuration.

In symmetry with this, while presenting the clinical picture of a man who murdered his girlfriend and whose immediate start in life meant that he had to accommodate a third into the relationship between himself and his mother (like a twin), you are to be asked to hold in mind another person into the relationship between yourself and the patient I am presenting: the convicted murderer Ian Huntley, who will be briefly discussed at the end of this chapter and is a public case that has distinct parallels.

The reader has been asked to hold in mind the fact that the Huntley circumstances will be discussed and, given its press and media coverage and that it is a more recent example than the patient I will be discussing, it may be that the Huntley issue holds more interest for you. Therefore your affective attachment to the Huntley case is greater, which creates the circumstances whereby the patient Mr G struggles to compete. This can put the reader in the position of holding two in mind, where there can be a tendency to eliminate one for the other. Moreover, in writing many of these chapters I have also had to hold a twinning in mind. This particular chapter was also the subject of a presentation at the IAFP Conference in Edinburgh in April 2004 on "Understanding persecution". I need therefore to relate to the twinship of "book" and "conference" by identifying their similarities and differences and having a relationship with both that is linked and yet separate. Should I merge the two then I would be murdering the benefits of a threesome for the sake of a twosome and while this would be easier for me (less thinking and work), I would be merely repeating the same crime I want to understand and think about. Indeed, this is so often our experience in the press and media when reporting a murder. The very crime the media are so drawn to describe is committed again in its reporting, in that the threesomeness represented by reflective thinking, especially concerning the complexity of the situation, is so ubiquitously eliminated in favour of the dyadic twosomeness of the good/bad scenario succumbed to in much crime reporting.

To begin with our patient Mr G, there were two significant areas of trauma in his early infancy. The first was the loss of his father five months prior to his birth. This was a trauma for his mother who was unable to come to terms with this loss and mourn appropriately. Research work, particularly by Bourne and Lewis (1984, 1992), has shown how difficult it is for normal mourning processes to take place around the time of birth. The denial and confusion involved in accepting "minus one" at the time of creating "plus one" has been further highlighted by the same researchers' important work on stillbirths, which demonstrates the hidden resistances that appear to take place both to mourning and to its subsequent remembering and recording in history. Their research work illustrates how difficult it is to sort out the emotional complexities of situations where births and deaths are found in close proximity.

When Mr G was born, not only was he given part of his father's name, it is also highly likely that in phantasy he became identified with his biological father by his mother through projective identification. Effectively he had forced on him, through the process of projective identification, the third dead other, as a compound image in the relationship between mother and himself. He therefore had to embrace another into himself, whereby a part of his own self was killed off, so that he was related to by his mother as if he was the dead husband/father who was now still alive, causing a part of his own self newly alive to be now killed off. It is suggested that Mr G's mother became traumatised by the loss of her husband who represented one part of the triangle (of mother, father, and son). His mother was unable to deal with her loss and thereby unable to hold her part in the triangle and therefore projected the loss of the father into her foetus/son. (This dynamic has deep resonance with the perpetrator of the Dunblane Massacre that I address in Chapter Nine.)

This gave rise to Mr G having to embrace his representation of father and he has consequently lived his life being persecuted by any tendency towards a threesomeness, which always has a tendency to carry the seeds of threats leading to eruptions of murderous jealousy. Such dynamics would have generated an underlying rage in having a part of himself wiped out and replaced with the dead father. This provides an inner world template, whereby a part of his own self has been killed off (not being seen wholly for who he is, but more of a composite figure with dead father) and it is this killing that he repeats in any triangular scenario that emerges externally, particularly emphasised in his index offence, which I will turn to shortly after a discussion of the particular transference experience.

A common theme countertransferentially in the work with Mr G was his struggle to embrace anything new—that is, anything other than that that existed between himself and me and his perceived control of our dyad. So I might say something and the moment that I began to speak his mind would shut down and he would be unable to accommodate the thinking. This was experienced by me in the countertransference as a persistent destruction of my reflective function (thinking), and my survival of this was one of the main therapeutic tasks.

Moreover, I felt that the dilemma that Mr G was faced with during the start of the relationship with his mother was similarly faced by me in our first session. Mr G informed me in the first minute of our first session that the timing of our session coincided with his weekly off-ward visit to the library, which was important to him. Given that Mr G was aware that this was the only time that I could meet with him and that his insistence that his regular visits to the library were a vital part of his week (he was an avid reader and he sought solace in childhood by visits to the library) I was faced with the potential destruction/killing off of our relationship together, in the face of the competing demand of the library. I also knew that this was the ward slot for visits to the library and felt angry that there was a competing attachment that was potentially destructive at the beginning of this new attachment in therapy. My response was to say "Perhaps we need to find a way that you can receive both", and I firmly took the stance that the time with me would not be compromised and that I would work with the triangulating third in our relationship within the ward structure (which was the clinical team) in finding a way to ensure his relationship with the library was also not compromised. He visibly warmed to this, although subsequently smiled, suggesting that I was mad when I commented that enabling him to have both books and therapy was as if he was being given the opportunity to have both parents in support of him.

In this opening session it was as if I was being put in the same affective field as he had been post-natally. Something historically was interfering with forming an initial attachment and forcing him to have to accommodate its presence. I believe my response to him, which was one in support of the real relationship between the two of us not being affected by the relationship he had with the "deadness" of the written word (while not denying the importance of it), provided him with something good.

An alternative solution would have been that the therapy or his library trips would have been lost (a potential of three being reduced to two) and when he introduced the dilemma this momentarily became a real option, as if a form of murderousness featured. It is this unexpected intrusion into the dyad that Mr G was originally faced with post-natally and which was a critical feature in his index offence.

Just prior to his index offence he learnt that his girlfriend was meeting with a male work colleague socially, under the auspices that she was helping him with a problem. His girlfriend returned with the colleague to the accommodation where she and Mr G were living and spent a while in the late evening talking together, while Mr G recalls feeling enraged and livid with jealousy. After this man left they retired to their separate beds (they were living in his girlfriend's father's house) and in the early morning Mr G strangled his girlfriend, after which he had the impulse to have intercourse with her, but was physically unable. This murder could therefore be viewed as a "solution", whereby he brought to an end the feelings he was having of jealousy which were persecuting him. In exploring the identifications/symmetries at the time of the offence, it is important to consider that at the time he believed his girlfriend was a few days pregnant with his child, so that effectively he believed he was killing a mother who was pregnant with child. Here I suggest that at the moment of strangulation he was killing his girlfriend (representing his mother) with a child (representing himself). This would place him in identifying perversely with his father. In essence he was killing off his own self while at the same time surviving (akin to his mother's experience whereby there was the survival of a death when her husband was recreated in her son, Mr G). That there was a killing off of a pregnant mother reverses the original scenario, where the pregnant mother survived the death of the father. The trigger for this murder was the jealousy he felt, creating the potential for the loss of his girlfriend to somebody against whom he felt he could not compete.

An additional factor that suggests that a reversal was taking place is that he and his girlfriend were staying in her father's house at the time and her father was asleep in another bedroom. Mr G had felt that her father had often related to his daughter as if she was his wife (a similar denial of his wife's death). In Mr G's mind his girlfriend therefore represented a twin figure, one who was dead (his girlfriend's mother) and the other who was alive (the child)—resonating with his own twinning. Moreover, her family circumstance was identical to his own, in that she had also lost a parent, and her other parent, in being unable to deal with the loss, had twinned her with the parent who had died.

Following her death, his girlfriend's father was left with the experience of having to deal with the feelings of loss associated with his wife/child, as opposed to the wife/child having to deal with the feelings of the death of the father, which points to an important reversal and projective identification of his own early experience.

Mr G's impulse for sexual intercourse with the dead victim was unsuccessful due to his inability to develop an erection (corresponding in equivalence to my feelings in the countertransference). Given that Mr G's life has been spent persecuted by being twinned with a dead other and has been an internal dynamic whereby he has felt impotent, given the deadness, to be able to engage in any intercourse, the scene of the crime represents an external re-enactment of that internal picture.

We can return to Matte Blanco's (1975) insights on the complexities of the identifications at work here and apply his understanding of unconscious process where gross symmetrisation takes place. To recap, Matte Blanco said that conscious logical thinking usually works within a framework of distinguishing things and that the unconscious that Freud investigated tends to unite and fuse everything. As we go about our business the human mind continuously classifies and this classifying involves the registration of sameness or identity, which Matte Blanco termed "symmetry". Relating to the world also/equally entails discriminating the relationships between things, for which he coined the term "asymmetry". The apparently inappropriate mixing or insertion of symmetrical thought into asymmetrical relations is called "symmetrisation". Symmetrisation is a feature of psychotic thought.

So, as previously stated, in thinking about psychotic processes, the psychotic sees symmetry where the non-psychotic person does not and the presence of strong emotion may inflate symmetrisation to an infinite degree. Given the strength of Mr G's feelings of jealousy (in addition to a life-long internal persecution) gross symmetrisation took place whereby subjects and objects became fused, merged, and reversible.

I would suggest that Mr G was faced with having to embrace a third into the relationship between himself and his partner. This resonated with his early experience in such a way that there became no awareness of time so that his current experience was symmetrised with his early experience and the rage erupted. In relation to the absence or elimination of time, Matte Blanco said that in symmetrisation there is no awareness of time sequence so that time as we know it (linear and sequential) disappears.

Persecution by the third remains a constant and hostile presence. This was exacerbated a few years after Mr G's birth when his mother remarried and was further magnified when she then gave birth to his half-brother. His rage regarding these displacements was demonstrated through his diurnal and nocturnal encopresis, lasting many years from shortly after his half-brother's birth. This soiling can be understood as angry attacks in a not dissimilar way to murder. So there is acting-out where there is an absence of reflective thought. Through the process of psychotherapy, Mr G is beginning to be able to understand some of this, which means that it puts a strain on his capacity to be able to contain any thinking around his feelings associated with rivalry.

This was particularly highlighted when one day he turned up for a session with bruises on his face. I learnt that the day before at 6pm in the evening, while watching television in his room, he collapsed unexpectedly, falling to the floor and injuring himself (he had passed out into unconsciousness). When I explored the circumstances at the time, I learnt that he had been watching an episode of *The Simpsons* on television and upon further enquiry learnt that this particular episode resonated deeply, in that its storyline was effectively autobiographical. While the clinical team were naturally keen to explore any other possible physical reasons for this unexpected collapse, Mr G felt that the psychodynamic understanding that we momentarily reached (before destroying it) in that session was as close to truth as we could get: that is that the sibling rivalry that was demonstrated in this episode by an older brother towards a younger sibling (which was murderous), resulted in reconciliation between the siblings and an acknowledgement of their true feelings. This linked deeply with Mr G's struggle in reconciling himself to rivalry that was unable to become fully conscious in him, causing his collapse into unconsciousness. We could say that this was a similar killing off of consciousness that took place in the index offence.

In living his life as the embodiment of a duality, in which one part of that duality is unable ever to compete successfully with the other, means that he is forever persecuted by its presence and seemingly unable to resolve the rivalry. This dead part of the duality (represented by his father) was always the victor in that father was experienced universally as an idealised figure when alive and so therefore somebody with whom Mr G could never compete (have intercourse with).

This dual figure was perfectly represented when Mr G attended a session more recently without teeth. Mr G has a full set of false teeth and apparently during the week between sessions his plate had cracked. This was being repaired, which meant that he attended his session toothless. We were able to think about the duality of varying ends of the spectrum of toothlessness (on the one hand, in infancy without teeth, and, on the other, in old age having lost all your teeth). This led on to thinking about his experience of feeling toothless in the face of a rival (father).

What I would like to emphasise is the feeling of deadness that can be pervasive in the work, given the destruction that can be experienced in relation to any reflective thinking. My attempts at an inter-personal/inter-psychic intercourse are often rendered impossible, in that I am put in the frustrating and enraging position of feeling impotent to engage with the deadness that he portrays—so that his intra-psychic impotence, in the face of this persecutory internal object, which cannot be related to because it is dead, is a persistent dynamic interpersonally.

While there is no direct and overt attack upon me there is an attack upon what I offer. There has been a slight shift in his reaction from initially killing off the intrusive other that comes into the room, represented by my thinking, to his capacity to begin to think about this destructive anger and how it becomes manifest.

An example of this arose when I had written in a report forming part of an annual review of our work that it was clear that he had not reached any position of remorse in relation to his victim (a conclusion reached largely on the persistent murderousness in the room). Some time later in a session he was talking about having seen a television programme discussing the issue of remorse and said how difficult it was for anybody to tell that somebody had reached that position. At the same time he was also talking about a particular patient who was leaving the ward (being discharged), making it clear that the two were very much linked in his mind. We were able to consider that he was angry with me for postulating that he hadn't reached a feeling of remorse which, in turn, was preventing him from leaving and being discharged. I commented that this was also anger with himself about the absence of remorse, that is, fundamentally his inability to come to terms with the jealousy in himself. He splits/kills off the murderer in himself and this gets projected out (he experiences me killing off his chances) and this causes the collapse of the potential for reflective thought into dyadic thinking. This was the scene post-natally, in that his mother was not able to triangulate within herself healthily between father, herself, and her son, so that one part of the triangle collapsed (was projected into her son, Mr G). In the same way, Mr G projected into me his own murderousness by making me responsible for him not being discharged as opposed to integrating the murderer in himself.

An understanding of these potentialities can highlight the observed rotations within triangles, which may correspond not only to the three real objects concerned, but may also allow complex movements of single intra-psychic contents or mixtures, in two-to-one variations of the different players in the overall triangle.

Melanie Klein, in her work on loneliness, mentions the longing to understand oneself and the need to be understood by the internalised good object (1963, p. 302). She adds that one of the manifestations of this longing is the universal phantasy of the twin soul, as shown by Bion (1950). This phantasy can be linked with the phenomenon of the double, studied by Freud (1919, p. 9) in "The Uncanny". Freud points out that the double was primordially a safety measure against destruction of the self. The creation of this double is intended to stave off annihilation and is said to present those split-off parts that the individual longs to recover with the hope of attaining plenitude.

Grinberg (1992) confirms that this phantasy was implicit in states of infatuation or extreme dependence of some individuals towards certain persons, who, by projective identification, are felt to possess those characteristics that correspond to the lost qualities. They sometimes behaved like real addicts of these objects whose company they sought desperately and compulsively with the unconscious aim of recovering those aspects (the stalking dynamic features here). He states: "[I]t is another expression, pathological in this sense, of mourning for the self" (Grinberg, 1992, p. 161).

I believe it is in this way that Mr G has developed a relationship in his therapy and the previous example I quoted is a case in point, whereby he is seeking to recover lost aspects of himself. In thinking about his capacity to integrate jealous murderousness, I am referring to his experience of my own capacity to be able to triangulate, using a reflective function, as opposed to my identifying with the projective identification and ending up with a re-enactment of the same destruction into dyadic thinking. Moreover, perhaps in this same way, Mr G was "created" as a twin (of his father) by his mother in an attempt to reconcile herself to her loss.

A central feature to understanding the roots of Mr G's psychopathology lay in his mother's inability to deal with the trauma of the loss of her husband. This, as we would expect, is being repeated in his identifications, represented by the attachments that he has had; no less so than with his victim. It also featured in his previous institution, where he had been in therapy with a female therapist, which came to an end when the therapist left the institution as a result of getting married and becoming pregnant. This occurred after a period of four years in therapy and we should note that this four-year duration "twins" with the four years that separated him from his next sibling. The feelings of jealousy and displacement were re-ignited with his mother/therapist and we might think that his previous therapist got caught up in the projective world of her patient and was unable to triangulate with sufficient reflectivity thus causing a re-enactment to take place. Mr G developed a strong libidinal attachment to this therapist who he continues to keep alive following the death of the therapy by pursuing a complaint against her. To date I remain unconvinced that he has reached the stage where he is able to let go of her, experience the loss, and move on.

It is perhaps relevant to now turn to the parallels with the recent case of Ian Huntley and the information I refer to is all available in the public domain. You will recall he was convicted for the double murder of two ten-year-old girls. The parallel I want to draw attention to will, I hope, become clear as I give you a very brief biography of Huntley.

He was born into a parental couple where it appears that the father had difficulty with his own jealousies, which interfered with his capacity to be able to triangulate with his first born. Mother and son, Ian, were very close. Soon after Ian's birth his younger brother, Wayne, was born, and given the proximity of their births, they were apparently dressed identically and related to as if they were twins. This twinning and identical dressing reminds us of the identical attire that his two victims wore with their Manchester United football tops (moreover, Ian was a Manchester United supporter). It became apparent as the sons began to grow up that Wayne was the more successful of the two, both intellectually and socially. It seems that Ian grew up feeling that he couldn't compete and in addition he was at the receiving end of an abusive relationship with his father.

When Ian was fourteen he exposed, to his mother, his father's sexual encounter with their childminder. His father responded with increased cruelty to Ian, which was linked to the situation of Ian's closeness to mother.

There were numerous examples where Ian felt unable to compete with his brother as they grew, while still being related to as if twins. His rivalry was exacerbated when on one particular occasion his mother chose Wayne over himself in relation to a job opportunity. The most significant example of his brother triumphing within the rivalry was when Ian's three-week-old bride left him, aborted their child, and moved in and subsequently married Wayne. His rage was such that there was no communication between the two for over a year. Apparently they reconciled approximately two years prior to the offence.

Circumstances surrounding the offence were that Ian Huntley was angry that his girlfriend, Maxine Carr, was away (from his control?) in another part of the country and socialising with others, provoking his jealousy. Minutes prior to the murder of the two girls he'd apparently had an angry telephone conversation with Maxine and we can infer from what has been reported that he was livid with jealousy. He was aware of the relationship that she had with these two girls, which was very close: so that unconsciously Maxine and the girls represented a mother and her twins, symmetrically matching his own mother with himself and his brother.

I suggest that his rage with his girlfriend/mother was such that he attacked and killed off the perceived rival to her affections, represented by the two girls, as if he killed off the double-headed figure within himself that was the twinning with his brother, while at the same time surviving the attack in an identical way to Mr G. Thereby, his life-long feeling of being persecuted by jealousy of his brother and of being caught up in the twinship, was perversely resolved through a displacement: killing off of the twinning and surviving.

In monitoring other "familicide" killings, I am further convinced of the importance of this dynamic. Not unlike the reference at the beginning of this chapter from *The Tempest*, surviving in a different form after being killed is the best way to describe my own countertransference experience with Mr G. It also represents what Mr G does with my contribution as well as describing his own early experience. Moreover, this quotation from *The Tempest* was referred to in a session by Mr G, when he commented that his mother had informed him that his biological father, who had died at sea, was a reader of Shakespeare and had thought about placing in the local church a plaque with this quote inscribed to mark his death.

In engagement, Mr G might say something that elicits a response from me, and while I sense that he has heard me, he appears to erase my contribution from conscious memory (so can forget it in an instant or after the session) but knows also that it hasn't completely disappeared. It's as if he re-enacts in the transference, transforming an alive third into a dead one, which is simultaneously kept alive but out of consciousness. It is a way of holding in storage a deadness that puts me in the position that he has persistently experienced himself—of not feeling able to engage with this third other, yet feeling persecuted by its presence.

Both Mr Huntley and Mr G had the early experience of being displaced by a rival and then being related to as if they were part of a twinship. Both experienced impotence in being able to openly compete with their rival, which meant that they were forever caught as the loser; that is, losing out to their rival's relationship with mother. Prior to the index offence, both Mr Huntley and Mr G experienced a jealous rage when their partners were out with others. Where the circumstances differ is that with Mr G his attack was upon his girlfriend/mother, ostensibly for the jealousy she had provoked in him by forcing him to embrace a rivalrous third. Mr Huntley, while he was similarly provoked by jealousy, displaced his attack on to his rival, these two girls, in Maxine Carr's absence, thereby momentarily resolving his conflict. In both cases there was, I believe, the fantasy of killing a double-headed figure of a duality of twinship. Mr G was killing the wife and daughter of his girlfriend's father while she was, in his mind, pregnant, and Mr Huntley was killing the duality represented by these two girls.

In both examples there is the attack on the child/children, representing the product of the union of the parents and thereby the third in the relationship. It is this attack upon the third that Mr G experienced post-natally, while at the same time surviving, which was in essence a feeling of being persistently persecuted by a third and not feeling free to compete with it. This was the case in identical form for Mr Huntley. This internal, intra-psychic, situation for Mr G is experienced by me interpersonally in our work whereby anything that is conceived from the union between us is automatically attacked by him. That which he takes in from the work he joins with in a dead form, so there is no open and lively engagement, interaction, or intercourse possible. Thereby he kills the child (foetus?) that is also a feature externally with his previous therapist, where his jealousy with a rival with whom he cannot compete (the person who took her away from him) has resulted in a perverse solution of denying the loss of her by holding on to her, via lodging a complaint. Similarly, we might think that Mr G has managed to hold on to his girlfriend by killing her (so no loss experienced) as indeed Mr Huntley did in his belief that the murder was the way that he could hold on to his girlfriend/mother.

Returning to Mr G, an incident occurred in his married life prior to conviction that serves to illustrate this feeling of persecution at having to accommodate threesomeness. (Mr G subsequently separated and moved in with his girlfriend who was to become his victim.) It was when neighbours called around unexpectedly and to all intents and purposes invited themselves in to his home. Mr G felt powerless to prevent this from happening, and his feelings were subsequently acted out on to the child in the home—his daughter, who was in infancy—whereby as a result of her crying he took her upstairs and began to strangle her. His rage at the displacement by the neighbours was then transferred on to his daughter (representing the third in the relationship between himself and his wife), which had to be strangled off. This all symmetrised with his experience of being forced to accommodate the intrusiveness of a third where he felt powerless to avoid feeling persecuted by its presence.

This was no less a feature for Mr Huntley in his life-long experience at having to embrace his brother and feeling powerless by the persecution of jealousy that resulted in murder. What I haven't had time to consider here was the possible part that both Maxine Carr (Ian Huntley's girlfriend) and Mr G's brother played in the provocation of jealousy, perhaps in an attempt to deal with their own. In this way Ian Huntley may have been a repository for a double dose of the jealousy in the family in the same way that Mr G may have done, perhaps for his own stepfather and brother.

Freud wrote:

> Actually we can never give anything up; we can only exchange one thing for another. What appears to be renunciation is really the formation of a substitute or surrogate.

(Freud, 1908, p. 145)

What is unavoidable in life is the experience of loss and what I am suggesting is the critical importance of the capacity to be able to triangulate, using threesomes in the process of reconciling oneself to the loss encountered. It is the monitoring of this area of functioning that for me is the key to his eventual prognosis. Engel (1975) raises the question of whether certain key losses in life can ever actually be completely resolved and Freud opined that a loved object is never really relinquished. What neither Mr G nor Ian Huntley had the opportunity and resources to affect at such an early age in their psychic development was the benefit of being able to triangulate. This, Mr G is in the process of working through. Whether Ian Huntley also has that opportunity remains to be seen.

CHAPTER FOUR

Crossing the divide*

"One of the beguiling aspects is the way that the finest bloodline to someone—who, a few hours earlier, you never knew existed—is enough to endear them to you in a way that you would never be drawn to a stranger in so brief a time."

—Joseph, 2004, p. 23

The distinction and separation between family members and others can be indicative of the inner divide separating dyadic and triadic thinking, or it might be said, paranoid-schizoid and depressive functioning (Klein, 1946).[1] A clinical example is presented whereby an inner divide could not be crossed in the mind of a mother to help her deal with trauma. Consequently, her trauma infected her children, who in turn dramatically acted out their unconscious content by casting a mix across the social divide between families and strangers in committing a joint murder. This act repeated the original trauma in a mirroring form in which there was no healthy crossing

*This chapter was first presented at a meeting of the International Association of Forensic Psychotherapy (IAFP) Conference on 20 May 2005 in Dublin.

of the divide from unconscious enactment to conscious reflection. From a trans-generational viewpoint, trauma can have far-reaching consequences, which suggests that while time can be a healer, it can also be involved in causing repeated and compulsive re-enactments.

The title of the conference where this chapter was first presented was "After Trauma—Within Families and Between Strangers". This draws our attention immediately to the affective difference implied by the word "within" as opposed to "between". I would suggest that the title would lose meaning (consciously) if the wording were changed to *between* families and *within* strangers. Given the context of the conference and my focus in this chapter, "within" refers to internal, "between" to external. It is the crossing of the divide from internal to external, from within to between, that is such an intrinsic and core part of forensic work where that which is internal and unprocessed becomes acted-out externally.[1] Moreover, there is a binding quality to the phrase "within families", which has a symmetrising dynamic (in that there is an exact correspondence of family members to one another), whereas the phrase "between strangers" has a separating quality, where difference is an intrinsic part and asymmetries abound (resulting in no obvious correspondence).

The idea of symmetry and asymmetry and their relationship are the keystones to the work of Matte Blanco (1975, 1988), as previous chapters have described. Fundamentally, he asserts that the unconscious treats asymmetrical relations as if they were symmetrical. Rayner comments that a patient once said, "I can't remember whether it was you or I who said it" and suggests that this is a symmetrisation of selves, which is a common occurrence and at the heart of all empathy (1995, p. 30). For my purposes in this chapter and its clinical example, Matte Blanco might say that strangers were related to as if they were family members and family members related to each other as if strangers. Logically, I know this is nonsensical and yet affectively this is no doubt familiar to us all.[2] Eric Rayner refers to Matte Blanco's thinking around symmetry, which led on to other profound ideas of infinite emotional experience, as *"A quiet discovery that contains genius"* (1995, p. 58; my emphasis).

The crossing of the geographical divide of the Irish Sea, which was necessary to present this chapter at a conference, represents a metaphor that for most separates family from strangers. This in turn helps us note the correspondence to the inner divide that separates dyadic thinking from triadic thinking, or as stressed in more recent post-Kleinian thinking, crosses the divide from paranoid-schizoid to depressive functioning, from an either/or to a both/and position. By extension, to use the language of Matte Blanco, I would stress the importance of being able to utilise the asymmetrical (between strangers) function when there is a powerful pull towards remaining purely in a symmetrical mode (within families).

I will present a clinical example that illustrates the effects of unresolved trauma within one generation upon a subsequent generation (crossing a time divide). This occurred because of the inability a mother had to cross the internal divide into depressive functioning, in order to cope with the trauma of loss. This resulted in her crossing the trans-generational divide with her trauma which, through the use of pathological projective identification, infected her children. The children in turn re-enacted the original trauma by crossing their own divide, from internal to external, in addition to crossing the social divide by enlisting strangers to commit a gang murder. In this act they attempted to resolve the original trauma. The critical importance that I attribute to the capacity to be able to create a reflective space to think is emphasised here. Such reflection facilitates containment, and is a prophylactic to an unthinking crossing of the divide, which is usually defined as "acting-out".

Before presenting my case material, I want to comment on the opening quote to my chapter, which was taken from the television review journalist Joe Joseph for *The Times* when he was describing his experience of reviewing a television programme entitled *Who Do You Think You Are?* (Joseph, 2004). This was a sequence of programmes that sought out various media personalities and helped each celebrity to trace his or her family history.

This fashionable interest in reflecting on historical backgrounds mirrors our growing hunt to find the specific personal and family theme of jealous murderousness.

The particular example that Joe Joseph reviewed was the story of the comedian Vic Reeves. In the programme Vic Reeves tracked down a cousin in Liverpool he never knew he had. She turned out not to recognise him in any of the aliases that he had used on television. Joe Joseph went on to say that it was amusing to watch a grown man (Vic Reeves), who is approaching the foothills of middle age, explain to a newly found seventy-year-old relative the tomfoolery he gets up to in public in order to earn a living. The fact that this cousin hadn't the slightest inkling about Vic Reeves' television fame highlighted one of the beguiling aspects of this series—how the thinnest bloodline to someone, who a few hours earlier you never even knew existed, is enough to endear him to you. Joe Joseph suggests that there is no real way to explain this. He comments that week after week encounters had been engineered between the celebrity ancestors and their unknown relatives, and *"[w]e have watched them welcome these apparent strangers into their homes, hug them, weep with them but nobody has put their finger on what makes us feel so welcoming"* (Joseph, 2004, p. 23; emphasis added).

Even Vic Reeves, who had earlier said he wasn't keen on meeting up with any living relatives he might unearth during his genealogical journey, seemed moved to have tracked down the daughter of a son born from the first marriage of his bigamist grandfather. Finally Joe Joseph suggests that it can be boggling and humbling to witness the way that even the youngest child is devoted to its parents and often will accept no other—even if the alternatives are richer, prettier, kinder, and more generous. To feel warmly towards someone who is, to all intents and purposes, little closer to you than a stranger seated beside you on a bus, is oddly unnerving.

I believe that it is Matte Blanco's understanding of the logic in the unconscious that allows us to really understand this dynamic. The moment that you are told, or are aware, that you share something that connects you or binds you and has the potential for an infinite binding and connectedness, perhaps back to the origins of human existence through the bloodline, then the potential for symmetry exists. Where there is symmetry, there is no differentiation; all is as one. Consequently, the affect associated with that thinking is a loving and binding one, in complete contrast to the asymmetry between strangers, where there is no immediate binding connectedness of a bloodline and symmetries have to be worked at in order to be achieved.

With specific reference to my clinical example, I also want to comment that all sexual intercourse with the potential to lead to the conception of children (apart from the perverse) takes place, whether in marriage or otherwise, between two asymmetrical individuals (hitherto strangers) as opposed to the symmetrical relationships within families. The fact that this has come from their asymmetrical relation provides an underpinning and reinforcement of the symmetrical family lines for each.

I was asked to carry out a psychoanalytic assessment on Jeff with a view to considering his needs for psychotherapy. He had been detained in high security for ten years and in that time had attended a number of therapy groups (approximately fifteen). Prior to meeting with Jeff, I was aware that he had had some significant contact with an experienced social worker and I was keen to speak with her and gain her reflections on her experience of him. She was able to recall that a core experience around him and his mother (whom she had also met on a number of occasions) was a preoccupation with death, as if all roads led to dying. One other important factor that emerged from her memory was that the death of the victim's foetus (the victim was three months' pregnant at the time of being murdered) was unacknowledged—so there was a general sense of a lost child. It is worth reminding ourselves that it has been found to be very difficult to hold on to the memory of a newborn dead foetus, even in doctor's records.

The index offence in our illustrative story is a gang murder, where two of the five protagonists were Jeff and his sister Jill. Therefore it is vitally important that the dynamics between the two of them are explored in relation to their histories, because it is clear that something malignant had brought them together (a mirroring had occurred) that could not be contained internally and became acted out between strangers.

Jeff and Jill were born quite closely together, and with our eye on the symmetrical process, we know that the closer the birth timing between siblings the closer the correspondence can be to twin dynamics (linking with the last chapter). Considering this, I am mindful also of the circumstances surrounding Jill's birth, given that Jill was the second pregnancy to her mother—the first pregnancy was lost after five months. Documentation suggests that the mother was traumatised by her loss, subsequently suffering from "poor nerves and the occasional blackout". This trauma for the mother (who demonstrated a lack of internal resource to work through the loss) provided the fertile territory whereby the birth of Jill provided a container into which her mother could project the trauma of her loss. Thus, for Jill's mother, Jill was identified as a plus one (as in a newborn) as well as a minus one, in relation to containing the experience of the previously lost foetus. Not long after Jill's birth, Jeff was conceived, and three months into the pregnancy Jeff's mother suffered three traumatic losses. The first was the death of her grandmother, who was a substitute mother for her. The second was the loss of her husband, who abandoned her. The third was the death of a new partner in traumatic circumstances, which I believe was re-enacted in the index offence, which I will come to. Again, documentation reveals that the mother was extremely distressed regarding these losses, and again the same picture emerges of a mother relating to both her existing child and her newborn as additions coexisting with losses (plus ones alongside minus ones).

The index offence is a complex picture around a group process. A few years prior to the index offence, Jill had provoked her friend's jealousy (Sue) by "stealing" her boyfriend and falling pregnant. (Sue would subsequently become the victim in our story.) Given this provocation, Sue, together with her brother and sisters (in a way that Jill and Jeff with others were subsequently to mirror years later), visited Jill while she was pregnant, beat her up, and caused the loss of the foetus. So Sue's inability to cope with the loss of her boyfriend, together with feelings of jealousy, because he was now with her friend Jill, resulted in a murderous attack. As a result, what had become a plus one through conception was now a minus one.

This created the background circumstances from which, some years later, Jill enlisted her brother Jeff to exact revenge for the loss of her pregnancy. Jeff was only too keen to help his sister in that one of the benefits, as he perceived it, would be to ingratiate himself back into his family (to strengthen feelings of symmetry), for he had felt distanced from the family since childhood. Jeff had been put into institutional care at the age of five, following a period of being sexually abused by his stepfather, and remained in care until the age of fifteen/sixteen. More powerfully underpinning the sibling relationship between Jeff and Jill was the mirroring experience whereby each carried the co-existence of loss and gain, life and death, as a part of his/her internal world.

Circumstances then arose that symmetrically matched not only Jill's recent history (in relation to Sue), but, for both Jill and Jeff, their own very early history in relation to their mother. Another of Jill's friends, whom I shall call Mary, was unable to conceive with her partner, because she had been sterilised. Arrangements had been made for Sue (the victim), a friend of Mary's, to act as a surrogate. A sex rota was set up whereby Mary's partner, John, would have intercourse with Sue and Mary at different times. As a result of this, John developed more of a liking for Sue than for his partner, provoking feelings of loss and jealousy in Mary—most acutely when Sue fell pregnant.

Conflict resulted between Sue and Mary, and Mary moved out of the family home, leaving Sue and John together. Mary then enlisted Jill (who was also an old friend) and informed her of the circumstances, which resonated with Jill's experience in relation to Sue. Jill then began to recruit people in order to kill Sue. There were five people involved in the murder: Jill; her partner at the time, Jack; Jeff, Jill's brother; Mary; and Mary's new partner at the time, a man called Mick.

The scene described to me by Jeff was that he went together with Jill and her partner Jack to Sue's address, where she was living with her new lover John (Mary's husband) and they all waited until John had left the house, leaving Sue inside. At this point Sue was three months' pregnant (mirroring the same period of pregnancy in Jeff's and Jill's mother when traumatic losses were sustained). So for Jill, Sue represented a mirror image of herself as a woman who had fallen pregnant (plus one) following a relationship with a "stolen" man (John). John was stolen from Mary, who had experienced the loss of John (minus one). Similarly, this plus one/minus one scenario hooked in Jeff, with his own history, and the two came together as one, in the way that that can happen over time. I am also interested that the offence took place after the father of the child (John) had left the home. This was indeed the picture for both Jill and Jeff's relationship to the departure of their biological father.

Upon entering the house, Jill and Jeff were to find that Sue was tending to her only other young child (Sue was a mother with one young child while pregnant with her second, by John). At a given moment, Sue was attacked by both Jill and Jeff, and during the attack they were joined by Jack (who had been waiting outside) in order to "finish her off"—she was stabbed, super-glued, and strangled. Once dead, Sue was wrapped up and driven in a car to the edge of a large river where Mick had been asked to dig a hole for them to bury the body in. However, he had not fulfilled his part of the plans, and so Jeff climbed to a high point above the river and threw the body in.

It is, I believe, highly relevant that after Jeff described the circumstances of the index offence, he went on to inform me of his home circumstances at the time. These were as follows: he was living with his mother, who was apparently quite ill and in need of a hysterectomy. He described that he became so concerned, the day after the murder, regarding his mother's loss of blood, that he contacted the emergency services who rushed her into hospital and performed surgery, which apparently saved her life. So again, I was being presented with the picture whereby one day Jeff was involved in a killing in order to gain a family (−one/+one) only for the next day to be involved in the saving of a life (+one) in circumstances of the loss of a womb (−one), that had hitherto contained the three successive conceptions from the stillbirth to Jill and then to Jeff. This reminded me too of the frequent occasions whereby my own countertransference experience could be described in the following way: whatever I had to offer by way of comment and/or interpretation was killed off, only for Jeff to save in some way something of what I had to offer, but in another form.

During the course of our meetings, Jeff mentioned, almost in passing, an incident that his mother had briefly referred to many years before, when she had been visiting him in prison. He recounted that when his mother was three months' pregnant with him, and following the abandonment by her husband, she struck up a new relationship with another man. One day they were apparently travelling on a boat on the same river and at exactly the same spot where Jeff many years later would dump his victim's body. While travelling across the river, Jeff's mother fell overboard. At the time not only was she accompanied by her new boyfriend, but we could assume that Jeff's older sister Jill, who would have been less than twelve months old, was also present (mirroring the index offence scene, a generation later, that is, three months' pregnant mother (Sue) with a young child of a year). Apparently, in order to assist her rescue, a dingy was thrown overboard and her boyfriend jumped into the river. Jeff's mother was subsequently saved by the dingy, while the boyfriend was killed by the propellers of the boat.

When Jeff presented this material, I commented on the striking coincidence that a pregnant mother should end up in the Thames in this way (and there has to be question marks around the circumstances of her falling) given that the victim of the index offence, also being pregnant, ended up in the same river in a similar way. Jeff rather unconvincingly suggested that he had also thought of that coincidence before and felt there was nothing in it. Indeed, following the session I had with him, it seems that he felt the need to speak with a member of his family to check out whether that relative felt there was any relevance to this. Both had agreed that there was no link that could be established at all and he was rather too keen to communicate this to me in our final session.

When I enquired where the victim's body had been thrown into the river, I learnt that this act was executed by himself alone and that the bodies (mother and her partner and Sue) were as close as within a twenty-metre area of where they had actually entered the river. So, while mother was pregnant with the potential of a plus one, she sustained a significant loss of her new boyfriend constituting a minus one, repeating the same pattern highlighted earlier. Moreover, I postulate that this trauma on the boat was re-enacted in the index offence, whereby the circumstances of a pregnant mother accompanied by a child symmetrically matched. In correspondence it is noted that Jeff said that, in relation to carrying out the killing, he did not feel anything about what he was doing: "It was like putting your hands in cold water."

So, not unlike his sister, Jeff provided the container for his mother's own losses and trauma, which meant that effectively a part of himself was killed off. Such dynamics remind me of the difficulty in differentiating separately when deaths and births occur simultaneously. Research work, particularly by Bourne and Lewis (1984, 1992), has shown how difficult it is for normal mourning processes to take place approaching or around the time of birth. The denial and confusion involved in accepting minus one at the time of creating plus one has been further highlighted by the same researchers' important work on stillbirths, which demonstrates the hidden resistances that appear to take place both to mourning and to its subsequent remembering and recording in history. Their work illustrates how difficult it is to sort out the emotional complexities of situations where births and deaths are found in close proximity. So that Jeff was the personification of minus one and plus one, in the same way that Jill had been prior to Jeff's birth (around similar losses that mother had sustained). Moreover, this was the family dynamic and highlights the significance in his family's inability to tolerate and work through feelings of loss. We might recall here the free associations of the social worker whereby "All roads lead to death". The complexity of the circumstances suggests that it may be that the arrival of somebody new is felt like a loss, at some level, between the two that have created the potential arrival (jealousy) so that in order to prevent the move from a two to a three, one cancels the other out and only the dyadic relationship remains.

I refer the reader here to the previous chapter "Murder: persecuted by jealousy", the thinking of which is extended here. The chapter postulates that "the persistent persecution at having to accommodate the third into a two-person relationship, particularly when the subject has not yet digested the dynamics involved in the two-person relationship, creates the environment for murderousness to be triggered when external circumstances mirror or approximate to such an internal configuration". Jealous murderousness is undoubtedly a feature of Jeff and Jill's index offence. The ubiquitous feature underpinning the arrival of feelings of jealousy is the challenge to the capacity to tolerate something new alongside the perception that a loss may be sustained.

A movement towards embracing the third position or reflective space, enabled me to identify, in the time that I spent with Jeff, that a re-enactment of the original trauma had taken place during our meetings. That is, after something had been conceived between us as a result of our meeting, where we might say he provided the necessary seed to fertilise the fertile womb of the space I was providing (in myself), I was then left with the experience of losing him (because he was being discharged). I then had to contain the experience of an addition to our engagement (a baby—the dynamic formulation reached) while having to contain the experience of loss of my partner (Jeff).

A reflective space allowed me to identify that this was an important communication. He was projectively identifying with me (so was crossing the divide from his internal to his external world) with the hope of seeking a resolution to the original trauma that had been passed on to him by his mother. I was left with feeling that I could very easily act upon the loss occasioned by his discharge by similarly relating to what had been conceived, between us, in a negative way. I was therefore susceptible to repeating history by allowing the experience of his loss to contaminate the experience of our meetings; that is, I could have quite easily written our exchanges up in a closure form, which would have been an angry and negative response to his discharge, as opposed to ensuring that the conception that occurred between us followed him and became a part of the thinking in his new home. We might say I crossed the divide to try to ensure that his new partner (in the form of his new treatment team) would join with him to take responsibility for previous experiences that he had had.

So, in conclusion, I am attempting to stress the importance of the capacity for an individual to develop a reflective function, that is, a thinking space, or, we might say, a third position, when experiencing a significant loss. Such a loss is traumatic, particularly if there is little capacity to contain the experience. It then crosses the divide from the internal uncontaining space into an external space, in an attempt to find containment. I again refer the reader to the exact links that this has with the perpetrator's history in the Dunblane chapter, where the community acted as the external container. Jeff became that container for his mother (as had his sister) where his mother unconsciously used her children to contain her experiences of the traumatic losses she sustained. The image on the boat of Jeff's mother pregnant with him while with a new man and her first born Jill, symmetrically matched the circumstances of Sue on the day of her murder. Only in these circumstances the loss that mother sustained on the boat that was then projectively identified into her children, born and unborn, was now reversed in the index offence. Therefore loss was going to be experienced by not only the father of the foetus and new partner, but also by the young infant who was present at the time. I am mindful of the extraordinary coincidence that at the time of the murder the original mother (of Jeff and Jill) was in grave danger of dying from the incessant bleeding of her womb.

There was a lack of a three-dimensional capacity in mother to deal with her losses, which resulted in her infecting her children. By extension, when circumstances arose in their lives which provoked feelings of loss and jealousy, symmetrisation with the original family trauma occurred. A sort of "psychic surrogacy" was again sought, to contain that which they were unable to contain by themselves. A dramatic re-enactment took place, where thinking was not possible, which meant crossing the divide (between internal and external worlds) causing history to repeat itself. We know from trauma research that if recent trauma picks up past trauma that hasn't been considered, thought about, and worked through, then the potential for a graver outcome increases.

Notes

1. Klein suggests that in developmentally earlier, paranoid-schizoid functioning, objects and the ego are split as a defence against persecutory anxiety. These splits are not perceived as parts of a whole, and separate qualities (e.g., good/bad) are attributed to each part. Depressive position functioning develops the capacity to appreciate the relationship of part to whole and the multi-faceted attributes of object and self. See Klein (1946).
2. There are lots of asymmetries and symmetries in any given relation— our work is stressing the way that our affect-driven minds focus primarily on one particular symmetrisation.

CHAPTER FIVE

The revenge involved in diagnosing untreatability*

"In the case of Reid, referred to the House of Lords, their Lordships took the view that whilst medical research and therapeutic innovation continues, it is difficult to say with confidence that any patient is truly untreatable or might not eventually benefit from care and treatment under medical supervision."

—David Morgan re Reid v Secretary of State for Scotland (1999)
1 all ER 481, per Lord Hutton T 515

In this chapter it is postulated that all criminality involves revenge and that revenge by being intrinsically talionic (an eye for an eye) is dyadic in nature and the results often represent the antithesis of creativity. By extension, when considering the roots of those deemed untreatable, their propensity for acting-out scenarios tends, in consequence, to obliterate valuable reflection, not only in themselves but all around. Extensive experience suggests that neglect of essential history

---

*This chapter was first read at a meeting of the International Association of Forensic Psychotherapy (IAFP) Conference on 31 March 2006 in Oxford.

taking of each individual is the ubiquitous casualty of the obliteration of reflection. An individual's history illuminates his particular pattern of revenge. A comparison will be considered between a male patient, with a high psychopathy rating, where anality features both in his index offence and in his object relations, and a female patient who poses problems in institutional care such that there is a highly infective charge of violent projective identification and concordant depression that mirrors her inner world. In different ways they have challenged a variety of clinical and non-clinical settings. Both have engendered powerful feelings, leading to the collapse, in those around them, of the capacity to reflect on that part of their unconscious processes that could understand what they are about, and formulate prescriptions for treatment. This chapter cements the progressive importance attributed to triangulation in thinking.

The opening quote was taken from an excellent commentary by David D. Morgan (2004) and it is indicative of the legal interpretation of treatability where the English courts have favoured a liberal interpretation when applied to psychiatric patients. In essence, as far as the courts are concerned, there are few, if any, mental disorders which are not treatable in a statutory sense. By contrast, it is the medical interpretation of treatability, that is, that there is a class of patients who are untreatable (as in the widely publicised case of Michael Stone, already discussed, who committed murder following a refusal by a psychiatric facility to admit him on the grounds that he was medically untreatable), that has generated immense anxiety in UK government circles. The bill to reform the Mental Health Act in England and Wales has recently been abandoned and replaced by amended proposals to the 1983 Act.

The UK government's position appears to be that the fault line in present legislation is the limiting requirement that patients have to present with a treatable disorder before they can be compulsorily detained. The feeling is that this exposes the public to dangerously disordered yet "medically untreatable" individuals, who pose a significant risk of physical or psychological harm to others. The perceived remedy is to place risk above the notion of treatability as the primary criterion for psychiatric detention, by introducing law stating that psychiatry *must* detain and provide treatment. Medicalising risk in this way will give society powers over the individual that the criminal justice system does not have.

The new proposals replace the treatability test with a requirement that "appropriate treatment" must be available. Louis Appleby, the government's national director of mental health, recently insisted that "appropriate treatment" would have to be of therapeutic benefit to the patient, although the Department of Health conceded that doctors would not be required to determine in advance whether treatment was beneficial or not (Alexandra Frean, *The Times*, 24 March 2006). In an article in *The Times*, Tony Zigmond, honorary vice-president of the Royal College of Psychiatrists, said that "[a]n important principle must be that we only deprive people of their liberty when we can offer treatment that will be of benefit to them". In the same piece, Michael Howlett, of the Zito Trust, welcomed the new measures: "Many successful therapeutic interventions are being used by people in the field" (Howlett, 2006). Government officials have insisted that this was not another form of preventive detention but a power of preventive intervention.

This is, I argue, a perverse solution to the anxiety created around treatability. In the triangulation between the state, the penal system and psychiatric care, there is, for all intents and purposes, a merging between penal policy (detention) and psychiatry that causes a collapse of the healthy triangulated relationship with the state into a dyadic structure. In this, psychiatry is forced into a dual role of handling penal policy alongside treatment and care. Moreover, the title of the conference where this chapter was first presented—"Revenge: Justice or Treatment"—also collapses a potential of three into two, with the use of the conjunction "or" as opposed to "and". In a preceding chapter entitled "Perverse triangulation" (Chapter Two), I explored this phenomenon that is no less germane to this discussion.

To recap again on the understanding of perverse triangulation: mathematically when one corner of a triangle collapses it reverts to becoming a straight line. As a result of such a collapse, this straight line would indicate a preceding perverse triangle.

Moreover, developmentally perverse triangulation could be presented in terms of a linked analogy occurring when the absence of recognition and inclusion of the father into the mother/child dyad takes place.

And finally, politically perverse triangulation occurs when in problem-solving a particular type of reflective thinking collapses or is eliminated in the pressure of seeking solutions (rather like what occurs around the "untreatable patient"). This results in the perpetuation of the original set of problems in a different form, so that one of the three factors involved is lost to view.

Thus in all of these three situations, the potential of three becomes an actuality of two, or one.

For the benefit of illuminating this dynamic, let us look at this triangular scene whereby the government can be symbolically equated with a patient (like Michael Stone), who fears being held responsible for a crime that might be committed, given that there is a perceived (unconscious) weakness in the capacity to contain this anxiety/threat/patient and a drive to seek external containment for that which is unfolding internally.[1] When the patient's (and/or government's) anxiety levels rise, as a result of this process becoming more conscious, the need for containment becomes paramount. The patient/government will then drive/provoke/force (act-out) any treatment team with the unconscious purpose of seeking to be safely contained, this being the unconscious purpose of acting-out. In view of the anxieties that can be generated and provoked in the treating team, a malignant mirroring can take place whereby an obliteration of valuable reflection is both a cause and a consequence. This results in the care and treating team prioritising penal policy, as in the form of safe physical containment, over any other treatment process, particularly reflective thinking. We must not ignore the potential for criminality (and acting-out) deriving from "unconscious guilt" (Freud, 1916) whereby in order to deal with an unconscious state of mind (self-condemnation) the individual, still unconsciously, acts to bring down a punishment on himself, and thereby finds containment.

For a while, both the patient and treating team feel contained in relation to their own immediate anxieties, until such time as they find themselves repetitively paralysed as the situation inevitably repeats itself. This is a repeating picture of a three-way process collapsing into a two-way process. In my experience a ubiquitous casualty in this includes the fundamental neglect of essential history taking (and subsequent linking with events) that always leads to this particular pattern of a three to two collapse emerging.

I am mindful here that I am effectively recognising one of the main conclusions reached by Isabelle Menzies Lyth in her chapter on "The functioning of social systems" (1959), that there is the potential for a social defence system to emerge in treatment teams to alleviate anxiety, and that this defence system represents the institutionalisation of very primitive psychic defence mechanisms. The main characteristic of these institutionalised defence mechanisms is that they facilitate the evasion of anxiety but contribute little to its true modification and reduction. In other words, the anxiety generated by the notion of "the untreatable patient" (which is an oxymoron) creates the environment for a defensive system to develop along the lines that Menzies Lyth suggests (1959). The primitive defence mechanisms of the paranoid-schizoid position (a dyadic/two-way dynamic) predominate, both within the patient and the treating team, rather than the triadic dynamic essential for the mature containment and treatment of the patient concerned. I am more than aware that this healthy triangulation is very susceptible to being made perverse, or having vital parts kept out, to reduce three factors in the situation to two or one.

To furnish this with a clinical example I want to describe the following, which took place with a clinical team in supervision in an inpatient setting. I was providing multi-disciplinary supervision to a unit who were treating probably one of the most severe forms of psychopathology in mental health, where anxieties were constantly generated around life and death issues. On the day in question the team were very keen to describe to me three noticeable features that had become issues of concern in relation to three different patients.

The first patient had absconded from the unit during the weekend and had been witnessed in a state of distress and dissociation moving from bridge to bridge in central London, as if contemplating throwing herself off and taking her life. Fortunately, this hadn't happened, and she was detained and returned to the unit. The second patient was described as having taken to wearing her night clothes all the time and not changing into day wear, as well as permanently wearing sunglasses on the ward. There appeared to be no rational explanation for this marked change in behaviour. The third patient was witnessed having scrupulously drawn on a large sheet of paper the old parlour game of battleships, whereby a grid was created and along both sides of the grid were written nurses' names. The patient had become preoccupied with this game.

Having been presented with this sequence of experiences, I might have been forgiven for addressing each individual one on its merits and providing various rational solutions to address each one—considering, for example, the policy of security to prevent any further break-outs from the unit by patient one; revising any medication that was required in addition to coercing patient two out of night clothes through a behavioural treatment plan into day wear; or engaging patient three in her preoccupation with the game of battleships onto other games. I chose instead to treat what was presented rather as I might a dream in individual work, and asked the team if they could freely associate to my following interpretation. I said something like, "What is the conflict on night duty that needs bridging with the day shift?", being mindful of potential unconscious content, particularly given that night duty can be that part of any twenty-four hour nursing care that can be split off and easily excluded by way of thinking. You will see my rather simplistic interpretation to the conflict (battleships), night duty (night clothes), and bridging (the bridges). The response to this was a collective relief from the team. It was identified that there had been a long-standing conflict between two nurses on night duty, extending over a number of years, which had been paralysing the team.

The two nurses had been caught up in a form of malignant mirroring, seemingly trapped in a relationship of attack and revenge, which was affecting the night duty team's effectiveness in safely containing the patients. The patients' only solution then was to act out this distress, in the hope that its unconscious meaning might be highlighted and understood and, thereby, safely contained and addressed. Moreover, as a consequence, in order to understand this conflict, it became necessary to explore the night nurses' own individual histories, and of course other beneficial insights emerged, in that their immobilisation was indicative of the frequently experienced lack of progress in the patient group. This reminds us of Freud's (1911, 1924) suggestion that many schizophrenic symptoms are attempts at recovery, a concept that Herbert Rosenfeld (1984) found confirmed again and again.

I mention this clinical example because I believe that it draws attention to the importance of being able to think in a way other than at face value, that is, to think in such a way that seeks to understand action and thereby truly contain the anxiety, as opposed to merely displacing (splitting off) the activity into something that momentarily feels less anxiety-provoking. Moreover, in my experience of working in the prison system, the resistance to understanding the actions of the criminals (their offending) is immense. Consequently, any thinking or reflective space provided is attacked (either passively or aggressively), which maintains the dyadic structure of crime and punishment, attack and revenge.

I therefore suggest that within the prison system there is a covert collusion that the prisoners are untreatable as such, and this also parallels and enables that part of ourselves to adopt an unthinking response to the crimes that they have committed by exacting revenge. A crucially important dynamic can also be missed, related to the previous example with the two nurses, in relation to criminality. The drive and impulse to (re)offend, if viewed as a form of acting-out, is ultimately in order to establish a sense of belonging (albeit perversely) to the criminal fraternity/prison/institution, whereby the perpetrator's dependent needs are met through containment, feeding, etc. This is all a way of compensating for deficits derived from having lacked a sense of belonging and secure attachment in early family life (and subsequently in the community). I return to this in subsequent chapters. By way of example, the next chapter offers an understanding of a patient whose feelings of loss of containment on release from custody had repeatedly resulted in almost immediate re-offending, and safe containment again.

I return now to my main discussion point of the revenge involved in diagnosing untreatability. It was the issue of untreatability which originally created such anxiety (and impotence) in the government that new amendments to the Mental Health Act 1983 had to be formulated. Given that the legal interpretation of the concept of treatability is not an obstacle to the compulsory admission or the continued detention of patients under the 1983 Act, it is to the medical interpretation of treatability that we need to turn. I have hitherto referred to the government being driven to a perverse solution, given the anxiety generated by feelings of guilt. This guilt (both conscious and unconscious) relates to feelings of responsibility for possible adverse events, through omission or commission. I want to add that in the triangle between the state, psychiatry (care), and security, if one part of that triangle—in this case, I am arguing, psychiatry—is in some way failing, this will lead to a collapse from a healthy triangulated position.

This reminds us, as I have already suggested, of the beneficial potential of the father's initiation of flexibility in a triangle involving mother and child and the necessity of the father having worked through his initial three-person jealousy about the newcomer breaking up the husband/wife, the duo. Gerald Wooster has previously postulated that "the father's initiation of flexibility in a triangle may be the later counterpart of mother's flexibility in the dyad" (Wooster, 1983, p. 38). I return to the Perseus myth, where Perseus' mirror (the gift to him by Athene, the

Goddess of Wisdom) creates a triangle which resolves his dilemma in being able to slay the Gorgon without himself dying in the process if he were to look straight at it. With the absence of the reflective mirror (father) the twosome can get caught up in a form of malignant mirroring, from which only one can survive. With this third lacking, the propensity is greater for a collapse from healthy to unhealthy and dyadic (paranoid-schizoid) dynamics.

In this context, is the mental health profession (psychiatry, and so on) providing an initiation of flexibility within the triangle with state and security (penal system)? I am suggesting that it isn't, particularly when failing to take sufficient regard of a patient's history. This loss of history can be a conscious and/or unconscious process. The UK government, through the anxiety generated by an uncontaining third, has acted to "make safe" by forcing the mental health profession to take responsibility for treatment within the newly amended proposals. This collapses the triangle into an unhealthy dyadic response. In essence, the government is saying that something must be done. This echoes not only the reporting that was taking place every night amid the horrors of Sarajevo, Srebrenica, and the rest (by Milosevic in 2006) whereby reporters on the spot were urging passionately that something must be done, but also far more recently the comments made by the mother of the convicted serial killer Daniel Gonzales, who said that she and her mother were at their wits' end and had been continually told that a crisis would have to occur before their son/grandson could be sectioned again and helped. They felt they were waiting for another crisis to prove he was ill. Max Hastings, in *The Guardian* of 13 March 2006, concluded: "We need to think much harder about what is needed to prevent mass murder, rather than congratulate ourselves on Hague trials of a few token perpetrators afterwards" (p. 32).

I am suggesting that what is primarily needed is attention to prioritising the history in the first instance; this includes the significance I attribute to critical dates.[2]

Psychiatry (father, developmentally) is not reflecting healthily and has by definition collapsed the clinically important dynamic of triangulating into a dyadic process by abandoning accessible relevant knowledge. The dyadic process by definition is revenge. I note with interest that starting next term on the academic curriculum at the Royal Military Academy Sandhurst (a close neighbour to Broadmoor) is a course on "Disordered passions", training officers in how to overcome the desire to abuse prisoners and inflict revenge on the enemy. The theory of disordered passions stems from the Just War theory of the thirteenth-century teachings of St. Thomas Aquinas. Cadets are taught to beware of responding to passions caused by hatred, and an overwhelming fear of death or capture, through a desire to inflict revenge or cold indifference. This course is being introduced by Sandhurst's new senior chaplain, who is the first Free Church minister to hold the post.

Baptist Padre Jonathan Woodhouse, who teaches the lessons, and is quoted in *The Times*, said: "[T]he disordered passion of being so cold and emotionally detached can de-humanise people … One has to be very careful to make sure these disordered passions do not surface and, if they do, that we manage them" (Woodhouse, 2006). I believe that there are many relevant parallels within psychiatry, in that the demands faced, particularly in forensic settings, can provoke similar disordered passions in practitioners. The *Oxford English Dictionary* (2002, p. 1,225) defines revenge as "retaliation for an injury or wrong".

Primarily I am suggesting that the government stance is one of revenge, that is, retaliating for a wrong that it feels psychiatry has perpetrated (through its complacency in not sufficiently taking a meaningful account of history), prompting it to introduce the recent amendments. I am in this chapter sympathetic to the amendments of the Mental Health Act 1983, while at the same time not condoning the solution to the difficulty that psychiatry has created, given that again the "solution" is a form of malignant mirroring.

I feel it is important to focus upon the suggestion that revenge is at work when patients are diagnosed as untreatable. A simple example here may serve to highlight the significance of history and the importance of allowing its place in creating true understanding of any events that occur. Recently I had reason to brake very sharply while travelling in my car and this caused the vehicle behind me to crash into mine. The driver of that vehicle emerged with considerable anger and was, I believe, about to attack me until he saw a young child a few feet from the front of my vehicle who had run out from the kerb, frozen in terror yet physically unhurt. Fortunately he was able to take account of the history to my need to brake so sharply and understood why this had had such an impact upon his own experience. We were both then able to attend to the child's distress.

I will be giving a couple of clinical examples in which the history of each individual patient became crucially important in formulating an understanding of his or her psychopathology and enabling a change towards containment and treatment. But before doing so, I want to comment on the notion of retaliation by psychiatry that may exist as a part of the dynamics involved in treatment. Any practioner/team/ institution diagnosing untreatability, following the definition within the *Oxford English Dictionary* (2002, p. 1,575), could be retaliating against a previously held injury or wrong. The definition is: "(of a patient, disease, or other condition) for whom or for which no medical care is available or possible".

I am of the opinion that such an injury or wrong can be a factor in any formative experience, including trauma. An individual lacking the father's "initiation" (analogous to the healthy reflective third) enacts a retaliation of sorts, in relation to that which the individual did not receive and lacked developmentally. That which is lacking is therefore not able to be given by way of treatment, reminding us again of the observations in Menzies Lyth's article (1959). Menzies Lyth suggests that the objective situation that often confronts the nurse can bear a striking resemblance to the phantasy situation that exists in every individual at the deepest and most primitive levels of the mind:

> [T]he intense anxiety evoked by the nursing task has precipitated … regression to primitive types of defence. These have been projected and given objective existence in the social structure and culture of the nursing service … and (the nurse) experiences the objective situations as a mixture of objective reality and phantasy … She then re-experiences painfully and vividly, in relation to current objective reality, many of the feelings appropriate to the phantasies. Successful mastery of the objective situations gives reassurance about the mastery of the phantasy situations.
>
> (Menzies Lyth, 1959, p. 49)

Ideally, we all vary in the extent to which we are able to modify or abandon our early defence mechanisms and develop other ways of addressing our anxieties. Methods include the ability to confront the anxiety situations in their original or symbolic forms and to reconcile ourselves to them, so that we can approach and tolerate psychic and objective reality. This allows us to differentiate between psychic and objective (internal and external) reality and perform constructive and objectively successful activities in relation to them both. Menzies Lyth suggests that every individual is at risk of objective or psychic events stimulating acute anxiety, leading to partial or complete abandonment of more mature methods of dealing with anxiety (1959, p. 75). Regression then occurs to the more primitive methods of defence, which may be vengeful, retaliatory, and talionic.

I now want to highlight two examples of patients, one male and one female, ostensibly deemed to be untreatable, following the experience they have generated in their treatment teams. Given that they are both extremely high in psychopathy ratings they can often generate intense loathing ("disordered passions") in any treatment team. Neither patient has been approached to give consent to be discussed in that in both cases informed consent could not be guaranteed. Therefore every attempt has been made to completely anonymise both patients to protect their identities while attempting to maintain clinical integrity in order to exemplify the issues. In the first case, the patient's psychic defence was the elimination, in his own mind, of his own personal history, given the degree of psychic pain associated with it, and its replacement with another history. In the second case, the defence in relation to her history was one of "identification with an aggressor" (Freud, A., 1993, pp. 109–121). The psychotic process in the latter case was that this patient took on the identification of her hated sibling (through the process of symbolic equation), because her sister had caused her so much pain in childhood, prompting her mind to adopt the adage "if you can't beat them, join them". She therefore protected herself from psychic pain by projecting her own intolerable early experience into other patients, by being the special patient on the ward herself. Other patients then experienced what it had been like to feel unable to compete for care with a special sibling.

In both cases, given the absence of a real significance being placed upon their own histories, custodial containment (dyadic) became the norm, and the temptation to dismiss both patients as untreatable was considerable.

The former case is of a male patient whose index offence was one of rape (per anum) against a teenage girl who was briefly known to him and with whom he was temporarily residing. In my sessions with him a familiar pattern emerged of a highly defended self in which he was presenting a false image and history to me of being the product of a significant criminal family fraternity—something that was very important to him. In addition, my countertransference experience was one of total castration around any potential thinking developing between us that could be meaningful. A ubiquitous feature was the revision of his own history, which had very little connection to the truth, and a very clear sense that he was in total control of himself and others. He adopted a classic and, for himself, a life-saving defence against the repeated trauma and experiences of his early life. This had resulted in him deluding himself that he had in effect given birth to himself, and had reinvented what is referred to as the "primal scene" (McDougall, 1972). In effect, he had fathered himself and created his own identity. This is understood to be a privileged form of manic defence against facing the truth of his existence and thereby preferable to developing other forms of madness. It became quite clear that he was the father of his own treatment plan and was clear in his own mind about what he needed to do in order to return to the community. Moreover, my own experience of him was that any attempt to engage creatively through a thoughtful and reflective intercourse was killed off and replaced by his own reality which was an identity and life of his own making, including hijacked material from his own personal history and environment. This attack upon his own knowledge and curiosity around his origins (his history) created a confusion which was designed to defend him against the painful feelings of rejection and annihilation by his primary objects. At one point, he was talking about his association with a notorious faction of a particular football supporters' club renowned for violence. I too happened to have an extensive and more in-depth knowledge of this faction and my reply immediately alerted him to this knowledge, which discomforted him intensely and had the effect of me establishing an authority beyond his own. I believe I became for him, in relation to this material, the real father in the room. His response to this experience was to recall an incident when he was detained elsewhere, where the leader of this faction was also detained and following a conflict with him (mirroring the one with me) his solution, he said, was to kill him by smuggling a handgun in and out of prison. In the transference and with a keen eye on his history, I understood this as his way of deluding himself that both I and his biological father and the delusional leader of this faction were all symmetrised and eliminated in his own mind in order for him to re-establish a degree of psychic equilibrium and control.

With the exercise of such primitive defence mechanisms (whereby the true history is defended against and has no place) two important dynamics featured. The first related to the confusion of his loving/libidinal impulses with his aggressive/hating and murdering impulses. He had not benefited developmentally from being able to establish a normal differentiation between these two impulses, given the absence of a triangulating capacity in his maternal object and the abandonment at birth by his biological father. By extension, his index offence of rape provides the image for this internal confusion, that is the anus of his victim, which was a receptive space that was commodious as opposed to creative and one that represents the deadness of the space in his mother's mind where there is no life-giving and creative space to engage with. In relation to the significance of taking account of history, it was no surprise to me that there was a symmetry in relation to the age of the victim at the time of the index offence equating exactly with the age of his mother when she gave birth to him. This suggests that at a deep level in his own mind, he felt he was the product of his mother's anus (given his commodious experience of her). His violent engagement with that part of the victim could have represented an attempt to get himself and his impulses safely contained, with his expectation that such a communication would not be understood and would both contribute to anal confusion as well as repetition compulsion (Rosenfeld, 1984).

This move from intercourse with a creative vagina to the deadness of the anus is indicative of the way that he relates to the world. It can often be treatment teams (the world) intuit the need for this massive defence and are drawn into colluding with protecting him from being challenged regarding his history and thereby avoid introducing any alternative to the identity he has created for himself. Moreover, this is also the environment where the social defence system, as formulated by Menzies Lyth, develops to deflect the emergence of individually held unconscious processes in favour of compliance with unconscious communal defensive systems (1959, p. 75).

Returning to the female patient, it was universally experienced in many institutions that she was untreatable and that she could command and preoccupy the minds of treatment teams to the point of exasperation and exhaustion. This inevitably resulted in her being moved on, whereupon the cycle repeated itself. In terms of self-harm she has used every imaginable form, as well as attacks upon staff and others.

Indeed, she has had the potential to bring an institution to its knees. She was therefore, upon reflection, repeatedly caught up in re-enacting a drama that was directly related to the traumas of her earlier experience and one that she compulsively repeated quite unconsciously, in order to seek understanding and the containment that understanding affords. Given the often life-threatening demands she places on any treatment team, it is not surprising that, in the first instance, the preoccupation is in making her safe. However, it would appear that in doing so, little further reflective activity takes place to gain some understanding about the activities she gets herself and others caught up in. Given the repeated nature of her acting-out, it is as if any treatment teams are just not understanding her unconscious communication. A mature reflection on her history had not been afforded any real significance in the treatment teams that she had encountered during her institutional life. In looking at her history it became clear that she had effectively identified with an aggressor within her family, namely a sibling with whom healthy competition was impossible because of the collusion by her mother, who was unable to see beyond the needs of the older and more demanding child.

I am reminded of the recent death of Ivor Cutler, the anti-intellectual poet, artist, and performer who attributed the life-long neurosis that shaped him to the birth of his younger brother: "[H]e took my place as the centre of the universe. Without that I would not have been so screwed up as I am and therefore as creative" (Cutler, 2006, p. 66). This is indicative of a creative response to rivalry, in contrast to our patient who, by forming an identification, re-enacted repetitively and compulsively the family dynamic. In re-enactment, she moved from the passive experience of being on the receiving end historically, to an active one, ensuring that other patients on the ward and staff were placed into the role of passively having to accept the inevitable experience that hitherto had been her own. This is understood as the mechanism of projective identification. Unmanageable feelings are split off from the self and projected or evacuated into others, so that the feelings become part of others' experience (Bion, 1959). Once the history was added to the mix for the treatment team, a clearer understanding emerged about the experiences they were having around this patient. This then provided an opportunity for a mature containment and a sense of being able to survive and progress in the treatment that was being offered. There was always a great danger that the cycle that had been repeated throughout her institutional life was yet again going to occur, by being moved on to another treatment team, who would again experience the same immense difficulties before moving her on as well. With the understanding based on her history underpinning the thinking, this repeating cycle could be interrupted, with a better prognosis. More recently I have learnt that this patient no longer preoccupies the treatment team in the same way, and that other patients have become more demanding, a scenario that could not have been envisaged by any of her previous treatment teams in her institutional life.

In conclusion, I am stressing the primary importance of including an understanding of an individual's history (grandparental and parental) in the links that can be made to any offending that has taken place and as an underpinning to the provision of a template for treatment and care. This robustly and potently combats the ubiquitous potential for corrosion of therapeutic effectiveness (into dyadic thinking), by addressing the deeply ingrained paranoid/schizoid functioning in us all, both as individuals and very particularly in the collective, that is, government and institutions. We ignore history at our peril; the alternative would be to impose rudderless treatment plans based more out of hope than expectation that benefits might be achieved.

Postscript

The UK government has recently announced, in response to the Offender Personality Disorder Consultation, a new pathway approach in a bid to ensure that the complex needs of high-risk offenders with personality disorder are addressed more effectively. As a result, Broadmoor will be the first Dangerous and Severe Personality Disorder (DSPD) unit to be decommissioned, by April 2012, and patients will continue to be treated in the level of security necessary for the risk they present. The aim is to address the complex needs of such offenders more effectively with intervention and treatment being provided earlier and in the most suitable location, initially increasing the number of treatment places in prison. In addition, there will be an investment in the early identification of offenders who present a high risk of serious harm to others and are likely to have a severe personality disorder. One of the keys to the success of the new proposals will be the extent to which the National Offender Management Service (NOMS) and the NHS can work together in support of the needs of the patient in a healthy triangulating process alongside the critically important need to take a full and meaningful account of history.

Notes

1. We must not ignore the potential for criminality deriving from uncon-scious guilt (Freud, 1916) whereby in order to deal with an unconscious state of mind (self-condemnation) the individual, still unconsciously, acts to bring down a punishment on himself, and thereby containment.
2. This refers to a phenomenon little known or used in contemporary psychotherapeutic assessment and treatment that links the timing of traumatic events in one generation to the next. This has been found by the author to be of universal value, particularly since it is significantly related to the arrival of a third through childbirth and the subsequent stretching of the mind to accommodate the emotion of jealousy along-side the numbers in the family. I return to these concepts in the final chapter on the Dunblane Massacre.

CHAPTER SIX

Boy do I exist!
The avoidance of annihilatory terror
through paedophilic acts

This chapter explores clinical material in the light of the patient's history from an extended assessment and subsequent treatment, to highlight some of the dynamics involved in paedophilic activities. It is suggested that what the paedophile hopes to achieve in his offending is primarily the elimination of anxiety emanating from the dreaded emotional experience of exclusion, isolation, emptiness, and non-existence. The paedophilic solution is rooted in his hatred of reality and the natural order of events, and is related to the ubiquitous importance of secrecy (notorious in paedophilia) that ensures that the relationship the paedophile has with his own knowledge (fantasies, thoughts, and actions) is not shared with himself or allowed to become known by another. Moreover, this is inextricably linked to the denial of otherness (the father, in the developmental model) by achieving early Oedipal triumph, as a corollary to the fears associated with accommodating/embracing in to the mind the malevolent experience of paternity, either directly through violence/hostility or indirectly through rejection/negation. This results in the relationship with mother becoming enmeshed and a perverse identification developing in an attempt to be at one with her, given the absence of a mediating, benign, supportive, and loving father. Authority (stereotypically the father) becomes compulsively undermined, giving the victims of such offenders the experience of authority (represented by the offender at the time of the offence against the child) as dangerous and to be avoided, thereby mirroring the early experience of the perpetrator.

Alex, my patient, has an extensive list of previous criminal convictions and while they include theft and burglary, my focus will be on his sexual offences. He has previously been convicted on ten occasions for up to thirty-one offences including two offences against the person in 1997, and twenty-three sexual offences from 1978 to 1997.

In September 1978 Alex was convicted of soliciting and failing to surrender to bail. He was imprisoned for three months, suspended for two years. In January 1981 Alex was convicted of gross indecency with a child, indecent assault on a male under the age of sixteen years, and soliciting. He was imprisoned for nine months. (Sixteen other offences were taken into consideration.) Further "theft" offences occurred up until December 1984 when Alex was convicted of seven offences of indecent assault on a male under fourteen years of age, one count of attempted gross indecency with a child, and one count of actual gross indecency with a child. He was imprisoned for seven years. In May 1989 Alex was convicted of soliciting, for which he was imprisoned for twelve months. In September 1990 Alex was convicted of four counts of indecent assault on a male aged sixteen years or over and one count of indecent assault on a female under fourteen years of age, which resulted in a further four years of imprisonment. In September 1993 Alex was convicted of one count of indecent assault on a male under fourteen years of age and one count of indecent assault on a female under fourteen years of age. Again he was imprisoned, this time for a total of five years.

His most recent offences took place in the beginning of 1997 when he was convicted of two counts of indecent assault on a male under sixteen years of age, one count of detaining a child without lawful authority so as to keep him or her from lawful authority, and one count of attempted kidnapping. This time he received a term of imprisonment of eighteen years, which was subsequently reduced to ten years on appeal.

I feel it is important to highlight at this stage a factor that I believe is inextricably linked to the underlying anxiety that drives his offending. When questioned about his index offence he had expressed feeling very lonely at the time and needing some comfort. This provoked his reoffending immediately following his release from prison. The initial offence was actually committed on the day of his release from custody for the previous offences. Indeed this was a repetition of what had taken place following his release on licence in 2003, when he was recalled to prison the day after having been seen by police to approach two separate males aged eleven and twelve years.

Alex had therefore had extensive contact with the penal system that resulted in his transfer to a high-secure hospital at the end of 2005. Prior to my seeing him in 2008, various assessment tools had reached the conclusion that his intellectual functioning was within the borderline range, although there were no specific deficits. He was not thought to be in the learning disability range either. There had not been any evidence of psychotic symptoms and Alex continued to express the belief that he did not suffer from any psychiatric illness. While there had been variation in his psychopathy rating, he was generally found to be on the severe end of the range, which was borne out in the general experience by the nursing staff of his abnormal behaviour, poor social skills, excessive preoccupation with cleanliness, fear of disease, complaints about his physical health, suspiciousness, rather grandiose ideas, and odd patterns of purchases, all resulting in huge demands on nursing staff time. His diagnosis was therefore considered to be that of a personality disorder consistent with antisocial and paranoid traits.

Alex was referred for a psychodynamic assessment given the difficulties he presented on a day-to-day basis and to explore whether greater clarity could be achieved in relation to his past offending and current behaviour on the ward. Prior to meeting with Alex on the ward I noted from his file that two different dates of birth had been recorded. Upon meeting him, he clarified immediately his date of birth (he is now over fifty) and this was particularly important given the significance regarding his adoption three days following his birth. I was also at the time very aware of what appeared to be an absence of any information contained on file relating to his early history. This was, not surprisingly, mirrored in my interview with him, when he registered his earliest memory at the age of six.

Alex's offending centres on a predilection for fondling young boys in the age range of six to thirteen, in and through their boxer shorts. The specificity of the fetish was repeated in the transference whereby, in his interactions with me, he would try to "stimulate" my interest and arousal (stir me up) behind the protective garment of my mind. I believe this ultimately served to compensate for the dreaded annihilatory possibility that he was not in my (his adoptive mother's) mind at all. Alex is a name changed by deed poll from that on his adoptive birth certificate of Brian. The name Alex was chosen to identify with the fore-name of a six-year-old fellow pupil/peer at junior school with whom he shared his very first intimacy, fondling each other inside their shorts. Given that at the age of six he also experienced the loss of his adoptive father who separated from his adoptive mother and left the family home (which he said "devastated" him) he was also told by his adoptive mother, for the first time, that she was not his biological mother, and it is therefore not surprising that he had a fixation linked to this period in his life.

Upon meeting him, his presentation had a manic quality (over-anxious) with a tendency to be verbose in needing to impress upon me how he had been misunderstood and misperceived in a previous unit. While holding in mind the universal traits familiar with the paedophilic pathology of secrecy, deception (self and others), and manipulation, the underlying and ubiquitous message he communicated to me was one of feeling unheard, misunderstood, and, in particular, not feeling that he was being given a voice that counts (a distinct lack of any potency).

To that end I sought to clarify in the time spent with him what the underlying anxiety might be that led to his offending. It would appear that, at core, he was terrified of the feelings triggered by the experience of feeling alone and being put in touch with his emptiness and feelings of non-existence, and that he sought to be found and lovingly touched/ fondled (re-connected) in a meaningful way. This was perversely acted out in his offending, and seemingly linked to the early trauma around rejection by his biological parents, compounded by the experience of a punitive environment in adoption, where not only was he subject to his adoptive mother's narcissistic preoccupations but he was also expected to comply with her nurturing style, which he described as a strict regime. It would appear that he felt the need to conceal any aspect of himself that he perceived would not meet with his adoptive mother's expectations and that this was all exacerbated by the absence of the mediating presence of a father whose mind was unavailable (due in large part to his alcoholism).

Money-Kryle considered that a "megalomanic delusion" of "parthenogenetic creativity" displaces the idea of the parental couple as the origin and historical precursor of the self (1971, p. 103). This is Alex's story and Money-Kryle was supported in his thinking by Franco De Masi (2007) who similarly stated that the paedophile's "inner world originates from a delusional nucleus in which an object (a child or an adolescent) is idealised and worshipped in place of the parents. This object promises all means of pleasure and happiness" (De Masi, 2007, p. 147).

Alex's story culminated in his adoptive mother's rejection of him at the age of thirteen (repeating his much earlier rejection after three days), in that, in his words, "she blamed me for allowing myself to get sexually assaulted". This was also the time in his life when his adoptive father, who had now been separated from his adoptive mother for some years, died. It is also likely that his adoptive mother may have been frightened of him becoming an adolescent with all that that entailed, as if communicating the message that adult relationships were untenable. Such an early experience would undoubtedly contribute to a stunting of healthy psychological growth, with the corollary that his development was held back, as if metaphorically concealed behind the boxer shorts that he was excited about engaging with.

I became increasingly aware that the very early environment and experience that he had emerged from and sought to avoid, he had paradoxically re-created for himself, in that he constantly experienced feeling alone and punished in the ward environment. This was particularly heightened when he felt he was not really listened to and heard, even though his often persistent and demanding presentation resulted in him driving people away. I considered that his reoffending when on licence (times two) following previous detentions was in part caused by being unable to reconcile himself to the feelings associated with being so alone (abandoned, rejected, uncontained, and unsupported) in the first few days of release, equating with the first few days of birth and afterwards through his adoptive experience.

Alex had an obsessive compulsive disorder around cleanliness; for example, he would only touch door handles with a tissue in his hand, and would be preoccupied with the cleanliness of the spout (breast?) of the hot water dispenser on the ward. This would seem to suggest a projection of his internal sense of badness/contaminants into his environment over which he can then have some "delusional" control. Moreover, he had gained some qualifications in cleaning and hoped to gather more in order to equip himself to enter the cleaning profession upon being discharged. I noted at the time that while this was commendable, he also needed to gain an understanding about the defensive nature of his choice of cleaning in relation to his own history. This highlighted that he was forever protecting himself from feelings that he was at core somehow wrong/bad and that this self remained hidden (under cover—in boxer shorts). During the initial assessment he did not deny his offending, although he wanted to insist that his paedophilic activities had always been non-penetrative and fixed at fondling boys to erection in their boxer shorts. He was excited by the prospect of engaging with the potency of the penis/boy that was concealed within his victims, representing himself.

As an aside, during this period of assessment on the ward I was made aware of his excitement and contact with a young male domestic cleaner, who was totally unaware of Alex's attraction to not only his youthful looks but also his profession as a cleaner. I recalled noting that this behaviour had taken place at a time when we were meeting and wondered whether this was indicative of the anxiety generated in the intimacy with me (as a potent male) becoming displaced into a perverse enactment with a younger-looking male.

In my conclusions and recommendations to the clinical team at the time I commented that his recidivism was clearly a serious concern. Further, I remarked that I felt that this would continue unabated in his ward-based and hospital-based activities, despite his attempts at deception (of self and others in his claims about having learnt his lesson), until he had been able to reconcile himself to the feelings associated with his early history. I suggested that he was therefore perversely acting-out, both via his offending in his past and in the way he relates in the hospital (indicative of his offending), in an attempt to find "the lost boy" standing for himself and represented by his adoption of the name Alex. I added that clinical energy needed to be applied to making contact with his adoptive mother, as well as his biological parents, to gather as much detailed history as possible with a view to bringing into consciousness that which had remained concealed and tantalisingly out of reach. I added that some significant thought needed to be given, particularly if he were finally to be released, about providing solid support and containment, given his susceptibility at such times to seek his own perverse containment by offending.

He seemed excited to meet me and I wondered whether this was a different experience for him and that perhaps I represented the "detective" he wanted to model himself on, in my emphasis on digging into the detail of his history. I further wondered whether he also felt that, in meeting me, important parts of himself had been found and "fondled" for the first time, in a way that gave him a different experience from the ingrained and perverse acting-out that he had engaged with via his victims. He gave me the impression that he could, once sufficiently contained, consider links in his mind, and as a corollary the minds of others could offer him something helpful. While he clearly demonstrated very poor anxiety management, I believed that he would benefit from individual work, particularly if there was the significant gathering of history taking that was recommended. He indicated to me at the time that he was happy to engage in both.

As a part of the normal progress through the hospital, Alex was subsequently moved to another ward and I was again contacted by his new Responsible Clinician (RC) asking whether I might be able to provide the team with further intervention, given the difficulties they were encountering in relation to his behaviour on the ward. It was decided that I would offer him an extended assessment which equated to twelve once-weekly psychotherapy sessions. Given my understanding of his psychopathology and growing awareness of his behaviour, I decided to introduce a model of treatment which from the outset was going to be undertaken with the patient's knowledge, with a view to addressing the endemic splitting which was such a feature around him. He was very adept at undermining/criticising/rubbishing one member of staff against another. I informed Alex that our work would be undertaken in a totally transparent way, whereby there would be a direct link with the ward and the multi-disciplinary team between our sessions, so that I could proactively review with him his perspective on the observations made by staff. In practice, this meant meeting individually with all members of the clinical team in order to robustly implement the model. Moreover, I made myself available to be contacted outside of sessions by email with his primary nurse/clinical team, in order to provide a holding and containing milieu. This I felt was crucially important with this type of patient in terms of triangulation. The aim and hope was to give the patient the opportunity to experience a metaphorical "parental couple", represented by myself and the ward/multi-disciplinary team/hospital, in support of his progress and development, while at the same time challenging that part of his functioning which was prone to undermine that whole process.

My thinking about the model is supported in "A psychodynamic look at paedophile sex offenders in treatment" (Drapeau et al., 2003) in which the authors conclude:

> [W]hat is interesting about such a setting [treatment for paedophile offenders] is that both a maternal holding function and a paternal law function are implicitly offered by the treatment … [I]t is crucial that all staff stand by this law … despite strong wishes to relieve a patient from the distress and suffering coming from the application of the program or institutional rules … [S]uch extensive representation of the law may be for the subject a rare opportunity to have access to, and confront, what may symbolically be a father figure for them.
>
> (Drapeau et al., 2003, p. 37)

It was quite clear that Alex's increasingly demanding behaviour on the ward was symptomatic and linked to his paedophilic psychopathology. The remit I set myself, in the extended assessment, was to establish the level of his curiosity, motivation, and capacity to engage with the thinking necessary to link his current ward behaviour with his index offending and ultimately his early experience. I believed that this would provide an opportunity to establish any potential he had to integrate these factors, which could act as a bulwark against any further acting-out, offence-related phenomena.

In addition, I asked two senior colleagues to undertake psychological measurements by way of interview and questionnaire, in order to monitor any possible change to Alex's psychological functioning as a result of the analytic work I was undertaking. I was of course very aware from the outset that the likelihood of any discernible/recordable change in relation to his psychological functioning was remote if not non-existent, given the limited frequency and duration of sessions.

The common themes that emerged during this period with him included his verbose tangential monologues whereby he would express lengthy complaints regarding perceived injuries. This would have the effect of my needing to bring him back to what was originally being addressed, as if he continually needed to be running away from the point of contact. In addition, he was always very keen to impress upon me his remorse for the crimes he'd committed, although this would often be couched in a way that suggested that in any event his victims in some way or another either colluded or acquiesced to his intentions.

I gained the view that he was experienced in talking about himself and his treatment, although I noticed that he had a tendency to over-anticipate a negative reaction to himself by others, which became no less a feature with me. His need on the ward was a constant feature and was extremely draining for staff. It was indicative of greed and a corollary to unmet needs, stemming from his early history. It is clear that he had a very weak/poor ability to control his impulses and as a caricature he represented a frightened little boy who was secretly seeking/searching for meaningful and intimate contact to compensate for absence and loss. In doing so he gets caught out and feels that nobody believes his tall stories and that he is generally considered to be up to no good and can't be trusted.

Given the model that I had adopted, he became progressively aware that all of his activity on and off the ward was being relayed to me and that any notable incidents were going to be taken up by me in the sessions. This had the effect of reducing to a considerable extent (although in no way eliminating) his annoying and persistent behaviours of pestering staff, as well as reducing, towards the end of the twelve-session period, the amount of running ward notes that needed to be made on file in relation to his ward behaviour. Alex certainly engaged with me and gave me indications that he was able to think, albeit fleetingly, about the various links that were put to him in relation to his behaviour on the ward, his offending history, and his early life.

At the very beginning of the work, it was brought to my attention that Alex had purchased eighteen pairs of underpants, and so I addressed this with him, curious to establish what his thinking was. He said that he liked to send pants to other patients in the hospital as a gift. I asked him to consider two dynamic possibilities. The first was that that he had somehow managed to convince himself that staff (authority) had colluded with him making the purchase of the pants and that they had therefore condoned the whole process, allowing him to remain convinced that the activity, linked as it was to his offending, was acceptable and permissible. This comment he refuted robustly. The second comment I made was that, by donating the underpants to other men he was able to hold images in his mind of the men wearing them, which would again convince him that they were also condoning his paedophilic activity and making it acceptable. Again, he refuted this suggestion.

While he continued to deny any truth to my thinking, he nonetheless informed me in the next session that he had decided to donate all of the remaining underpants to charity because "I don't want people still thinking I'm a paedophile". This reaction was of course unconvincing, in that it represented a behavioural/practical solution, lacking any depth and meaning to his actions and solutions based on his offending and history.

While he said that he trusted me and felt supported by me, this was often difficult for him. When I challenged him on certain issues he immediately felt that I was aligning myself with the ward, in believing that he was telling tales. Therefore, in our model of triangulation and his vulnerability, he could very quickly feel that I was drawn into taking sides against him, as opposed to joining with the ward in support of him. One particular clinical example serves to highlight this.

Prior to a session I was informed by a member of the nursing team of a comment by a patient from another ward regarding a very brief contact that he'd had with Alex. Apparently they had met on a stairwell and, in briefly exchanging pleasantries, Alex offered to shake the other patient's hand, which for all intents and purposes for observers, was merely a gesture of greeting. However, the patient commented afterwards to a member of his team that the manner in which his hand was shaken was more indicative of a caress/stroke than a clear handshake. This was fed back to Alex's ward and consequently relayed to me. I challenged him about this in our next session and he was predictably angry in his response, probably feeling that the other patient had betrayed him when he had been secretly attempting to seduce him. Characteristically, his initial response was to claim that the staff had made it up. Given the rapport we had developed, he was able to stay with this challenge and, to his credit, he was able to return in the following session having reflected upon the possibility that the paedophilic part of his own mind could not be trusted, before admitting that he had indeed intimately shaken hands with another patient in the way described.

This was an example that serves to underline the importance of maintaining very clear boundaries, and providing Alex with the experience of a firm but fair challenge to his behaviour; as well as underlining that I and the clinical team were united in joining that "healthy" part of his own functioning that could challenge the other "malevolent, paedophilic" part of his own mind that he is forever needing to conceal and make excuses for. He agreed with me that the paedophilic part of his own mind could not be trusted and that he felt he had no control over it. This served to emphasise that he couldn't trust the "authority" within himself to comply with the law and prevent the paedophilic impulses from being satisfied—in other words, the (stereotypical) father in him was absent. By extension, if his paedophilic activities were successful, he would be able to triumph over father (authority) and exact his revenge upon all fathers who abandoned him. He agreed that his experience with me was one of a father figure who was fair, firm, supportive, and benign, while challenging. He expressed that this was a new experience and, while ambivalent, one that he hoped would continue.

This constant law-breaking and undermining of authority (fathers) was a constant feature experienced on the ward, where he sought to undermine/deceive and avoid any of the hospital protocols through various means. On one such occasion this was demonstrated by his non-compliance with the "law" that I had introduced, which was asking him to make notes of the session in his spare thinking time and to bring these notes back to the next session so that we could ascertain his level of thinking and reflection about the work. This is by no means conventional psychodynamic practice and this flexibility with the therapeutic frame I address in due course. He returned the following session without having made any notes and so had "broken the law", also demonstrating a total absence of thinking and reflection. I interpreted this as an attack upon the third, represented by reflective thinking and the father in our developmental model, in which one and two are mother and child. While he agreed, it was clear that this dynamic would require some considerable working through over time, which was not, on this occasion, a resource we had. This is again reflected by Drapeau et al. (2003) when their research showed that paedophile subjects

> don't want someone who doesn't know what he's doing as my therapist ... that the therapist was the most important factor of the therapy [in being] strong, capable of leadership and even authoritarian ... strong enough to contain attacks, trustworthy, predictable and reliable ... with a therapist's weakness and hesitation reason enough to quit.

> (Drapeau et al., 2003, pp. 34–38; emphasis added)

I personally have always adhered to the crucial importance of trustworthiness, predictability, consistency, and reliability, and perhaps to an obsessive degree, but it saddens me to have to say that, in contrast, on occasions I have despaired when I have witnessed some (often senior) clinicians treat some of these characteristics too lightly.

Overall Alex attended the sessions on time and remained throughout. When he was able to consider any comments and interventions that I made, he would give the impression that these were important and meaningful insights, although I remained unconvinced that they were in any way digested by him to make a difference. In addition, any interventions and comments that I sought to make were hard-earned, in the sense that I often had to intervene quite assertively in his verbosity in an attempt to make it possible for him to consider a different way of thinking. At no time did I feel that there was any real continuity between each session and that he had in any meaningful way spent time reflecting upon the work that had been undertaken, which was why I introduced the homework. The homework he subsequently presented was strikingly thin in content and gave the impression that he was merely complying with an expectation on my behalf.

The two psychological tests that were conducted independently, interviewing him both before and after my twelve-week intervention, produced the following outcomes. The first was a child empathy test and addressed his ability to read (decode) children's reactions to adult sexual/affectionate advances. Prior to the therapy, he endorsed a comparatively normal set of scores, and was clear in his narrative that he must be extremely cautious not to overlook any kind of distress. After the therapy, he endorsed an even greater sensitivity and on occasion reported anticipating distress where others did not rate it as present. The assessor's overall interpretation was that while the test had significant limitations, it did serve to underline how hard Alex worked to try to convince himself and others that he was able to empathise with the distress caused by his offences in an attempt to present in a convincing way to others that he had changed. Indeed, he worked very hard with me in the sessions, as he did persistently on the ward, to try to present a sensitivity that he had to the victims of paedophilia which could often leave you with the feeling of being unconvinced.

The second psychological test was a tape-recorded Adult Attachment Interview (AAI) together with a semi-structured interview of personality disorder (SCID11) and consisted of open-ended questions designed to tap into the patient's view of his index offence and illicit the narrative around the individual's representation of their index offence.

The interviews are specifically designed to access the patient's capacity to understand his motives and those of his victim(s), and to reveal any narrative variations in the presentation of the offence history and errors with respect to how the patient inferred their own and others', particularly the victim's/victims', state of mind. The significance of the open-ended nature of the questions and the way that the interviews are rated is that there are no "right" answers and it is difficult for the interviewee to fake a socially desirable response.

The assessor concluded (with interest) that before treatment there was a greater discrepancy between Alex's score on what is referred to as the "agency" scale and his score on the "perception of self" scale. The former indicated that he was able to take some (but not full) agency and responsibility for his role in his offence; however, he also represented his offence as discordant to his sense of self. This combination of representations was not consistent and suggested that, at some level, Alex distanced himself mentally from a more realistic view of himself in relation to his offending. The assessor concluded that the shifts on two of the scales were in a healthy direction indicating that, post-treatment, Alex had a more respectful mental representation of his victim and saw his offence more in keeping with how he perceived himself. The report ended stating that there were clear psychological links between Alex's early experiences and his offending, although he was not yet able to make deep and more complex links between his early life, his relationships with his current carers, and his offence.

Despite the significant limitations of both tests and the short duration of the therapy, there were nonetheless perceptible shifts in his functioning to suggest that he could potentially benefit from a more intensive form of intervention.

Following this period of treatment, I felt able to offer the clinical team the following understanding regarding Alex's behaviour and how it was linked to his offending and psychopathology. I suggested that Alex compensated for a grave sense of disconnection emanating from the early experience of being given up for adoption and that this had been exacerbated by his experience of his adoptive parents. His adopted mother related to him for her own narcissistic needs, usefully described elsewhere as a mother treating her child as a form of "narcissistic doll" (Bailer, 1993, pp. 573–589; Drapeau et al., 2003, p. 37). His adopted father had not wanted to adopt him, but acceded to his wife's wishes for an adopted child, to fill the vacuum in her life. Alex defends himself at all costs against feeling and re-experiencing an annihilatory experience of rejection (originally by his biological parents and then, at core, by his adoptive father and, in her use of him, by his adoptive mother). By maintaining a fixation in his mind upon an intimate experience that he'd had with a six-year-old boy (when Alex was also six) he seeks to fill his own vacuum of not feeling meaningfully attached. This experience with another child was one that gave him the feeling of being wanted and loved and that he sought to recreate and be at one with when feelings of disconnection and of being alone were again experienced. This important memory and incident at the age of six coincided with the time in his life when he was left/ultimately rejected/ abandoned by his adoptive father (which you will recall left him feeling devastated). It thereby cemented identification with the adoptive mother who engaged with young children in order to meet a need regarding her own feelings of emptiness.

I have considered before that the paedophile defends against the natural triangular family order by destroying (through rage) the reflective potential of the bridge from the parents to himself. He attempts to eliminate all difference so that the natural possibility of accommodating all three is reduced to two and then to one. Therefore, at the point of offending, the paedophile deceives himself by annihilating key differences between himself and his victim (object).

I have found a deeper understanding of this frequent powerful mechanism to eliminate difference best expressed by way of Matte Blanco's symmetrisation (1988). There is thus a denial of the essential asymmetry, and by extension the asymmetry between subject and object, whereby the perpetrator is at one with the victim. This also affects the time dimension, whereby a development of the sequentiality of difference also affects the situation in which the perpetrator (Alex) eliminates the significant asymmetry between himself and other by a denial of difference. This puts out of court all difference, thereby convincing himself that "the victim wanted it", as he "wanted it". I feel that these patients are leading us into dynamic considerations of symmetry, which suggests more investigation.

Alex's recidivism indicated a total inability to contain his anxieties about a disconnection (which occurred when he was released from institutional care in 1989, 1996, and 2003 after his licence was revoked and he was re-arrested within days of being released), so he sought to recreate the experience of feeling connected with a young male child. The trigger to the impulse to offend was considered to be the unbearable reminder of his emptiness, inadequacy, and non-existence (a sense of being nought, in the one, two, and three referred to earlier), which is compensated for by joining up with a fixated period of connection in order to feel included, moving from nought to one. I am postulating that what Alex hoped to achieve, in his offending, was primarily the elimination of both uncontainable anxiety and underlying feelings of annihilation. This is achieved through the elimination of difference, with an identification with a "perverse" mother. He "became" his own internalised mother, at the time of offending, by giving his victims his own early experience, via the process of wholesale projective identification. The alternative resonated too closely with the dreaded emotional experience from childhood of exclusion, isolation, and emptiness. I would like to say at this point that having some time ago heard (at the Institute of Psychoanalysis) Rob Hale's very detailed work in this area at the Portman Clinic, I feel that there may be room for consideration of an important factor that needs to be included regarding the transgenerational family history of the perpetrator and its contribution to understanding the paedophilic psychopathology.

Alex's general way of relating on the ward was indicative of his inability to contain his impulse to get his needs met appropriately. By trying to get others to accede to his persistence to do this or that, he used others in a way redolent of his victims, to satisfy his impulse for connection, which was ultimately unsuccessful.

He had a constant drive to seek an identity for himself (he had changed his name on numerous occasions), which I understood as an attempt to metaphorically adopt another version of himself redolent of his adoptive mother's narcissism.

I informed the team that the task, therapeutically, in the long term, would be to facilitate his awareness of his need to feel wanted and loved and that he existed in their minds, which stemmed from the deficit in his history. Growing awareness would enable him to begin to provide containment for his impulse to reoffend. Containment was based both on this knowledge and awareness of the consequences of his actions (guilt), that is, by complying with the law/authority/father with whom he was paradoxically seeking a healthy engagement while also feeling enraged. His maternal identification was with an object who selects young children for its own narcissistic gain. Alex had made it abundantly clear to me that if he were released from the secure hospital he would re-offend within twenty-four hours, emphasising that his own paedophilic functioning could not be trusted. Not uncommonly, this also suggested that his own dependent needs were being met in institutional care and that to separate away from this into independent living was too anxiety-provoking and would be resisted at all costs (referred to in forensic circles as "gate fever"). He had perhaps gained a perverse sense of belonging, which is a feature we see all too often in the penal system whereby the prisoner's own history illuminates an absence of a sense of belonging, which is then compensated for by feeling a sense of belonging to the criminal fraternity. In general, he over-anticipated the mistrust and negative reaction towards him by others and while not wanting to be rejected by others, he was nonetheless potentially deeply rejectable, stemming from his history and compounded by his offending and way of relating. He was seemingly caught up in a repetition compulsion where he drives people away, which was the reverse of what he was seeking to achieve. It appears that his symmetrical engagement with a six-year-old boy was the only refuge and relief, when his anxieties and terrifying feelings of disconnection threatened his sense of existence. The compensating experience of an intimate physical engagement provided an island of security in the sea of rejection and insecurity that existed in his internal world.

Given the transparent nature of the work with him, I was aware that my report might be experienced as a rejection as opposed to providing him with an understanding of the paedophilic part of his own functioning (which he couldn't trust) and of his need to act out repeatedly. Fortunately, we had developed a good enough working alliance for him to be able to communicate that he could consider this thinking, even though it was not possible for him in such a short period of time to in anyway integrate it in a meaningful and mutative way.

Following this piece of work, discussions were held to consider his future treatment, with clinicians' minds preoccupied in trying to reach a consensus about whether Alex required ongoing high-secure containment or whether he could be appropriately treated in a medium-secure setting. Clearly there were deep anxieties regarding the risk he presented and debates ensued regarding the viability of placing him on anti-libidinal medication and/or further psychotherapeutic intervention. Given the complexity of his case and the protracted clinical and legal negotiations, it was nonetheless decided to offer him a more intensive period of treatment following the same model as before only this time with a greater frequency of sessions over a longer period of time.

I want to highlight and stress the importance I attribute to the model that I used in working with him, in that his propensity for splitting and undermining processes was enormous. This propensity coupled with the demands he would place on nursing teams, both on the ward and in his many various off-ward activity areas. I believed it was therefore crucial to again meet with everybody he came in contact with, and inform them of the psychotherapeutic work that was being undertaken and to urge their engagement with the process by communicating to me any aspect of their involvement with him which they felt would be of importance. This included not only overt actions that were witnessed but also intuitions and feelings. To that end, I met with every member of the clinical/nursing team, together with staff in all other areas he visited in the hospital, to ensure that there was a transparency and free flow of communication. Such a context enabled me in our sessions to take up with him any of the observations that were made. This had the effect of challenging him in the way that he related outside of the sessions and to give him the experience that his splitting could be contained, held, and worked with.

I was of course very aware that this approach did not fit the conventional analytic/therapeutic frame, although I and many of my forensic colleagues so often feel that we have to be extremely flexible in our approach in order to reach and connect with such complex and damaged patients; Drapeau et al. have concluded: "But as the common interest of all clinicians working in this field is to—at least—reduce recidivism, efforts to adapt interventions must be constantly made" (2003, p. 38).

It was not uncommon for me to feel that Alex was in some way enjoying being caught out by me when I challenged him about a particular behaviour that had been observed, for example, subtle contact with another known paedophile. This would then be followed, again with some pleasure, by an admission on his part. It was as if he was somehow manufacturing circumstances repeatedly and compulsively whereby he would be found out for being "a naughty boy". I believe that what he took pleasure from was being able to invite my involvement (arouse me) if he needed to, not trusting that I would want to be actively involved in his life without his manufacturing such opportunities. It was also paradoxically indicative of him coercing me into stripping him almost naked, which gave him a sense of excitement, of feeling alive, and that he existed, while at the same time not becoming fully exposed, reminiscent of the modus operandi of his offending, with regard to underpants.

The importance of taking account of his early history to enable an understanding of the root causes of his offending and by extension the way he related generally should be highlighted. In identification with his adoptive mother he used young boys narcissistically to compensate for any abject sense of loss and non-existence. While it momentarily offered relief it failed to address the core dynamics and needed to be repeatedly and compulsively revisited.

There were many examples of the abnegation of an identification with adult maleness (stereotypically and perhaps intrinsically, representing authority) with his ubiquitous undermining of all authority. These examples represented a triumph (elimination) over the father, and regression to identification with mother. So the drive to offend was to reduce the relationship between himself and his parents from a three-way relationship to a two and then to a one. First there was the elimination of father (three to two), and then the need to symmetrise with the object (mother) and become at one with her (two to one). In that way, all anxiety and difference was erased.

The hatred in relation to such paedophile offenders, with its attendant denial of the full picture, is something we feel as observers precisely because it is so denied in the paedophile perpetrator, as if he assures himself that he isn't doing anyone any harm. Hope can be achieved if we hold in mind the full history of the perpetrator, to ensure that there is a full empathic and dynamic understanding by all those involved within his therapeutic treatment and prevent their becoming infected by the adoption of defensive secrecy so characteristic of paedophilia. The perpetrator needs to find a more living and virile image of a good father. In the absence of Alex's potency being supported and developed, particularly through his relationship with his father, this then led to power closing down into secrecy (legendary in paedophilia) as if things have to be driven underground in defence against annihilatory / severe authority.

My own view is that this type of psychopathology requires intensive, long-term therapy to ensure that a real working through of the processes can take place and to give the patient the experience of a supportive, benign, and authoritative intervention that he can introject. Such introjection creates a part of his internal world to mediate and act as a bulwark against the internal malevolent paedophilic force that seeks to undermine authority by seeking perverse solutions to unmet needs.

At the end of our time together, Alex continued to impress upon me that he would not reoffend because he was very aware of the harm he had inflicted upon his victims. He followed this up with the following comment, however: "I don't want to go through all that again, with the police and courts, etc." It seemed that he was emphasising the effort and inconvenience of that process more than any integrated sense of guilt and remorse, illuminating his lip service to the victims alongside the absence of a reflective position in relation to his history and offending.

With this particular type of patient and psychopathology, applying a modified model of treatment whereby all activity and observations outside of sessions (only of course possible within institutional settings) is felt to be crucial. It has the specific aim of addressing the compulsive splitting, that is, the drive to reduce three to two and two to one, and eliminate deception and secrecy within a truly transparent therapeutic process. This ensures that the "third" is very much a part of the work and not split off/undermined in the way that is so typical of this type of pathology.

CHAPTER SEVEN

Digesting history as a lifesaver*

Dedication

"Learning from fatal experience."

This chapter is dedicated to the memory of a patient whose death from anorexia nervosa has enabled life to be given to the understanding of its causes.

My gratitude is extended to both the clinical team led by

Professor Janet Treasure

for their dedication and professionalism, and also the patient's family whose availability and generosity in providing me with the relevant facts following their loss was invaluable and humbling.

"What's past is prologue ... "

—Shakespeare, The Tempest, Act 2, Scene 1)

---

*This chapter was first presented at the International Association of Forensic Psychotherapy (IAFP) Conference on 11 April 2008 in Venice.

This chapter seeks to clarify and establish a definitive position that has been progressively developed in the collection of chapters in this book, which is that without a meaningful engagement with the past, whether in relation to the individual, family, group/institution, or state, the capacity to understand any terrors involved and thereby safely understand and contain them is irreparably disabled. Failure to engage with the past also creates the huge potential for those terrors to become manifest (displaced) in a different way, thereby perpetuating the original problem/conflict in another form. The clinical case of a patient who developed anorexia nervosa to solve her own early terrors will be discussed. Concomitantly, this patient cut out her own history from her mind, culminating with the perverse pyrrhic victory in bringing about her own death. Her terror stemmed from the annihilatory experience of feeling excluded and unable to compete with an idealised sibling, which became fatally re-enacted at ward level. Her resistance to meaningful engagement with her past, given that it was too painful, infected and affected the capacity of the treating team to include it. This resulted in her earlier terrors being projected into the treating team regarding the prospect of her death, while they endeavoured to keep her alive. It has already been suggested that it is vitally important to be a good detective in relation to history taking—that is, taking a meaningful account of a history in order to provide the maximum opportunity to contain the associated terrors.

Estela Welldon, the Honorary President of the International Association for Forensic Psychotherapy (IAFP), explores the idealisation and denigration of motherhood when she comments in the prologue to her seminal publication, *Mother, Madonna, Whore* (1988), that "[t]he children's problems are traced to the problems of the mother and these, in turn, are traced to the problems she [the mother] had with her own mother". Welldon concludes her epilogue by commenting upon the apparent paradox in (Western) society of linking perversion with motherhood. She says:

> To them I would like, in conclusion, to say two things—the first is that knowledge is the beginning of wisdom; to treat patients you must act on evidence, not pre-suppositions. The second has to do with power, the status of mother ... and that the clinical evidence

[*identifying perversion*] supports the maxim never underestimate the power of the mother.

(Welldon, 1988, pp. 157–158; emphasis added)

My chapter will unpack in detail the evidence that Estela Welldon refers to. My evidence is the detailed history of a patient who tragically died from anorexia nervosa and I trace this patient's difficulties to the unresolved/unprocessed trauma that occurred in her own mother's history relating to acute jealousy, loss, and displacement. Moreover, it was the re-enactment of that trauma on the hospital ward that contributed to her acting-out (by causing a small fire) and subsequent death. I suggest that insufficient knowledge of her history was available both in fact and in the minds of the team to underpin thinking and reflection in order to make safe the terrors and insecurity that her condition was rooted in.

At this point in time it is worth noting that the patient, while in a specialist setting, was not a forensic patient, although she crossed the divide when she acted-out and set the fire as opposed to and in complete contrast to turning-in on herself. Stereotypically, acting-out can be considered to be associated to the male, while turning-in more to the female.

Given my extensive clinical experience I have become all too aware of the grave deficiencies in clinical formulation that affect patient care and subsequent rehabilitation either through the absence of a detailed history and/or the way in which a patient's history is related to when it is taken, together with the subsequent application of it. I have detailed this is in previous chapters. In not only my own training, but particularly in Dr Wooster's (at The Maudsley Hospital) in the 1960s, comprehensive histories were taken by cross-referencing in interviewing different members of families of patients. This function has waned and its loss is detrimental to patient care and rehabilitation.

Unfortunately it seems to have become familiar to the point of ubiquity that a mature intercourse with the patient's history is replaced by it being rendered irrelevant and effectively killed off. A meaningful intercourse would be represented by concentrating on the situation at and around conception and birth into the family and then the world. All too often now, this mature engagement is replaced by the clinician/clinical team performing a task that is stripped of meaning and attachment through compliance with some internal and/or external expectation, by, for example, ticking a box that it is done. Moreover, further problems can occur when histories are taken if the experience for the patient is one in which the clinician just walks off afterwards without a word to the patient, which can have the effect of leaving a gaping hole for the patient.

In this chapter I seek to demonstrate that the denial of terrors associated with birth and subsequent development (history) within a family go on to infect clinical teams resulting in displacements, perversions, and psychosis, and, in my example here, ultimately the death of the patient. In relation to birth, I would want to apply this to all birthing, including that represented by becoming consciously aware of something for the first time. This "giving birth in the mind" equates to recognition by a younger sibling that an older sibling had already been around in existence prior to his birth. Moreover, I also discuss later the idea of giving birth to the anorexic condition, which is then perversely nurtured as a way of competing with another.

I am presenting the tragic case of a woman who suffered with anorexia nervosa. During her contact with psychiatric services there was a continual problem of security and terror which created great difficulty keeping in touch with her, psychologically, and blocked reflection on her family history. Since her death, I have been extremely fortunate to have had the full support of the patient's older sister in establishing a detailed trans-generational history, and as a result feel that my observations can make a significant contribution to the understanding of the genesis of her anorexia nervosa.

Before proceeding, I want to provide you with a clear template in relation to the complexity of the story to work with as I unfold the detailed case of a patient called Margaret, and as I do so you might want to refer to the family tree shown in Appendix 1, where the crosses signify death.

I postulate that Margaret's mother's traumatic feelings of being displaced from her closely enmeshed dyad with father by "a wicked [sic] stepmother" at the age of nine, were repressed (see Appendix 2). I would identify these repressed feelings as acute jealousy, rage, displacement, and annihilation. These were then trans-generationally transferred into her own family, such that her close enmeshed relationship with her father in her own generation was replaced by her relationship with her daughter, Elizabeth, whom she conceived and gave birth to in the same year that her father died. On the subsequent arrival of Margaret, mother's primary maternal preoccupation with Elizabeth, the elder sister, was not relinquished (not going to be interfered with) and her dyadic bond was not going to be displaced by the arrival of somebody who became equated with stepmother, that is, Margaret. Margaret's deep feelings of being unloved, unwanted, and insecure created an unmet need that I am suggesting caused a greed that was insatiable.

This greed would have been felt to be shameful; this shame giving rise to a reaction formation to starvation.[1] Margaret was subsequently diagnosed with dysmorphophobia, an obsessive fear that one's body or a part of it is repulsive. What was known was that she was twenty-eight years of age, married, with a young son aged six, who had been diagnosed with autism. The realisation that she couldn't compete with her elder sister was profound, and examples of Margaret trying to emulate Elizabeth occurred, ushering in the defensive reaction of "If you can't beat them, join them". A re-enactment as an inpatient occurred, whereby her rage in relation to being jealous and unable to compete was triggered and this culminated in her death.

Had the foregoing history been known and available, then the clinical team would have been much better equipped to help Margaret understand her feelings. Understanding would have provided the potential to reduce and/or weaken acting-out scenarios, through which Margaret repeatedly communicated her unconscious feelings. As Freud comments in "Remembering, repeating and working-through": "[T]he patient does not *remember* anything of what he has forgotten and repressed, but *acts* it out" (Freud, 1914, p. 150; emphasis in original).

From the moment that our patient Margaret was known to psychiatric services, she was reluctant to provide any background history, which remained the case throughout most of her period of treatment. She first came to notice in the autumn of 2001 when she was referred by her GP for self-inflicted lacerations to her head, which occurred as a result of her shaving her head to remove all hair—she had been pulling her hair out, literally, for the previous three years.

In hindsight I attribute much significance to Margaret's son's age (six), in that when both of his parents were born they had an older sibling aged six. This would therefore represent a time when significant events can occur, which indeed it did for this six-year-old boy, with a sick mother.

As I have previously highlighted, significant time-linked events can be an invaluable way of identifying significant periods in family dynamics.[2] Margaret's hair pulling had begun when her son was three which coincided with him being diagnosed with autism. Psychoanalytically, we might factor in the symbolic association of penis and hair and consider this as a "removal" of Margaret's relationship with her son, linked to his "imperfection" as autistic.

It was felt that in her own attempts to be perfect she was progressively failing, and later I attribute the need for perfection as part of her desire to be as good, if not better, than her perceived perfect sister (a common feature in eating disorder patients). Not only had she conceived out of wedlock, in the context of a very religious family, but the son that she gave birth to and on whom she doted was to be less than perfect because of his diagnosis.

I recall Margaret's primary nurse on the ward saying that the only thing she could now perfect was her anorexia. Her striving to be perfect, I argue, has a strong competitive dynamic, so that if in her mind (as I earlier noted) she had given birth to her anorexia, her need to ensure that she had perfect control over it and that it was perfect in itself, created something that could not be interfered or competed with.

Margaret had become fixated with her hair and was to become bald and recognisable by wearing a woollen hat to conceal her shaven head. She subsequently had three admissions to an Eating Disorders Unit, the first between September 2003 and February 2004, when she was taken to her local accident and emergency department by her husband following a fall. She was in an emaciated state. Her weight was 33 kg (5 st 2 lb), with a BMI of 11.4, upon admission. (A healthy BMI is normally considered to be in the range of 18.5–25.) She was originally sectioned, although this was rescinded as Margaret agreed to comply with treatment as an informal patient. So in February 2004 she was discharged with a plan to attend community meetings with health professionals.

Following discharge, her weight reduced again from 42 kg to 37 kg, and so in line with an agreed strategy she was referred back to the Eating Disorders Unit for further inpatient treatment. She was re-admitted in April 2004 and progress was made in regaining weight. However, she was unhappy with the emphasis on the weight gain, and discharged herself against medical advice in July 2004.

Ongoing multi-disciplinary discussions took place regarding the significant concerns to her physical health. Moreover, Margaret and her husband were avoiding contact with professionals, including home visits, on one particular occasion claiming that they were on an extended holiday in Bournemouth. The risk of her relapse and potential death was discussed amongst the team. In a visit to her home address, while there was no reply to knocking, a child's voice could be heard inside. Police were called, who managed to get a response from the patient's husband, who said that Margaret was not at home and still in Bournemouth (I had at the time powerful associations linked to her own history with the combination of words "born" and "mouth"), even though he had apparently temporarily returned home to deal with an emergency. Given concerns about Margaret and her health, as well as the child protection issues in relation to their young son, a S135 (2) Search and Remove Warrant was obtained from the Magistrates Court which was executed on 13 September 2004. Despite there being no initial response, cigarette smoke could be smelt emanating from a small open window, which was perhaps prophetic given the later arson attack. Eventually her husband opened the door, denying that Margaret was in, only for her to be found cowering in an emaciated state under a bed. Of equal alarm was the fact that police discovered what amounted in the end to four truckloads of ammunition together with firearms in the property owned by Margaret's husband. At this moment in time Margaret could not stand up without help and weighed 27 kg (4 st 3 lbs) and had a BMI of 9.8. Following hospitalisation she was transferred back to the Eating Disorders Unit for treatment from January 2005.

There was clearly collusion between the husband and Margaret that I would consider to be a form of malignant mirroring. I would also consider that Margaret represented the husband's own sister in his internal world, with whom he was also conflicted.

While Margaret initially reached a BMI of 16.0, by the summer of 2005 her weight continued to fluctuate. Her weight was noticed to reduce every time plans were proceeding to discharge her. She was re-detained under Section 3 of the Mental Health Act in November 2005 but continued to lose weight, while her husband supported her request to be discharged from Section. The difficulties the clinical team experienced in dealing with Margaret and her husband cannot be over-estimated. It appeared that she was very able to recruit him to complain about her treatment, as well as interfere with it. He was often contacted by her by mobile telephone and would then complain on her behalf. In hindsight (as mentioned previously) his collusion perhaps enabled him to pursue his own vengeance against his sister, transferred as it were on to Margaret.

Given the difficulties with her admission, in June 2006 the Trust sought legal advice regarding her treatment under the Human Rights Act, particularly Article 2, "The right to life", and Article 3, "The right to not be subjected to inhumane and degrading treatment" (Human Rights Act, 1998). The Trust was advised to apply to court for a formal declaration if there was doubt about Margaret's best interests. The issue was that Article 2 indicated that the Trust had a positive obligation to protect her right to life. However, Article 3 protected the right that she had as a patient not to be subjected to inhumane or degrading treatment (forced feeding, etc.) that should be balanced against her right to life. The point in law was: "Is there therapeutic benefit in continuing to treat or would the only impact be to prolong her death in a manner that would be degrading to an objective person? [and therefore] … only if treatment was particularly invasive and not in her best interests would it breach her right." The dilemma created by Margaret was therefore how to respond to her as a very sick patient when she was rejecting the procedures that were there to support her. Her perverse gain by pursuing this would have been to triumph over the team and that part of her own mind that supported health.

The Resident Medical Officer (RMO) decided to re-assess her for a Section 3 of the Mental Health Act in order to assist-feed her (which was a last resort to keep her alive). Her husband objected to the Section, and an application was due to be made to the County Court to seek his displacement as the nearest relative. He changed his mind before this took place, and she was made subject to Section 3 of the Mental Health Act in June 2006. Improvements were noted, although she remained a concern throughout. Within her final year, the team felt that she had made some real progress at times with her weight, but more importantly, in how she was experienced on the ward. However, events were to occur on the ward that resonated deeply with her conflicted internal world, causing a significant deterioration in her health and subsequent loss of life.

In terms of supervision, this patient first came to my notice following the search of her home and subsequent detention in September 2004, just prior to her third admission. At that time I was providing psychodynamic supervision for the lead nurse individually, in addition to multi-disciplinary team supervision twice a month. There was a deep double anxiety and terror in the clinical team with regard to the perceived dangers of admitting Margaret with her desperate condition alongside her husband's association with firearms. A range of measures were being considered by the Trust to alleviate anxieties and make her admission possible by, for example, financing the cost of twenty-four hour security guards on the unit. Given this reaction, it was decided that I would facilitate a reflective group to include all professionals within the service, and this took place in September 2004, which fortunately resulted in a significant reduction in anxiety and eliminated the need for any overt security measures to be implemented. It was understood that the team's own countertransference was indicative of the terrors that were unable to be contained in, not only the patient, but those within her immediate circle.

Our fortnightly multi-disciplinary team (MDT) supervision meetings began to be minuted in order to ensure that the thinking that took place was not only recorded but made available to those clinicians who were unable to be present to try to overcome the difficulties of communication within the clinical team. In reflecting upon the history of the discussions that took place around this patient, I therefore had the rich resource of a file containing the minutes of the discussions that were held. This practice of minuting the MDT supervision meetings still continues and is an invaluable aid to triangulating with absent members of the team.

In January 2006 Margaret was first presented to the group. She had therefore been on the ward for over twelve months. While she was experienced as a tortured woman and had a ghost-like quality on the ward (she was completely unable to verbally communicate any aspect of her suffering), nonetheless at times a warm and sometimes humorous side was also experienced. What had become clear is that the clinical team had not been able to gather any information at all about her history. Indeed, all that was on file was one short paragraph. While this had been largely due to Margaret's own resistance to that process coupled with a degree of unconscious collusion by the team, it was also indicative of Margaret's capacity to ensure that clinicians' minds were taken up with other matters. For example, she ensured that she kept the spotlight on the team and her complaints regarding their malfunctions, which, by getting the team to look at themselves, ensured that she didn't have to look at herself. In addition, the team had experienced ongoing and persistent interference from her husband in their attempt to treat Margaret. What became apparent was that she ensured that she retained a weight that was low enough to keep her on the ward, while at the same time making accusations and complaints about her treatment, and making contact with her husband, who would support her in criticising the clinical team. Nonetheless the burden of his circumstances, whereby he was the sole primary carer for their autistic son who at this point in time was eleven years of age, together with responding to the demands of his wife, led him to quietly comment that he wished he had ended the marriage a long time before and that he found it difficult to cope with both his wife and their son. Moreover, he did not want her to return home.

Margaret, through her husband, was able to engender a litigious environment, and, in addition, the Community Mental Health Team (CMHT) had expressed their own terrors of Margaret and her husband by the fact that she, in their view, might die, with the corollary of being sued. It was noted that the patient had become significantly isolated on the ward and did not try to integrate herself and she was experienced by the nursing team as extremely controlling, closed, and detached.

This emotional stance is referred to by Emma Corstorphine (2008) as the "detached protector", which she describes as "a maladaptive coping mode characterised by emotional withdrawal, disconnection, isolation and behavioural avoidance. It functions to shut off emotions in order to protect the individual from the pain of feeling" (2008, p. 87). Young et al. identify a detached protector mode of functioning, which stems from the young child's need to detach and avoid feeling when living with unmet needs in a harmful environment (2003). A concept that seems particularly important to the development of the "detached protector" is the invalidating environment, which Linehan describes (1993). This leads to a core belief based on the expectation of being left alone and abandoned such that the detached protector mode (primary level of avoidance, e.g., food restriction) serves to protect the individual from an anticipated pain of being left (Linehan, 1993). It was this sense of abandonment that was to be borne out when Margaret's history was gathered.

Margaret could be very manipulative and classically deceitful. It was universally agreed within the service that she was the most difficult patient they had ever had to treat. Margaret created the reaction in others that they didn't want to be with her. This was always interpreted as important countertransference information that helped inform the team of aspects of her early experience of not feeling wanted.

The discussion opened up to consider her history, and examples were given regarding the pressures that Margaret applied to her husband, preventing him from being able to communicate any history to the clinical team. All that was known at this point was that she had lost contact with her family around the time of the birth of her son and, more particularly, after his diagnosis of autism at the age of three, when she was aged twenty-two. Other than that, there was no history.

I felt deeply that this absence was profoundly significant, and impressed upon the team how essential it was that we pursued her history with the utmost vigour. Given that the team were feeling that any attempt to explore a history with Margaret was futile, the example of the Perseus myth (see p. 26 and p. 69) was used to enable the clinical team to see that her husband could act as a mirror in being able to establish some history. The supervision meeting concluded that the team would take up this issue more robustly than hitherto to try to obtain details about the family from Margaret's husband and for the ward administrator to pursue other medical contacts via her GP and other agencies.

The clinical team were increasingly feeling that Margaret's history was the key to understanding her condition and provided the best chance that the team had to develop a formulation and treatment plan to help her. Given her condition, the lead nurse discussed sectioning Margaret and because Margaret was so against being sectioned she agreed to provide her parents' address (without a postcode, although this was subsequently traced) as a compromise to prevent being sectioned under the Mental Health Act. The team registered some shock, although were also pleasantly surprised, to learn that Margaret's parents were still alive and living not far away, and were very amenable to making contact. The team were to learn that Margaret was the youngest of three siblings, with an older brother by eight years and an older sister by six years.

Given that Margaret had broken off all communication with her family some eight years previously, to re-engage her with her family on the ward met with significant resistance and protest. Moreover, a number of allegations were made by her, which included one of being sexually abused by her father. This allegation had, of course, to be taken up and dealt with seriously (an initial police statement was taken, although no further action followed), while at the same time holding in mind the possibility that this was yet another attempt by her to prevent her relationship with her family from being rekindled and to detract the clinical team away from that important part of her treatment.

In a further meeting in May 2006, staff expressed the feeling that they were just keeping her alive, and that Margaret's husband was as obstructive as ever. In hindsight we were to learn that in addition to his collusion with her eating disorder, the complaints about her treatment, and not wanting her to return home, he was having an affair. Consequently, his attendance on the ward and continued involvement in her care, particularly from a litigant point of view, was in part, we now believe, in order to try to ensure that she remained on the ward.

Professor Janet Treasure (the head of the service) had drafted a letter to Margaret and had asked that it be presented for discussion and possible amendment at our supervision meeting. It informed Margaret of the view that she had "a fatal form of this illness". It set out the team's exasperation with treating Margaret and said that they had reached the stage where they had accepted that she might end up killing herself, and felt that she was effectively giving up.

This was indeed a powerful communication to the patient and certainly matched the dynamic in the room, where feelings of despair, hopelessness, and stuckness pervaded. There was universal agreement that Margaret was the most difficult anorexic case they had ever experienced, and the feeling was that she was impossible to treat. The letter contained the comment that "all attempts at treatment had failed". This particular phrase was reflected upon and it was felt that it did not fully take into account the relevance that was progressively being attributed to the significance of the patient's history in understanding the current events. The draft letter was amended, in order to take account of this thinking, and to inspire the team to use their energy in reconnecting the patient with her past. I found myself suggesting that Margaret perhaps needed to get the staff to the very point of giving up, so that they were able to experience how it had been for her, as if this not only represented a point in her earlier experience where she gave up on her own life but also that staff were faced with powerful projections to collude with her, as opposed to fighting for life. The staff were able to see the identification processes at work and to engage a more reflective stance. I believed it represented a potential turning point in her treatment. Perversely, it seemed that Margaret was elated by the attention of the whole of the clinical team and of the other patients, when a community group meeting attempted to discuss what her plans might be in the event of her death.

As we started to learn more about her history, what began to emerge was a clear understanding of the importance and centrality of the relationship between herself, her sister, and their mother. The impression we got was that her sister Elizabeth had a very special place in their mother's mind and was idealised. The idea that Margaret had always struggled to find a way of being included took root and then began to be identified as a repeating dynamic on the ward, where other patients would be perceived by Margaret as being favoured, particularly by the lead nurse.

A corollary to feeling excluded is the experience of unbearable psychic pain/anxiety. Kalsched (1996) has commented that experiences of this magnitude emanate from the cumulative traumas of unmet dependency/needs and mount up to a devastating impact on some children's development. He says: "To experience such anxiety threatens the total annihilation of the human personality, the destruction of the personal spirit … (and) this must be avoided at all costs" (Kalsched, 1996, p. 1). He refers to the necessary psychic defences that emerge as a result to protect the mind from experiencing the "unthinkable". He suggests that such primitive defences both characterise severe pathology and also, once in place, cause it. That is, the victims of psychological trauma continually find themselves in life situations where they are re-traumatised, in repeated self-defeating re-enactments. The supervision meeting concluded:

> We need to establish contact with her sister and see what the response is, and then see what her sister's experience was of Margaret as a child, and then hopefully it can be arranged for Margaret to meet with her sister and then finally for the parents to be brought in as well.

(Supervision Minutes, 11 May 2006)

Contact with Margaret's sister Elizabeth had been made and she was very keen and excited to become involved in her sister's care as much as she could, despite having her time taken up with a young daughter. We revisited Margaret's case a month later, in June, and it was reported that her sister had attended the ward but that Margaret had refused to see her. Then, given Margaret's protest and dire weight, assisted feeding was considered together with the opinion of a consultant gastroenterologist regarding the possibility of PEG (percutaneous endoscopic gastronomy) feeding, which is a form of tube feeding through the abdomen wall into the stomach. His opinion was that there was no hope for her and that we had to accept that some people just want to die. At this stage assisted feeding was introduced.

Feelings were expressed in this meeting that Margaret evoked both compassion and revulsion, as if she draws you into her and then pushes you away at the same time (again an important countertransference reflection, giving staff the experience that might have been her own with carers). Margaret had registered poor blood results over the preceding weekend, and it was confirmed that her body was now eating its own liver.

In addition at this meeting it was reported that Margaret was at a loss to understand what relevance her history had, particularly her relationship with her sister and family, to her eating disorder. We found ourselves progressively considering the importance of Margaret's feelings of isolation and exclusion from the relationship between her mother and her sister, through examples being given whereby Margaret had felt that she had never been really seen by her mother. This was, not surprisingly, also the experience of her on the ward. The meeting concluded to pursue further contact with Elizabeth and to set up further visits.

Margaret was again discussed at the end of June, when there was a team acknowledgement about the importance of persevering with the family work and the ongoing reminders that Margaret provided of her attempts to interfere with that process. Opinion was shared that her protests against meeting up with her sister should not be taken at face value, given that there was the sense that she was trying to save face and wanted to find a way of re-engaging with her sister. Now that the family were very much on board, that is, Margaret's parents and her sister, the clinical team felt mobilised and for the first time able to be proactive as opposed to reactive, and had something of clarity around a formulation to work with.

As we moved towards the end of the year and into 2007, it was clear that the relationship between Margaret and her sister had been renewed, and by the May of 2007, Margaret had agreed to meet with Elizabeth off the ward with an escort for a day visiting a historic site. This was felt to be a considerable breakthrough, and enabled the team to reflect on the time when they felt that they had given up on Margaret and were reconciled to her dying. It was recorded in the minutes of this group that in her last Care Programme Approach (CPA—an assessment of her needs) she had improved and was much better with her family.

Then on 4 September 2007 a significant sequence of events occurred. In the early hours of one morning Margaret crossed the divide into forensic enactment by setting fire to a waste paper bin on a part of the ward where the psychology offices were located (sending psychology up in smoke!), causing some damage to a wall and more generally smoke damage to a part of the ward. This caused a part of the ward to be locked off for a number of days before it cleared.

The antecedents were that Margaret had absconded from the ward the weekend prior to the incident. Upon return her weight had fallen. Predictably Margaret and her husband were angry and critical of the service. That same evening, Margaret had demanded cigarettes and wanted to go out of the unit to smoke. This was not unusual, although her request was refused, given that it was now in contravention of a new ward policy. Although she went to bed at her usual time, she was observed to wake up at 4am. She was described as having rushed into the nursing station complaining about her care plan. Staff reported that she tried to tear it up, before leaving, and about fifteen minutes later the fire alarm went off and smoke was seen in the corridor. Margaret claimed that the fire was an accident. When Margaret left the ward she stated to a team leader: "If you'd only given me what you gave _____ [the other patient]."

Consensus on the ward was that the fire setting was deliberate and that Margaret had been complacent about any danger to life. This was based on the fact that ordinarily she had been noted to be extremely careful about ensuring that her cigarettes were put out properly, to the point of obsessionally crushing them and testing the butt on her lip. The natural concern at the time was that Margaret could set further fires and that these could occur not only in hospital but also at home, presenting a risk to her husband and child.

Following police involvement, Margaret was removed from the ward and placed in a Private Intensive Care Unit (PICU), which enabled the ward some time to reflect on the incident and try to return to a state of normality. Meanwhile, Margaret was temporarily detained in the PICU, whose experience of working with this type of disorder was minimal, and consequently Margaret's weight dropped to very dangerous levels. She was consequently transferred to a general hospital for feeding.

In the meantime, I held a group on 11 September 2007 in relation to the events that had occurred and to discuss and reflect with the group about the best way forward. The team generally agreed that in the three years that they had been treating Margaret, there had been fluctuating progress, and that the fairly recent deterioration as well as the persistent provocation from her and her husband (which had been immense), had all led to feelings in the team of wanting to get rid of her again. They were able to express very clearly that this incident had given them the excuse they needed to get rid of her. This was a very powerful and extremely difficult, although honest, expression of the feelings that this type of patient can provoke in clinicians, and the team deserve credit for being able to express such profound feelings of rage and hatred towards a patient, which was reminiscent of D. W. Winnicott's article on "Hate in the Counter-transference" (1947). Moreover, once the foregoing feelings had been expressed, we then began to be able to think and reflect upon the background (history) to the incident.

A few days prior to Margaret's absconsion, which had been the prelude to the incident, another older patient Anne (equating with Margaret's older sister Elizabeth) had absconded from the unit. As a result of the absconsion, Anne, given her low weight, had generated a considerable degree of anxiety, which in turn had led to some significant media attention on her absconsion as well as a very active response in setting up search teams, which included a police helicopter. This reaction had in large part been generated by Anne's mother's involvement. In stark contrast, when Margaret absconded, her mother was completely uninvolved. This disparity was known to Margaret. Anne was subsequently found and returned to the unit with some fanfare, receiving a huge amount of attention on her return. As a result a new no smoking policy at night was implemented on the ward, given that Anne's absconsion occurred while she had been taken out of the unit during the night for a smoke. Moreover there was a growing awareness in Margaret that Anne was not only able to get what Margaret could not get for herself (a mother responding to her needs), but also had been instrumental in the implementation of a revised no smoking policy that impacted hugely upon the one activity that Margaret had a real passion for, which was smoking. In terms of Margaret's relationship with the team, her cigarettes were an ersatz third, and it was a third that was under her complete control—only now that control had been dangerously interfered with. In addition, it was noted that prior to Anne's original arrival on the ward, Margaret had been more pleasant. The lead nurse also mentioned that she had seen more of Margaret (in a demanding way) since Anne had arrived on the ward, and especially recently, begging for a change to the cigarette ban and blaming Anne for its implementation.

Therefore upon reflection it became clear that Margaret had absconded from the unit (not dissimilarly to the way that Anne had), but had not generated anywhere near the same reaction that Anne had. After approximately a week she returned, under her own volition, accompanied by her husband, and in the early hours of the morning, after voicing criticism of her care plan, set the fire in the way described. The team reflected further that Margaret had been conscious that Anne was getting far more attention than herself (including psychological intervention), and that this had clearly provoked significant feelings of jealousy in her. We are reminded here also of her parting comment, mentioned earlier: "If you'd only given me what you gave _____ [the other patient]." We then linked this "ward sibling dynamic of jealousy" to her sibling relationship with Elizabeth, and there then became a clearer understanding for the team in relation to the incident. It was felt that the fire setting was indicative of her rage at feeling jealous, unable to compete, and of feeling almost irrelevant. Feelings of guilt and remorse were then expressed within the team and a desire for reparation, and they were very keen to want to secure Margaret's return at the earliest opportunity with a revised treatment plan in place, so that they could continue to help her overcome her eating disorder.

Within five hours of returning to the ward from the general hospital, Margaret died.

Margaret's husband was notified of the death, and eight days later he had a pulmonary embolism, collapsed in the driveway of his house, and died in the ambulance on the way to hospital. Their son has since been placed successfully in good foster care.

I now want to turn to the gaps in her history that have been filled through contact with Elizabeth, Margaret's sister, which I feel provides clinical clarity to the rudimentary formulation. They link Margaret's difficulties with her own mother's unresolved conflicts in terms of her relationship with her own mother and father, and how this, given the re-enactment that occurred on the ward, led to Margaret's untimely death.

Critics could rightly comment that there are likely to be many thousands, if not millions, of youngest siblings in families who feel that an older sibling is favoured by mother, who don't end up feeling so excluded to the point of developing an eating disorder as a perverse solution. This is the point at which I feel the need to emphasise the significance of incorporating our patient's mother's own history (trans-generational) so that any significant events/dynamics can be included in the picture. The question that arises is: What might it have been in mother's own history that contained such powerful affective loadings to cause repression to take place and for that to then be trans-generationally transferred? Before answering that question, I want to draw attention to the first celebrity anorexic, who died in 1983 from her condition, who was Karen Carpenter of The Carpenters, the famous popular music duo (with her brother Richard) of the 1970s. There is such poignancy to the lyrics of The Carpenters' hit song "Goodbye to Love" in its reference to living without love.

Karen was the youngest of two siblings with an older brother Richard (plus four years), and Richard was described as the "apple of their mother's eye". From available sources my research has established that Richard's pre-eminence in the family dictated decision-making by the parents (not unlike Anne with the clinical team), for example, moving to California in 1963 so that Richard could pursue a career in music. Richard was the talented musician, and while Karen apparently hero-worshipped her brother (again "If you can't beat them, join them") she became very tomboyish as a young character. She moved into music herself by mastering the drums (partly mischievously since it was not a traditional instrument for women in those pre-liberated years) before then joining her brother in performing. The uniqueness of her voice, unparalleled in pop music, many would say, led to significant success. I am therefore wondering whether similar trans-generational factors are involved here; of course we are not blessed with any detail of The Carpenters' mother's own history, but I do hold open the strong possibility that Karen, not unlike Margaret, felt unable to compete with her brother Richard, and that feelings of shame, rage, jealousy, and loss became rooted in Karen, which eventually led to her anorexia and death.

I now want to turn to Margaret's trans-generational history, and draw out what I believe are the significant factors, and it might be helpful to again refer to your copy of the family tree. Margaret and Elizabeth's mother was born in 1932, and her mother died giving birth to her through loss of blood. She had been the third pregnancy, the first two having been miscarried.

Fortunately her father was a relatively wealthy man and was able, unusually in those days, to nurture his own daughter alone for the first nine years of her life. They shared a very close relationship until such time as her father became close to another woman (who had been a friend of his wife's) whom he subsequently married when Margaret's mother was nine years of age. The stepmother was unable to accommodate and embrace her stepdaughter (Margaret's mother) and the decision was made by her to send her stepdaughter to boarding school. So Margaret's mother's experience, at the age of nine, was of the significant loss of the closely enmeshed dyadic relationship with her father, following the arrival of her new stepmother (and mirroring the traumatic earlier loss that was the dyad with mother). From that point she was not included in the triangular relationship in any way.

We then fast forward to Margaret's mother's marriage at the age of twenty-eight whereupon their first born, a son, developed Asperger's syndrome and an itinerant lifestyle with some mental health problems. We might say he became "miscarried", analogous to the earlier miscarriages. Not unlike his sister, Margaret, he has similarly cut off from his family. As I mentioned earlier, in 2004 in Edinburgh I discussed the case of a patient who had been in treatment for murder, and my thinking related to his internal conflict (in feeling persecuted by jealousy) originating from the very early experience of containing toxic projective processes from his traumatised mother. Simply put, while his mother was carrying him in pregnancy she suffered the traumatic loss of her husband and had been unable to mourn the loss appropriately, subsequently relating to her newborn son as if he was a replacement for the un-mourned husband. When Margaret's mother was pregnant with her elder sister, Elizabeth, her "beloved" father died. I would therefore be remiss in not considering the strong possibility that mother replaced the loss of her father (a powerfully important, closely enmeshed dyadic relationship) with Elizabeth. In Elizabeth's own words, she certainly felt that she became favoured in her family to the point of acting as a close confident and solace to her mother during some very turbulent early years. I would then need to factor in Margaret's birth as a potential re-enactment for mother of the arrival of her stepmother in her own generation. Margaret therefore represented a rival who potentially threatened mother's relationship with Elizabeth, just as the stepmother had threatened mother's relationship with her beloved father.

Margaret's parents' relationship deteriorated significantly following Margaret's birth, and there was the experience that she represented an unwanted child. Given that I am suggesting that Margaret represented stepmother (in her mother's mind), alongside her mother's inability to relinquish her primary maternal preoccupation with Elizabeth, I believe that this was experienced as a sequence of cumulative trauma of unmet needs. Malan (1997) identifies that it is the mother's inappropriate response to the infant's expressed needs that lies at the core of situations that can emerge in anorexia. I agree with this and want to further highlight the sequelae.

By the age of three, Margaret was displaying unusual behavioural characteristics with a particular daily ritual of wanting her small dress pulled very tight at the back. Elizabeth's understanding of this was that it was in order to make her feel secure. Margaret's insecurity extended to her inability to attend school (she was diagnosed as a child as having a school phobia); the family were threatened with legal action, which resulted in Margaret receiving intermittent education in a specialist unit.

Prior to getting married at the age twenty-one, Margaret was to experience two profoundly upsetting losses provoked by jealousy. At the age of eighteen she learnt that her boyfriend had been unfaithful, and second, while Margaret was courting her fiancé, she was informed by her older brother that her fiancé had said that he found Elizabeth extremely attractive. This is indeed powerful dynamics around jealousy and is not dissimilar to those I discussed in Chapter Three of this collection, regarding the history of Ian Huntley who murdered the two school girls Holly Wells and Jessica Chapman. You may recall that Ian's girlfriend had left him and set up home with, and subsequently married, his brother some years before the murder.

Following Margaret's marriage at the age of twenty-one, she gave birth to a son on whom she apparently doted. Margaret's husband, not dissimilar in his sibling position, was the youngest by six years, with an older sister. He was described as having a dependent relationship upon his parents who both died within three months of each other in 1986—the father from cancer and the mother from a heart attack. He was not himself averse to the idea that history would repeat itself in his own life, which in fact happened when he died eight days following the death of his own wife.

Following the birth of their son, whenever Elizabeth would visit Margaret she would, not surprisingly, dispatch her husband out of the home, which in hindsight can be seen as Margaret's efforts to ensure that she protected herself against any likelihood of a relationship developing between her husband and Elizabeth. Elizabeth can identify the time when Margaret chose to distance (eliminate) her and the rest of her family from her life, and it occurred when Margaret's son was approximately three years of age following a diagnosis of autism. Elizabeth particularly felt that it followed a "special" meeting whereby, as sisters, they were able to discuss their own memories (histories), and they had become close and connected, almost for the first time. Following that visit all further contact was stopped by Margaret until the time eight years later when the Eating Disorder Team were able to reunite them.

It would appear that from that moment in 1999 Margaret's health began to deteriorate. This started with her pulling her hair out—culminating in her shaving her head completely—and, all accompanied by a significant weight loss, resulted in her first referral to hospital by her GP for self-inflicted lacerations to her head in 2001, leading to her admission to the National Eating Disorders Unit.

Margaret's lifelong feelings of insecurity and terror, particularly in relation to primary attachments and to those that held the risk of being lost to rivals, infected the clinical team through projective processes. It has to be said that the Eating Disorder Unit is a very skilled and professionally led specialist department whose experience and expertise in working with this most difficult pathology is renowned not only within the UK but beyond, particularly through Professor Janet Treasure's excellent pioneering work. This patient remains the most difficult that the unit has had to encounter and treat. It was Margaret's need to cut off from her history, because of its trauma to her, coupled with her husband's mirroring psychopathology, that prevented the clinical team from being able to formulate a clear understanding from the transgenerational picture of her acute susceptibility to feeling that she was unable to compete and have her jealousies provoked. In the end this led to her death as a result of the re-enactment on the ward, as described. Moreover, coupled with facts that emerged after Margaret's, and her husband's, death (avarice and hoarding) I would want to consider that Margaret's powerful sense of shame in relation to a greed that was a corollary to her unmet need, caused in her the reaction formation of starvation.

I am mindful that there might be relevance to the following: this was Margaret's third admission to the unit, equating with being the third born; she lasted three years before she died; there was a conscious awakening at the age of three years that her sister had pre-dated her, which also equates with her son's diagnosis of autism at the age of three (he was born after thirty-three weeks of pregnancy) and with feelings, aged three, of deep insecurity in needing her dress tightened.

Before concluding, I want to return to Estela Welldon's work, where she comments on her gratitude to Zilbach (1987) in understanding the importance for a woman in reaching adulthood that "actual procreation will start deeply within a woman when the sperm is 'actively engulfed', and not passively received as previously thought. This 'active engulf-ment' is the core, the beginning, and the growing essence of being female" (Welldon, 1988, p. 32). Given the very high female incidence of eating disorders, it is a universal experience in caring for this type of patient that their relationship with food is one in which one needs to move from passively receiving to actively engulfing food. Clearly this refers to the relationship with food and all its meaning, and I would want to extend that not only to the importance of history taking, but also to this chapter—that is, that you actively engulf (engage and digest) as oppose to passively receive it. Moreover, it is that level of engage-ment in history taking per se that I believe is essential to any optimistic prognosis.

In focusing attention in this way I join with Julia Buckroyd and Sha-ron Rother in their recent publication entitled *Psychological Responses to Eating Disorders and Obesity*, where they say:

> We by no means discount other related factors which have them-selves been the subject of a great deal of research. Genetic, physi-ological, nutritional, social, cultural, class and gender issues are undoubtedly relevant. However, we are surprised by the lack of attention to underlying psychological factors ... We have repeat-edly been made aware of responses to disordered eating from health professionals, which ignore or take little notice of emotional issues.
>
> (Buckroyd & Rother, 2008, p. 4)

I want to stress that through the detailed history taking of a patient suf-fering with this disorder I believe I have been able to identify the core issues promoting her anorexia. She was, I believe, at the receiving end of such powerful trans-generational processes that she was rendered acutely sensitive to feelings of overwhelming shame, jealousy, and exclusion. Consequently, in order to have a degree of control over those and the associated feelings of terror and insecurity, she foreclosed on taking anything further into herself, symbolically represented by food, to the point of her own demise.

Notes

1. Reaction formation is a defensive process by which an unacceptable impulse (greed) is mastered by exaggeration of the opposing tendency (starvation). It is regarded as an obsessional defence and it is assumed that the unconscious rejected impulse survives in its original infantile form.

2. I am drawing attention here, as in previous chapters, to the important work of Averil Earnshaw in her short publication *Time Will Tell* where she emphasises that emotionally unmetabolised residues of family catastrophes erupt in subsequent generations as precisely age-linked events. Moreover, she also refers to the autistic child and links the birth of such a "psychologically dead" baby to the traumatic losses of babies in previous generations through miscarriages and/or stillbirths (Earnshaw, 1995, pp. 50–51). If we look back in Margaret's history her grandmother had two miscarriages prior to giving birth to her mother.

APPENDIX

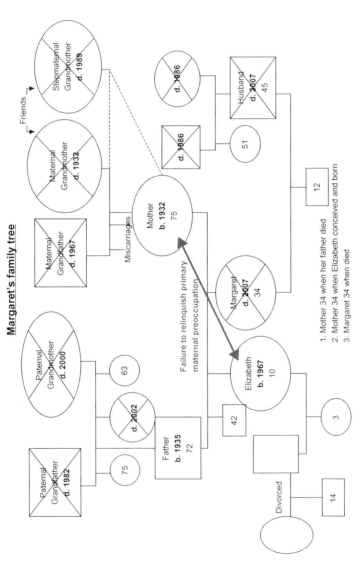

Margaret's family tree

Paternal Grandfather d. 1982
Paternal Grandmother d. 2000
Maternal Grandfather d. 1967
Maternal Grandmother d. 1932
Stepmaternal Grandmother d. 1989

Friends

75
d. 2002
63
Miscarriages

Father b. 1935 72
Mother b. 1932 75
d. 1986
d. 1986

Failure to relinquish primary maternal preoccupation

42
Margaret d. 2007 34
51
Husband d. 2007 45

Elizabeth b. 1967 10
12

Divorced
3
14

1. Mother 34 when her father died
2. Mother 34 when Elizabeth conceived and born
3. Margaret 34 when died

Appendix 1. Margaret's family tree.

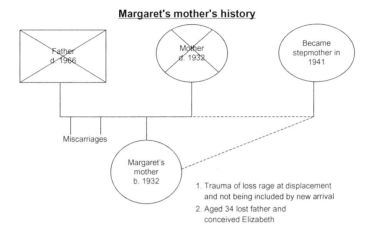

Margaret's mother's history

Appendix 2. Margaret's mother's history.

CHAPTER EIGHT

In defence of the realm … of emotion*

Personae

Adam	Patient
Temitope	Fiancé
Ruki	Victim/Confidante
Bella	Victim—two-year-old daughter of Ruki and Audu
Henry	Victim—eight-month-old son of Ruki and Audu
Audu	Husband of Ruki
Cannie	Sister of Audu, and friend of Temitope and Bubby
Erika	Girlfriend
Fatima	Half-sister of Adam
Ricki	Ex-girlfriend and previous fiancé
Ama	Girlfriend/Confidante
Bubby	Girlfriend of Temitope

This chapter explores the defences and identification processes used by a man during the homicide of a woman (a close friend) and her two young children, which enabled him to protect himself from an

---

*This chapter was first presented at a London Bi-logic Meeting on 31 October 2009, and subsequently on 6 November 2010.

awareness of his feelings in relation to original family members, whom they represented. The patient was seen both during an extended assessment and subsequently for treatment following a specific request from his Responsible Clinician (RC), given that his defences continued to challenge not only the treating team but also the holding institution. He placed powerful demands on all clinicians to collude with his defences to the point where at times he was experienced as if he was a member of staff and not a patient. This was understood to represent an acute level of denial (from psychic pain) with a manic defence that ultimately protected him from his own vulnerability and early experience.

In 2009, after spending twenty years in a high-secure hospital, he was geographically relocated to another high-secure hospital following a national reorganisation. His new treating team sought a psychodynamic assessment on the complex aetiology behind his homicidal offending and to explore any dynamic factors linking his history to his ward/hospital behaviour and his index offence. The assessment had been prompted following a mental health tribunal who were seeking further explanations to his index offence. I met with him for seven assessment sessions, and also felt it to be vitally important to meet with his nearest relative, his sister, so that I could accurately triangulate the history provided by the patient with another family member.

The patient, of Nigerian descent, I shall refer to as Adam. He killed a married woman (Ruki) and her two young children (a two-year-old daughter, Bella, and an eight-month-old son, Henry) in a homicidal attack which resulted in the near decapitation of Ruki and Bella. Adam was subsequently arrested and convicted in the 1980s of three counts of manslaughter on the grounds of diminished responsibility and detained in a high-secure hospital. Since then he has remained in high security and undertaken numerous therapeutic interventions. Prior to our meeting, I had heard a lot about him from the ward staff in that he tended to preoccupy the weekly multi-disciplinary team discussions in the reflective practice group I facilitated on the ward.

The impact that Adam had upon his treating team cannot be overstated. While he was generally liked in that he was not an overtly hostile and aggressive patient, he was nonetheless extremely adept at pulling professionals out of line through a range of very clever, manipulative and psychologically seductive techniques. This resulted in him effectively controlling the patient group and, if the staff were not mindful, the ward itself. Unchecked, this could all result in him being related to as if he were a member of staff. Countertransferentially staff often expressed intuiting a real fear, and while his physical presence and frame was dwarfed by most other patients, he was generally perceived to be one of the most dangerous. In conclusion, he was regarded as a most difficult patient to treat, given the universal experience that he somehow managed, in his interpersonal contact, to create a situation where he held the authority.

Given that Adam had been in hospital for over twenty years when I first met him, there was consequently an enormous amount of material in his personal file. I therefore triangulated the information held on file with my own experience of him, together with the interviews that I'd held with Fatima (his sister).

For the most part, Adam presented as extremely courteous (bordering on the sycophantic) and verbose in feeling the need to ensure that he explained himself fully and, more crucially, was understood. From the outset I want to highlight and stress the significance of a particular characteristic that pervaded our exchanges together, which was his inability to agree/concur with anything I might say, even when I was merely mirroring back in exact detail something that *he* had just said. I believed that this was representative of his total resistance to authority, and the authority in another, which he found psychologically intolerable, and sought to undermine and triumph over to ensure that *he* was the authority. I felt this was exemplified when he reversed the dynamic between us, whereby I would be kept waiting for him at the start of our interviews rather than the other way round. This, not unfamiliar, defensive characteristic had both cultural and developmental stressors, which may explain why "heads" seemed to be important, whether by almost severing the head of his adult victim (Ruki) or by the retention/collection of cut-out heads in photographs that were found in Adam's wallet (which he used to talk to) at the time of arrest. I am suggesting that the cultural/developmental stressors combined to burden him with the need to be the head of any family (relationship/group/ward) and that if this aim was frustrated then, at its extremity, the corollary could be, as it had been, fatally catastrophic.

In relation to the index offence, I believe that while he attacked and killed Ruki, Bella, and Henry, the hidden and perhaps more important agenda was a passive aggressive attack upon the authority and head within that family, namely Audu (Ruki's husband and the father of Bella and Henry). In Adam's rage at who Audu represented (his own biological father) he also emulated, in a delusional manner, the revered head of his own family, that is, his grandfather. This underlying passive aggression was a pervasive experience in all who encountered him.

In understanding the complexities involved in his index offending, it is important to be grounded in an accurate understanding of his history. I will highlight what I believe to be the key areas, being very mindful that the devil is in the detail. Of crucial importance was Adam's attempt to emulate, as a revered and almost iconic figure, the head of his family, his grandfather. His grandfather was an extremely wealthy and powerful man, referred to by Fatima (Adam's sister) as the head of one of the top three families in Nigerian society. He advertised/demonstrated his professional and social standing there by having six wives. His second wife, Adam's grandmother, was unable to bear children and so adopted a girl, Adam's mother, who became the grandfather's favourite daughter.

Adam's mother was to become (as described by Fatima) a very glamorous and educated hostess. She was the one survivor of a twin birth and was given the nickname "heart of the diamond", given the perception of her strength as a survivor. She grew up in very favoured circumstances, was apparently spoilt, and perhaps not unsurprisingly had significant difficulties around sharing and reconciling herself to feelings of jealousy.

One particular example given by Fatima of their mother's jealous rage was when, in early adulthood, she was unable to prise a man away from his wife in her attempts to become his mistress, and became very distressed at this challenge to her narcissism, which was seemingly intolerable. In effect, she struggled with the authority of this man's wife, who was English and not only unfamiliar with Nigerian customs around mistresses, but also unwilling to compromise her values to accommodate it.

While Adam's mother had been the spoilt daughter of Adam's grandfather, her attempts to secure herself an honourable husband were to prove problematic and shame-laden. The man she was betrothed to originally was given substantial financial support by Adam's grandfather to gain a recognised qualification in chartered surveying in the UK. While they were apart during his studies in the UK, he eloped with a British woman, which left Adam's mother traumatised, humiliated, and ashamed. In order to save face, Henry's mother was sent on a "rehabilitation" cruise, financed by the grandfather. On the cruise she met and then subsequently married the man who was to become Adam's father. However, it was progressively believed that Adam's father primarily married to exploit his father-in-law's wealth and position (it is worth noting that Adam's father was seen as the black sheep within his own family, in a not dissimilar way that Adam would later mirror, through his offending). Adam was soon conceived, but not long after his birth his parents separated. It is this separation of his parents that Adam was later able to reverse, from being a passive experience of "being done to" to a pro-active one by "doing to" through his index offence where he came between Ruki and her husband Audu.

This separation between Adam's mother and father added further shame to Adam's mother who, given that she was in such high standing in Nigerian society linked with the grandfather, had to begin to live with the stigma of being a single parent with a young son. Fatima informed me that there was an expectation in such circumstances (separation and divorce), in contrast to the West, that the son would follow the father, which would have meant Adam leaving Nigeria and returning to live with his father in his country of origin, elsewhere in Africa. This was powerfully contested in a number of ways, most notably through the courts by the grandfather, at considerable expense. He was ultimately successful, thereby securing Adam in Nigeria with his mother under the grandfather's "harem", and I will go on to suggest that it is this sequence of events that Adam repeated through his offending—as if he were the grandfather (see Appendix).

It is worth reiterating that for Adam his grandfather was a very powerful, influential, and revered figure, and I believe represented a "head" that Adam sought to emulate to disastrous effects. The following is a quote taken from my meeting with Fatima: "Adam wanted to be the powerful grandfather, bring back honour to the family in circumstances where he was always the only man of the family ... it was expected that the son would look after the family as he grew older." As a result of Adam's mother's difficulty in relationships, she and Adam became progressively estranged from her family and grandfather. She felt the need to become self-sufficient financially, which apparently prompted her to move into the masseuse profession, particularly given that she was described as a very attractive woman who had often been the subject of media attention, given the links to her father in high society. Her poor circumstances were exacerbated when, as a result of another relationship, she conceived and gave birth to Adam's half-sister Fatima, putting further pressure on her to gain financial security, either through marriage and/or through her profession as a masseuse.

While I am addressing other dynamic factors in Adam's history, it is also worth mentioning the potential impact and ramifications regarding his sister's birth (Adam was four at the time). It is a given that such a displacement can have the effect of promoting all sorts of defensive responses following the anger and jealousy that can be experienced. I have therefore held in mind that, at some level, Adam saw himself as his mother's partner given the responsibility he assumed (and was perhaps expected of him). In seeing himself as mother's partner, he offered himself and his sister a "paternal" presence, in the absence of a father. Furthermore, taking on the position of a parent defended him against the need to reconcile himself to the presence of a sibling.

A further attempt to marry was successful for a brief period to a man who helped her to migrate to the UK when Adam was seven and Fatima was two years old. Their emigration was apparently inevitable in that circumstances had become desperate. This proved to be a significant culture shock to Adam, given that in Nigeria he'd attended a private school (all boys) and recalled being chauffeur-driven to it on a daily basis. School life in the UK was completely different as he attended a comprehensive school in the suburbs of London. Adam recalled the private school in Nigeria as a time when he felt acutely ashamed that he didn't have a father, unlike all of the other boys. He went to great lengths to ensure that the fact remained concealed, always needing to give the impression that he was no different from anybody else and that he had a father too. Moreover it was as if he became the father to himself in the same way that it had often been felt that, as a forensic patient, he had become the father to his own treatment plan and to the ward. There was therefore for Adam (at the Nigerian private school) a considerable self-imposed pressure to give the impression that he had a father, which it seems he became adept at, while having to tolerate the feelings of anger, sadness, shame, and jealousy in relation to the reality of an absent father. During this early period, and particularly prior to the UK, Adam and his sister repeatedly experienced the absence of their mother while she secured income via her masseuse practice, which presumably gave Adam in particular the experience of being "adopted" by others (his extended family who were predominantly female) to look after him during his mother's repeated absences. In the UK, following the loss of this extended family, he became, in effect, the man in the home, looking after his sister. It became clear that Adam's early infancy and formative years in Nigeria were spent almost totally in the company of women (the various grandmothers, aunts, etc.) while the only masculine presence was the somewhat distant figure of a grandfather, who provided status and credibility to the family and who was successful in eliminating Adam's father.

Adam arrived in the UK at the age of seven with both the cultural expectations and the developmental stressors for him to be the head of the family. He also had the experience of losing a father who had been triumphed over by his grandfather, and the cumulative experience of an abandoning mother, who was taken up in her chosen profession as a masseuse in meeting with other men; she was choosing to be with other men as opposed to the growing man that was Adam. Rationally, Adam could progressively understand that this was in his and his family's best financial interests. Nonetheless he had to develop the resources to survive her absences and to contain his feelings of jealousy, particularly if he also held the belief that, as the only male, he was effectively her partner. During one period, he described himself and his sister being babysat by an uncle who became extremely abusive, without his mother ever knowing; "I was so powerless yet knew I couldn't say anything because mother was earning money and looking after us." We might consider that the shadow side of Adam's mother (her jealousy and early experience of abandonment/adoption, repeated in her later rejections) were revisited (projectively identified) upon Adam. He grew up needing/wanting to be the all-powerful grandfather figure (as a defence against his vulnerability and needs) with an intolerance for having that authority challenged. It is these factors that I believe contributed to the commission of the index offence that I will now go on to describe.

The significant events leading up to the index offence were as follows. Adam was driven, as I have said, by a combination of both cultural expectations and developmental factors, in identification with his grandfather, to become successful, particularly in the Nigerian community in London. A relationship with a young woman called Temitope developed in his mid-teens. He then became a part of Temitope's social circle of girlfriends, which included Cannie and Bubby. In addition to Cannie being a friend of Temitope she was also the sister of Audu, the husband of his adult victim, Ruki. Adam progressively became a part of this social network, and quickly established that Ruki (Audu's wife) was very much looked up to by his fiancé, Temitope, and her two friends, Cannie and Bubby, because of her standing in the Nigerian community, primarily as a result of her marriage to the businessman Audu. His relationship with Ruki slowly became closer, to the point where he says he became over-dependent on, and powerfully attached to, her. More importantly for Adam he could see that by ingratiating himself with Ruki, he would be able to develop his business opportunities and financial standing through Audu. So that, in effect, Audu became a very important man and Adam admitted that his development of a relationship to the household of Ruki and Audu was in order to secure better business and networking links with Audu. He was later to add that Audu loved him and trusted him like a brother.

It is worth repeating the similarity here with his own biological father, who sought through his marriage with Adam's mother to gain financially and in business through the links with the grandfather. I understand that Adam was successful in securing some insurance and property purchases for Audu and believe that he managed to secure the trust of Audu to the point where he became a respected member of the family.

In relation to authority and the struggle that I felt Adam had with that issue, an interesting dynamic developed between us when Adam felt that I was being disrespectful and discriminatory by referring inappropriately to Audu as Mr Boro, which was Audu's formal, Western, title and name. This issue resonated with my experience of feeling acutely monitored by Adam, as if he were seeking to establish a weak spot in me that he could then exploit. While it is almost a universal given in psychotherapy that a patient will initially establish (consciously and unconsciously) how safe and containing their therapist might be, this dynamic felt particularly pronounced with Adam. Adam insisted that I refer to Mr Boro as Audu because he said that it would enable him to free his mind up from having to continually interpret one name for another and to be more spontaneous! This became an area of some conflict between us, and resulted in me acceding to his request that I refer to Mr Boro as Audu in any ongoing discussion. As a corollary I felt, as I did on many occasions, that I should apologise to him for the misunderstanding and explain myself, as if being pulled into subjugating myself to his authority. On reflection, I wondered whether this represented outstanding feelings that Adam might carry (feeling the need to apologise and explain himself) in relation to Audu, following the killings. I was, however, more struck by the fact that using the forename Audu had the effect of equalising the relationship between Adam and Audu with the implication that they were brothers, which ensured that any connotations associated with the title of an adult/parent by using the formal title of Mr was removed. He left me wondering whether this was significant and a means for Adam to be able to deal with the imbalance of his relationship with Audu, so that he was then able to change the relationship he had with Audu in his mind from one of Audu being the "head" to more of an equal relationship, around being a sibling/brother. The conflict between us on this issue had the potential of destroying the assessment process. Adam had become considerably aroused and angry about this issue—to the point where he made it quite clear that he would not continue with the assessment process were I to not change from referring to Audu as Mr Boro.

I was subsequently able to refer to this difficulty that we'd had around the importance of using the right descriptive words when he became angered by my reference to his murderous rage in relation to the index offence. He challenged this from the rational position that it was not legally murder and there was no aspect of the offence that was premeditated given that it had been proved in law that he had had a brief psychotic episode, from which he was now free. To his credit, despite again becoming angrily aroused and threatening to "walk" from the assessment process, he was able to hear that I was describing a feeling state as opposed to asserting a concrete diagnostic fact. I was asking for his consideration and flexibility in accommodating the thinking that his offence was a demonstration of his murderous rage, which was a descriptive term, in the same way that he'd been asking me not dissimilarly to accommodate Audu as a descriptive term in the place of Mr Boro. The reduction from parent to sibling that had been so important to him resonated with the need to reduce murder to manslaughter; I found myself reflecting upon the mirrored abnegation of responsibility. I also took up with him his angry assertion in the exchanges that I was discriminatory and disrespectful. He was able to think that, because of his arousal and anger, he was acutely susceptible, from previous experiences he'd had, to feeling misjudged, and that asymmetrical time ("then" was different from "now") disappeared and I became the same as previous clinicians with whom he'd felt he'd been incorrectly evaluated.

Returning to his identification with his grandfather, who had six wives in Nigeria, I was able to identify in my discussions with him that at the time of the index offence he had six girlfriends/confidantes; hitherto he had also described having six different personalities. The six girlfriends were as follows: Ruki, Erika, Ama, Cannie, Ricki, and Temitope. While there is enough complexity to Adam's story, I would nevertheless want to note that at the time of the commission of the index offence there were potentially six identifications at work:

1. identification with grandfather as head of the family
2. identification with father (Audu taking his son away—as Adam's father had attempted)
3. identification with a sibling (Audu as "sibling brother" to Adam—equating with his own sibling, Fatima)
4. identification with mother (Ruki)
5. identification as the eldest child (Bella)
6. identification as the eight-month-old son (Henry). (Unlike all other family members Henry and Adam are the only ones to share Westernised names.)

It is worth noting that three years prior to the commission of the index offence, a not dissimilar (although not fatal) incident to the index offence occurred with his fiancé Temitope. The trigger point was the painful feeling that he was losing her, generating acute anxiety (possibly linked with his past experiences with his mother). Apparently, while he had been seeing her on a daily basis, she needed to move some distance away to North London in order to secure employment (with all of the possible resonances with mother leaving him, also for employment purposes), and this had the effect of significantly reducing the amount of time that they could see each other.

Temitope's family were from a culturally different part of Nigeria from Adam's. This prevented him from being given ready access to her family home where Temitope was now residing in North London, which meant that on the infrequent visits that he used to make, late at night after she'd finished work, they would apparently grab an hour or two together on the streets in North London before Temitope returned home. This arrangement was very unsatisfactory to Adam, and increased his anxieties that he was losing her. In particular he felt that she was becoming progressively influenced by Cannie, whom he felt was adversely affecting their relationship, and this was coupled by the anxiety that Adam felt that Temitope was planning to return and visit Nigeria to explore her family roots, adding to his feelings that he might lose her.

On one given night, an argument ensued between the two of them about his anxiety, and while he could rationally understand the reasons both for her need to be in North London for employment purposes and for her need to return to Nigeria to trace her family roots, at an affective level this felt like a real and permanent loss. The anxiety this generated ended up with the following scenario: after parting with her following the argument, en route back to the train station, he purchased a pack of knives and went to her home address where at the front door he alerted Temitope and her parents to the fact that he was holding a knife to his throat. He stressed that what had provoked this was that he was deeply worried that she did not love him anymore and that Cannie would corrupt her way of thinking. He said that he placed the knife to his throat in the manner described to indicate that "she was killing me". Despite being very shocked, Temitope was able to ask him to go home and Adam said that it was the gentle, caring, and loving way that she had said this that prompted him to drop the knife and place the pack of knives through the letterbox and go home.

Later on in the week, Adam returned to Temitope's house and much to his surprise was welcomed in by her parents only to be told that Temitope had left and gone to Nigeria. He said that he was angry and sad, and felt that he had lost her for good. He said that he returned home, talked to his mother for a few hours, then asked his mother to leave the house before conducting some Nigerian invocations, summoning up a Goddess to help him ("foolishly", he said), and through a number of coping strategies was able to continue his life without Temitope. He said it was six months before he next saw Temitope, and during that time he became engaged to Ricki, who, he said, forced the engagement upon him! This was not an uncharacteristic assertion by him, for he often felt at the receiving end of predatory and seductive activities by women. Some six months later, when Temitope returned to the UK, he was able to meet with her and they forgave each other for what had happened. He then ended the engagement with Ricki, who it appears was subsequently adopted by Adam's mother as a goddaughter in order to help Ricki save face. Adam said that his relationship with Temitope then became stronger than before, and the concerns that he'd previously held had changed. Since that time, he said, "All of my jealousies have been cured".

This incident in relation to his fiancé and the knives and the anxiety of losing Temitope, particularly as a result of an influential other (on that occasion Cannie), had deep resonance with the index offence. Ruki, together with Audu, Bella, and Henry were also planning to travel to Nigeria for a protracted period, in order to celebrate the birth of Henry eight months previously with the extended family there. The clear link here was that while Adam had hitherto felt that he was losing Temitope this was again being repeated with Ruki. This was an anxiety that was barely survivable previously with his arrival at her house with the knives (let alone in infancy when left by his mother), and on this occasion was exacerbated by other significant factors.

A further alleged incident is worthy of note. Apparently four weeks prior to the index offence Adam had indecently assaulted Cannie, although Adam had felt there had been a complete misunderstanding about what had happened. He claimed he went into the bedroom where Cannie was sleeping and sharing a bed with Temitope, his fiancé. In the same bedroom was Cannie's mother, sleeping in another bed. Adam felt that Cannie misunderstood his attempt to tidy up the duvet on her bed as an attempt to fondle her bottom. The timing of this misunderstanding is interesting, given that Cannie was on the cusp of her wedding with a man called Levi, but I believe the more important dynamic was that Cannie was also the sister to Audu. Therefore this alleged incident could have been viewed as an indirect attack upon Audu. The timing may be important in that this was potentially an issue that might have disrupted the arrangements for the marriage. Certainly on the day of the wedding, while Adam still attended, he never felt that there was any possible reconciliation between himself and Levi. He had undermined and triumphed over Levi by assaulting Levi's fiancé and, if true, effectively coming between the couple in perhaps the same way that defined his infancy in coming between his parents and splitting them up and later coming between Audu and Ruki, via his killings.

Adam made progressive attempts to become an important and established member of the Boro family (with Ruki and Audu). However, he felt that his relationship with Ruki, whom he had established as one of his confidantes within the Nigerian culture, had become distorted some weeks prior to the index offence when he alleged that she had made sexual advances towards him. He felt an obligation to comply with her demands, and proceeded on one occasion to have reciprocal oral intercourse and on another to have vaginal intercourse. While he claims he was excited about the sexual part of that relationship, he was also excitedly alarmed that he was doing this to the wife of Audu. I am reminded that we only have Adam's account of the existence of this activity, and of course whether it occurred in reality or not is to some extent irrelevant, given that I am stressing the importance of this being in Adam's mind, particularly as it links with the jealous relationship he had with Audu and all its meaning. Moreover, the foregoing alleged incident with Cannie in her bedroom that followed this "sexual activity" with Ruki could be understood as an unconscious way of seeking to get caught out and punished to allay his feelings of guilt in relation to Audu.

The burden that Adam felt in needing to pursue a successful career and social standing to restore honour to his family was exacerbated by his developmental experiences. He had a revered grandfather, an eliminated father with all of the subsequent possibilities of promoting an identity as father's replacement, particularly around the arrival of his sister, and a narcissistically preoccupied mother insensitive to the jealousies provoked in her children around her nefarious masseuse activities. Such underlying factors led Adam to be susceptible to acting-out, via offending, in the following way. The night before the index offence he met with Erika, one of his girlfriends, who was returning to the Midlands that very night to be with her family for her birthday the next day. This may well have resonated with Adam about somebody close to him (mother/Temitope/Ruki) leaving him to be with important others. He then chose to take the train to the Boro family home, to try, he said, to clear the air between himself and Ruki, following his feelings that she was controlling him, and to try to address the difficulty that he felt he had about her jealousy of his relationship with Temitope. It is of course very possible that this was a projection on his part of his jealousy of Ruki's relationship with Audu. Either way the following factor is, I think, of profound significance in contributing to the explosive murderous rage that was to result in the deaths of Ruki, Bella, and Henry.

Historically (through both projection from his mother and his actual life experiences) he was extremely susceptible to feeling abandoned, rejected, and jealous and needing to find the resources within himself to contain the experiences and cope. An intrinsic part of this process was the added experience of unreliable paternal figures who, in their absence, had denied him the opportunity to healthily triangulate such experiences, whether through the absence of his own biological father or later a man called Mr Ismail whom mother briefly married and who sponsored the family to come to England, or finally another partner of his mother's (unnamed), who was also experienced by Adam as exploitative.

After Erika's departure on the night of the index offence, on top of his previous experience of losing Temitope (which had triggered his threats to kill himself with the knife), he was not dissimilarly facing the possibility of losing Ruki, who was about to embark for Nigeria for an extended period, at a time when he was feeling particularly vulnerable and exhausted. This was compounded by the issue of authority both in himself and with that commanded by Audu, who was taking his family to Nigeria which Adam could do nothing to prevent. Moreover, Adam had informed me that he was the godfather to Henry, Audu's eight-month-old son, and Henry was the reason that the family were travelling back to Nigeria. Adam said he was deeply honoured to be made godfather and stressed to me how he learnt of Henry's conception from Ruki before anybody else, including, critically, Audu. I believe his envy/jealousy of Audu was such that Adam needed to triumph over him (and had perhaps recently attempted that possibility with the alleged indecent assault upon his sister Cannie) through his destruction of Audu's family. Adam told me that on the train journey up from London, on the night of the index offence, he recalled holding his head in his hands repeatedly saying, over fifty times, "Audu will forgive me... Audu will forgive me..." Adam asserts that he believes that the conscious reason for seeking Audu's forgiveness in this way was in relation to the concocted story he'd prepared for himself should Audu be at the house when he arrived. While Adam anticipated that Audu wouldn't be there, he nonetheless ensured that he'd got a very good reason in place should he be present. The cover story was that he was attempting to construct a mock burglary for Audu so that Adam could claim against Audu's insurance company on Audu's behalf for a burglary that had happened, in order for some money to be realised. At another level Adam may have been seeking forgiveness for other murderous unconscious impulses.

Adam was able to describe the index offence scene, and his need to emphasise that he was so desperate in his desire to free himself from being controlled by Ruki (in transferential terms, his mother), which was also a dynamic I often felt he was struggling with in our interactions. His stated aim was to attempt to re-establish the relationship with Ruki on a more comfortable setting, but that he unfortunately reacted explosively to her feelings of jealousy about his relationship with Temitope. He said he felt she was blackmailing him with the fact that she would mention to Audu the sex that they had had if he were to finish the relationship with her, and so he felt completely trapped. He then repeated the same scenario that he'd previously carried out with Temitope, by holding a knife to his throat, again communicating to Ruki that she was killing him, and to demonstrate the degree of desperation he felt. He claimed that he then offered her the knife to do it for him, and in the exchange that occurred in passing the knife to her, she inadvertently cut his hand with the blade. This was apparently the moment when the total sum of the complexity of his murderous feelings took over and triggered a reaction in him of a feeling state that I had earlier described to him as murderous rage. He told me: "I thought why would the very person who is there to protect me actually hurt me? ... I was deeply pained by the person who I entrusted my whole life with." Not unsurprisingly, I immediately thought that this would be an assertion he might have made of his mother, and at that moment in time both Ruki and his mother had become symmetrised. All the rage that he felt towards his mother, coupled with the rage that he felt towards his abandoning father, together with an envy of the head of the family (whom he wanted to triumph over and become), coalesced in a violent attack upon the body of his adult victim. This culminated in an attempt to sever her head, a not dissimilar attack on her two-year-old daughter, Bella, who was in the room at the time, followed by the asphyxiation of Henry.

What I want to highlight here is that at that moment in time he had a complete identification with his grandfather as the head of this family; he was the godfather after all. His grandfather was successful in preventing his biological father from taking him (Adam) out of Nigeria and by doing so managed to retain his relationship with his wife, daughter, and grandson. This was then mirrored by Adam who, in slaughtering Audu's family, prevented Audu from taking his son out of England to Nigeria (in identification with grandfather) ensuring that Adam, as the godfather/grandfather, was able to prevent the biological father from taking his young boy away and secure for himself through their deaths, Ruki (his wife/confidante), Bella (the daughter), and Henry (his godson/grandson)—see Appendix. These two mirroring events are identical, particularly given that Henry was around the same age that Adam had been when his father had attempted to take Adam out of the country, that is, eight months. In the index offence, Adam draws our attention to the attempted severing of the "head", which I viewed as an externalisation of the importance of "heads" from his internal world in triumphing over the father by preventing the young, very important, son from leaving the country.

Following the killings, Adam took some intimate photographs of his victims, which were later found by police. His photography, he said, was apparently an attempt to deceive the police that a sex crime had been committed. It was this aspect of the crime that has concerned clinicians regarding the sexual motive there may have been in the enactment of the offence. Adam tentatively agreed in treatment that there may have been a sexual component to his offending, although stressed that this did not lie at the core of his intention to take photographs. The multi-faceted identifications that I believe were at work at the crime scene included another aspect in relation to his identification with his mother who ostensibly as a masseuse was engaged in one activity while at the same time discreetly and covertly engaged in another, namely the sex trade. As a masseuse and/or mistress to a number of clients, there was a taboo in speaking or referring to any sexual aspect of the relationship. Not dissimilarly through Adam's identification with his mother and her professional life, it may be that the covert nature of the sexual component of the index offence must remain just that. We might also say that it was only at that moment in time following Ruki's death that he had complete control over her (Ruki/mother), free from ownership by any others. The sexual component of the crime alerts us to considering whether Adam falls within the domain of sex offender, although I would want to state that the primary motive for the attack was not in my view sexual, if applying the spirit of the diagnosis. In particular, it would be important, in the long term, for Adam to have a full understanding about his unconscious need to photograph the victim in the way that he did. Further identification with his mother's profession was perhaps also highlighted by his attempts to put Ruki's clothes back on following her death, which apparently is customary practice by Nigerians in the masseuse industry, on completion of an intimate activity. As a postscript, Adam is very aware that it is a useful survival tactic not to be perceived as a sex offender by other patients while being detained.

Adam's continuing assertion is that this was a brief psychotic episode whereby evil spirits in the room at the time were seeking to take over the bodies of his victims, and that he needed to prevent that from happening by attacking them. This led me to suggest to Adam that those evil spirits that were seeking to take over the three victims were in fact a part of his own functioning that was seeking to own them and separate them from Audu (as in a projected part of his own internal world). It was that part of himself that he was seeking to attack, that is, an internal world conflict that became externalised.

Adam's response to this was to liken the events of the index offence to the thriller film *Eyes of Laura Mars* (1978). I was struck when viewing the film recently that the perpetrator of the killings in the film was, before killing himself, was seemingly struggling with his own early experience of being left to survive using his own resources, following repeated abandonment by his mother who was a prostitute working on the streets in New York. There are indeed significant resonances in relation to Adam's history and index offence, as well as in relation to the photographs that Adam took.

Film and photography have been a thread running throughout his life (you will recall that his mother was frequently photographed as a young attractive woman in high society). His particular interest in film was apparently shared with many patients and he once ran a film club on the hospital ward. In addition, there is a link with his grandfather, who invested significantly in Nigeria with three other businessmen in one of the major film companies of his time.

I stressed earlier that Adam can often be experienced as if he is not a patient but a member of staff, and this equates with the idea that he has of himself, which he externalises, of being in a position of authority and control as opposed to feeling vulnerable and impotent. This represents an acute level of denial (of psychic pain) with a manic defence that cuts off everything else, particularly his vulnerability in relation to women, where his own needs and desires get projected and he therefore becomes the passive victim to predatory females. Interestingly, when I explored with him the issue of a pornographic video that had been found in his room, he went on to talk about his penchant for mild pornography, stating that he's not interested nor is excited by any hard-core pornography of any violent nature, and that he is only interested in "big-breasted blonde women that feature in videos where no men are present". I attributed more of an importance to the fact that there were no men present, and that he was the only male amongst the women. This elimination of the male (authority) ensured that he established the position as the granddaddy of them all, which I believe strikes at the core of understanding his psychopathology and index offending.

In my time with him I told him that I was less interested in establishing any diagnostic criteria and more driven to wanting to help him understand the meaning behind his offending. Having said that, I would not be averse to agreeing with the diagnosis that included a severe narcissistic disturbance, indicative of a fragility regarding trust in relation to attachment figures, as well as an underlying delusional matrix that he is the ultimate authority. The latter is a manic defence against not only loss, but also envy/jealousy, with the attendant identifications that drove him to such a disastrous conclusion. I struggle with the diagnosis that this was a brief psychotic episode, given his behaviour immediately following the killings, which was very rational, almost reflective, and thought through in an attempt to cover his tracks, highlighted by indicating to the cab driver (who was called to the house by Adam when he had finished there) that he was waving goodbye to someone in the house while shouting something in Nigerian.

Following my assessment of Adam, he was reviewed, and a decision was made to send him on trial leave to a less secure institution. While there, his new RC requested a further intervention by me, given difficulties encountered regarding his continued resistance to thinking about his offending from any other perspective than it representing "a brief psychotic episode", alongside his constant challenges to authority. Given the cost implications, it was agreed that I could offer a maximum of eight sessions. I wrote to Adam making it very clear that, in our work together, we would be seeking to establish the level of curiosity that he could demonstrate regarding any unconscious factors in the complex aetiology of his offending, alongside the monitoring of his willingness, motivation, and capacity to reflect on any significant dynamic factors involved. In addition, I informed him that I hoped to meet with his sister, so that she could again be included in the same way that she'd been included during the previous extended assessment work. This I achieved and in meeting with her she expressed her full support of the treatment plan and understanding of the rationale.

Despite considerable communication, both verbal and written, Adam was (unconsciously) late for our first session, which resulted in his immediate apology (sycophantically expressed). However, this very familiar, somewhat masochistic presentation, quickly changed when he felt that in my response to his apologies for lateness, I lacked a warmth, acceptance, and accommodation. I reminded him that his lateness was a repetition of what I had hitherto experienced in our previous assessment and that I understood this as an attempt to reverse the power ratio in the room from one in which hitherto he was waiting for me to arrive and now I had to wait for him. I added that his experience of my "hostility" was a projection on his part, in terms of his angry feelings with me, rooted in his anxiety about not being the authority in control of the situation. His anger with me continued throughout the session and apparently afterwards on to the ward, although we were subsequently to agree, in the next session, that his feelings had become displaced, not unlike in his index offence, on to the computer in the room, which had then become a ward issue. The allegation he had made following our first session (which had not at all featured in that session) was that by my unplugging the computer from the wall and moving it to the back of the room in preparation for our first session, I had damaged it, rendering it unavailable to the other patients. My interpretation to him in the next session was that he was also saying that he had felt damaged by me in a way that made him less available, too; his anger towards me had been displaced on to the computer. The importance of the meaning in this is that displacement lay at the core of his index offending, in that in part his attack upon Ruki was a displacement of his murderous rage towards his mother and indicative of an inability to process his feelings appropriately, in that they became split off and projected into his environment.

This example of his initial attachment with me served to highlight and provide understanding of how he managed his feelings in that they become displaced, which then affords him an opportunity to intellectualise and rationalise in such a way that the recipient is left somewhat confused and often angry and dismayed. The listener therefore experiences the very feelings that Adam finds difficult to process in himself.

He attended all sessions throughout, although there came a moment during session five when he threatened to walk out of the room (mis) perceiving that I was seeking to psychopathologise him as a sex offender. This was indicative of an acute sensitivity in this area (of sexuality) of his functioning and one that I was able to subsequently explore at some length and help him understand. He had been susceptible in his development to powerful cultural dynamics that suppressed his emotional life into subservience to authority and, by extension, his sexuality often needed to be disguised by being played out in the socially acceptable form of confidante relationships. More importantly, I agreed with his repeated assertion that at core he was not a sex offender, although he agreed with me in a later session that, not unlike his mother (in her activities akin to the confidante role), there was a sexual component to the offending that he sought to disguise from not only the police but also from himself, which took some considerable time for him to reconcile himself to.

Adam exhibited deep anxiety regarding his emotional life in general (of which his sexuality was a part) and, while his intellectual and rational functioning was quite advanced, it was often in the service of protecting (and disguising) the somewhat infantile and regressed emotional part. This was ubiquitously apparent in that when he was feeling insecure about exploring any aspect of his emotional experience, he would take flight into an often confusing intellectual and verbose rationale that would protect his vulnerable/emotional self. I associated this process to the decapitation of two of his victims, in that by separating out the head (intellect) from the rest of the body, he was demonstrating this internal split in himself (thinking and feeling) and externalising it into his environment. This had occurred at a time when he was so taken over with murderous feelings that his intellectual and containing mind was unable to cope, resulting in a parallel decapitation.

I had learnt that his ambivalent relationship with authority was a crucial area of his functioning. My formulation, which I presented to him during this treatment and to which he agreed, focused upon his identification with his grandfather or we might say his delusional belief that he *became* the grandfather (at the acute moment of distress at the time of the index offence) by competing with Audu and successfully triumphing by securing ownership of not only Henry but also the rest of the family. This identification/delusional necessity was designed to defend himself psychically from any exposure to feelings of weakness, vulnerability, and loss and a bruising to his narcissism. So, not unlike his grandfather, his sense that his perceived authority within the Audu family was being undermined and humiliated was defended against, resulting in the murderous attack that took place. His identification as the ultimate authority had much resonance in the way he related in general, no less so than in the opening sessions with me, but also more generally in the relation to the Trust managing his care.

During this treatment, a judicial review was being undertaken at his behest to challenge a decision to handcuff him on an escorted visit to a hospital for some medical treatment. He was specifically objecting to what he perceived as unnecessary security measures being imposed. I addressed this challenge to authority purely from the perspective of his psychopathology, as opposed to any agenda in overturning the judicial review, and suggested that while mirroring his grandfather's challenge through the courts in Nigeria, it ultimately resulted in his own real needs for medical attention not being met, as he would not be taken to hospital without handcuffs. I commented that he was again caught up in repeating trans-generational history and that, if he could allow himself to accede to the conditions imposed and not challenge them in the way that he felt drawn to, he would get his own needs met. He responded by saying that the legal process was now too far down the line to reverse it.

He was nonetheless able to see that his constant challenges to authority worked to ensure that he remained stuck in institutional care, counter to his claim of wanting to move on. This is redolent of a disguised dependency and a part of him which, unconsciously, sought to remain in safe care. Often, as clinicians, we can miss this crucially important dynamic, as if the dependent culture in institutions compensates for unmet dependent needs and this oversight adds additional problems to the rehabilitation goals.

It is an old debate about whether jail/confinement in institutions works, and what is so often missed is that while many offenders are seeking punishment to alleviate feelings of guilt (both unconscious in relation to developmental aggression and conscious in relation to their crime) they are also more crucially seeking a sense of belonging. This can be achieved through criminality whereby all dependent needs can be met once in institutional care. This sense of belonging (even to the criminal fraternity) goes some way to compensate for life-long deficits but unless the offender understands his own history and the part it has played in his offending then the cycle merely repeats itself. Jail therefore works but not for the reason it is intended and often acts as a spur to reoffending.

In Adam's infancy there had, historically, been a rivalry between his grandfather and biological father for ownership of Adam when he was in his infancy. I therefore felt it was important to ensure that there was awareness of what was possibly a similarly competing dyad, in his doctor/Responsible Clinician meeting with him for a small number of sessions, in parallel to the sessions that I was conducting. I ensured that I raised awareness in both his doctor and in Adam that the sessions were not competing, but were running in parallel and that liaison occurred in support of his overall progress, in contrast to his early history. Moreover, this intensified my own reflections around who I might be representing in the transference at any given time and I remained very watchful of the ebb and flow of merging with unconscious material to re-enact object relationships and conflicts: at once the grandfather (given my seniority and experience) and the father (in potentially using him for my own "business/career" opportunities). It was not uncommon for me to feel that I was mis-handling his communication(s), exemplified on the occasion when he was offering an apology to me (for being late) and I became caught up in injuring him by my response, which enraged him. This represented a re-enactment of the dynamics surrounding the index offence. It was as if he was holding a knife to his own throat, in communicating his need to be heard and understood, only to then hand it over and be cut in the exchange, triggering a murderous rage: "… why would the very person who is there to protect me actually hurt me? …", with all of the resonances with a maternal transference.

While the foregoing issue with authority was linked to the importance that might be attributed to the decapitation of his two female victims in that it symbolically represented the importance of becoming the head of the family, it also represented a separation of the intellect from the rest of his functioning. In-between our sessions, an incident occurred on the ward that highlighted this split. Apparently a knife had gone missing from the ward and Adam was the last patient who had been entrusted with it. With the knife missing, he characteristically became verbose and quite manic in convincing himself and others that he was not responsible for being complacent about its security and/or for countering any suggestion that he might be concealing it. His reaction was indicative of an ultimate mistrust of himself with regard to his own feelings of dangerousness. I helped him to consider that his verbosity was an attempt to reduce his anxiety concerning the fear that he could not trust himself and to eliminate the likelihood of any propensity, in his or others' minds, that he had feelings similar to those held during the index offence. He was certainly uncomfortable with the idea that his behaviour demonstrated a deep anxiety that danger-ousness still existed in his own functioning. The decapitation that took place was a flight into an intellectual discourse in an attempt to take control of situations where his anxiety and feelings are out of his con-trol. Moreover, the missing knife had deep resonance with two signifi-cant incidents in his history, the first of course being the index offence where he said that he handed the knife over to his victim Ruki, which then provoked his murderous attack. This was predated by the incident with Temitope, three years prior to the commission of the index offence, when, suffering intolerable feelings of loss, abandonment, and humilia-tion, he bought a pack of knives, apparently with suicidal ideation. It did not escape me that the missing knife was in some way representative of the missing dangerousness in his own mind.

Before concluding, I want to comment on a dream that Adam pre-sented to me in his final session. I am conscious that, while in analytic circles there is considerable credibility given to the interpretation of dreams, in other professional domains it might not sit so comfortably. The significance I attribute to it is that it appeared to represent a shift in Adam's internal functioning (coming straight from his unconscious) that cannot be ignored. He informed me that the dream he had was of being on escorted leave and visiting the gift centre in a shopping mall. However, once in the gift centre (and in the dream he had the sense that he was considerably younger, almost as if a young boy) it was decided by his hospital escort that he would be left to carry out his shopping alone, while the escort did his own shopping. This left him feeling both excited and of course a little anxious. The escort left him and he had all sorts of thoughts about what he might want to do in terms of shop-ping and after a short period of time his escort returned and everything was fine. I could not ignore the wish-fulfilment aspect of this dream, in that it carried association to his judicial review and conditions applied therein. However, more importantly, the dream suggested that escort-ing his infantile/repressed (feeling) self by the rigid intellectual and authoritarian part of his functioning was no longer necessary and that he could quite happily and safely survive without it. I also attribute relevance to his reference to the gift shop, in that it was as if he had been given a gift by way of the formulation in relation to his history and index offending. He had been presented with my formulation during the work, particularly emphasising that Henry and Adam were symmetrised by not only holding the only Westernised names in the family but were at the same age (eight months) when the respective parents split up. Their fathers had sought to take a son away to another country, and, to prevent that from happening, the grandfather/godfather had intervened triumphantly. He expressed to me that, for the first time, he had been fully able to understand his offending and felt that my formulation had provided him with a real insight that had hitherto been missing. The therapeutic challenge, if the appropriate resources could be found, would be to offer him a prolonged psychoanalytic intervention to help him fully digest his new understanding.

This chapter demonstrates how crucial it is to take into account transgenerational history, cultural beliefs, and developmental factors. Adam clearly had the intellectual capacity to engage with ideas, albeit largely through rationalisation to defend himself against being in touch with his affect world, and by extension the traumas and conflicts of his early history. His use of the mystical in Nigerian culture was, I believe, defensive and understandable, in that it allowed him to protect himself from the enormity of his crime and enabled him to explain his index offence as a brief psychotic episode that quickly passed. He has always been adept at asserting that he has knowledge of the cultural/mystical and that the Western world either will not or cannot embrace such knowledge, which leaves him feeling prejudged when insufficient account is taken of such belief systems. This is akin to the split represented by his parents belonging to two different countries and his belief that one is not understood by the other. While I believe he has used such issues to defend against reality, he did indicate a possible availability for accommodating a different way of thinking about his life and offending towards the end of our time together, more redolent of the West.

My remit was to challenge his own thinking and to explore his capacity to consider other factors (unconscious) and despite considerable and perhaps characteristic resistance he was able to embrace this different perspective.

I believe that as a result of our interaction he developed a greater understanding of himself and his offending, which had the potential to be built on. This would enable him to really begin to digest the importance of his history and how he had been caught up in a complete repetition (by identifying with grandfather) as a defence against his inability to handle his feelings maturely. Reconciling himself to the foregoing understanding is a considerable therapeutic task and would represent the equivalent of giving up on the judicial review around the issue of handcuffs and all that it represented. The outcome to such a process would be living his life in relation to his own needs, as opposed to repeating history.

I have emphasised how he decapitated his thinking from his feeling in an attempt to find a degree of control and authority in any given relationship. I learnt in my time with him that he clearly benefits from persistence in engagement, to ensure that the decapitation is unsuccessful and that thinking very much remains attached to the feelings. I was particularly struck that, at the end of our work together, he was able to express sadness and also guilt. In relation to the guilt, he was able to comment that he had been aware of his aggression towards me in the exchanges that we'd had and was aware of his guilt as a result of that. While there were discernible shifts in him in the work that I undertook, I really have to stress that in order for there to be a fundamental change in Adam's internal world there would be no alternative in the long run to "working through". This is the process by which a patient discovers repeatedly (rather in the same way that an infant digests and introjects) over an extended period of time, the full implications of some insight. I was, however, not optimistic at the end of our time together that he would be accorded that opportunity, in that in the setting that he was in there was no psychoanalytic therapy being offered. The lack of any psychoanalytic therapy being available increased the likelihood that Adam would return to his engrained way of functioning, with all of its potentialities to infect his treatment team. History would then be repeating itself in the absence of the opportunity for fundamental change.

My cup is, however, half full, in that it may be that our interaction together provided enough of a shift, however small, in understanding based upon his history to ensure that the likelihood of any repetition of murderousness was reduced. As a postscript I met with Adam and Fatima to read through this chapter prior to publication (Adam had made this a requirement before giving his written consent to go to print) and they both expressed their deep gratitude for being offered such an in-depth insight and understanding into the offence and said that it had accorded both of them a grounding and template to work with in Adam's attempts to bring about changes in the way that he relates and functions.

APPENDIX

Identification with grandfather by Adam at time of index offence

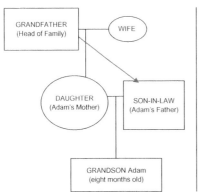

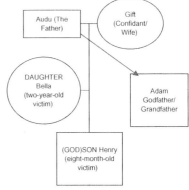

Elimination of rival to secure ownership of wife, daughter, and grandson

Elimination of rival to secure ownership of wife/confidant, daughter, and godson/grandson

CHAPTER NINE

Understanding the Dunblane Massacre*

In memory of all victims of the Dunblane Massacre

> Gwen Mayor, teacher of Primary One: 45

Victoria Clydesdale: 5	Emma Crozier: 5
Melissa Currie: 5	Charlotte Dunn: 5
Kevin Hasell: 5	Ross Irvine: 5
David Kerr: 5	Mhairi McBeath: 5
Brett McKinnon: 6	Abigail McLennan: 5
Emily Morton: 5	Sophie North: 5
John Petrie: 5	Joanna Ross: 5
Hannah Scott: 5	Megan Turner: 5

> and
>
> Thomas Watt Hamilton: 43

---

*This chapter was first presented at the International Association of Forensic Psychotherapy (IAFP) Conference on 29 April 2011 in Edinburgh, and subsequently at the Group Analytic Society 2011 Symposium on 2 September in London.

"I do not believe in a fate that falls on men however they act; but I do believe in a fate that falls on them unless they act."

—G. K. Chesterton (1922)

Introduction

This chapter presents an understanding (it is believed for the first time) of the causes of the largest mass killing in Scotland's recent history at Dunblane Primary School on 13 March 1996 where sixteen children and two adults (one of whom was the perpetrator) lost their lives. It portrays the powerful picture of a man destined to act out the unresolved conflicts of his family history at a critical time, given the absence of a meaningful intervention into the historically perverse and enmeshed dyadic relationship with his mother. This absence of another dimension (ordinarily the father) to mediate between the two ensured that through repetition compulsion he went on to relate to his environment as a re-enactment of his personal history, resulting in the massacre of innocence of infancy that was originally his own.

The fact that this incident is always referred to as the death of sixteen children and one adult draws immediate attention to the exclusion of the life/death of the perpetrator Thomas Watt Hamilton, whose feelings and experience of exclusion were profoundly characteristic factors throughout his life. This dynamic of exclusion (and its antithesis, the need for a sense of belonging) lies I believe at the core of humanity's struggle with itself. That is, the ubiquitous impulse to exclude difference and create a foe (which can represent a projection of a part of ourselves) is responsible not only for incidents such as this one at Dunblane but extends outwards, fundamentally influencing all mass killings, crime, and conflict whether between individuals, nationally, or internationally.

This analysis reveals the unfolding process whereby uncontained feelings associated with exclusion and loss seek to get contained in the wider community group, given the experience of an absence of containment by the primary attachment figures within the family.

In relation to the Dunblane killings, the "who", "where", "when", and "how" is known and yet the "why" has remained unanswered in that the perpetrator Thomas Watt Hamilton shot himself at the scene and he is not in a position to tell us (assuming that he would know himself) or to confirm any theories. There has been considerable speculation in the press and in the public inquiry undertaken by Lord Cullen in 1996 regarding his motives (Cullen Enquiry, 1996).

This chapter augments the public enquiry, in that there appears to have been an absence of psychodynamic thinking, linking the perpetrator's history with the offence, somewhat mirroring the unfolding story of the perpetrator, in there being an absence of another (reflective or third) dimension. Psychological and psychiatric reports explored a diagnosis of sadistic personality disorder alongside psychopathy and mental illness. Thomas Watt Hamilton was described as a loner, unmarried, living in a ground floor council flat, unemployed, on benefits, with significant debts. Hitherto he had owned and managed a DIY store for a number of years and run a photography business, before relying upon some income from the running of Boys' Clubs. He was neither a drinker nor smoker and no drugs were found in his body at the autopsy. He last visited his general practitioner some eighteen years prior to the offence and was considered to be a reasonably fit middle-aged man. While he had no previous convictions or charges he was known in the area largely as a misfit. He had been expelled from leading a Scout group when aged twenty-two, given concerns about his "moral intentions towards the boys" (Cullen Enquiry, 1996, 4.6). Following this expulsion he ran a number of Boys' Clubs (which occupied his time). The clubs raised yet more concerns, given his predilection for inappropriate, "old-fashioned" discipline, and his penchant for photographing the boys at his club while they undertook their gymnastics routines dressed only in black swimming trunks that he had provided and ensured they changed into, ostensibly as a form of uniform. Despite paedophilic suspicions, at no time could anything be proved. He was, in response to rumour and allegations, a prolific letter writer (getting them typed at Stirling University) in which he challenged and rebutted all allegations and innuendo, often with erudition. What has come across clearly in my research is that concerns were often raised regarding his "parenting" at his Boys' Clubs of vulnerable children. An objective observer would naturally be drawn to focusing upon the potential perpetrator in him. This focus ensured that any vulnerability and "victim" in him from his past history (which he was blinded to) was mirrored by being completely overshadowed by the concerns about his relations with vulnerable others.

We know how crucially important it is in forensic work to take account of the victim in the perpetrator and that fundamentally this proposition ordinarily translates into taking account of the perpetrator's personal, family, and trans-generational history. This is one of the core tenets in working with forensic patients and the one that is the most likely to face resistance, in that it really challenges our own capacity for empathy with a perpetrator, particularly if heinous crimes are committed. "Empathy is like a universal solvent … any problem immersed in empathy is soluble" (Baron-Cohen, 2011, p. 128).

What I am wanting to stress is that at no time has Thomas Watt Hamilton's trans-generational family history been taken into account with any seriousness.

Once one does consider this history, it becomes clear why a time bomb had been waiting to explode at a critical moment in his life, linked directly to his mother and her own early life. Indeed, I would wish to add that these factors need to be taken into account in order to truly understand all similar incidents, and I have deep concerns that they may not be included in attempting to reach a full understanding of events in Norway on 22 July 2011, the largest peace-time mass killing in Europe.

My main focus will be on the innate drive in human beings for a meaningful sense of belonging (the ideal being autonomy in the context of attachment to society) exemplified by its opposite, which is the feeling of being excluded and emasculated and the concomitant shame associated with this most painful of feelings whereby violence is so often perceived as the only solution. This investigation will incorporate the effects of the absence of fathers and by extension, what they represent, particularly if the mother/child twosome requires an intervention to facilitate the child's separation and individuation and to prevent an unhealthy and perverse enmeshment. Lastly, the crucially important area of the transference of trauma across generations will be highlighted, whereby unresolved conflict gets played out (displaced) along the generational line—what I describe as the most uncomfortable of "hand me downs". Is it not a maxim that extreme human behaviour is always determined by the nature of the society in which its perpetrator lives?

An abiding memory of my mother was her passion for the detective novel, the whodunnit, and I recall the frequent visits I made to the local library in the 1960s to borrow three more books for the week. I particularly recall the feeling of exclusion in sitting for hours with her while she read her books as I perhaps quite unconsciously took in her cigarette smoke as a way of feeling a part of her life at that moment in time. I used to be intrigued at her interest/relationship with this genre, so perhaps it was an inevitability that I would pursue a life seeking to belong to the world that was my mother's—one from which I felt excluded. My life-long involvement first in the detection of major crime and latterly in its understanding and treatment has, however, left me feeling enormously frustrated and dismayed.

I feel that unless society can fundamentally address the issue of exclusion, in all its forms, but particularly of, and also, by the male in the mother/child twosome, then we will continue to experience the levels of violence and murder that are so familiar today. This family paradigm of mother, child, and father I am using as a template for all aspects of our lives in the way we relate (as I hope will become clear). It represents the crucial importance of triangulating in all we do, the one, two, and three, with the third position in the triangle being the most susceptible (like father) to being eliminated and killed off in our minds and in the way that we live our lives. This is akin to killing off the father in the mother/child dyad and it is this exclusion that lies at the heart of all violence, exemplified I believe in this study of the Dunblane Massacre. As I earlier stated, given the strength of feelings provoked by such a crime it is, perhaps understandable that at no time in the life of Thomas Watt Hamilton was consideration given to the victim in him (the third part of his own functioning in the triangle of perpetrator, witness, and victim). That is, he lived a life that drew attention to concerns (through witnessing) about his conduct as perpetrator and I have said and want to stress that we know in forensic work how essential it is to factor into our thinking the victim (his own personal trans-generational history) as well as the perpetrator; unless we do so the root of the problem will not be addressed.

The third in the one, two, and three, has many forms and also factors in the crucial area of sibling dynamics. It is also the experience of exclusion in sibling dynamics, in the way that often one sibling can feel totally unable to compete with the other, thereby feeling jealously excluded in the minds of parents, that can so often lead to murderousness as a response. It would be deeply remiss not to include this dynamic. In my scanning of recent campus-based mass killings, Cho Seung-Hui, who was responsible for the largest mass killing by a lone gunman in America, killing thirty-two people in April 2007, had a high-achieving sister. Tim Kretschmer, the seventeen-year-old German who killed nine students at his younger sister's school (in Winnenden, Germany, on 11 March 2009), eight female and one male aged from fourteen to sixteen, before going on to kill six others, had a sister who was, like many of his victims, fourteen at the time. Closer to home is the mass killing by Derrick Bird in Cumbria in 2010, where his twin brother David (his first victim—shot in the face at point blank range) was felt to have been favoured by their father with a "secret" donation of a £25,000 gift. I have hitherto presented at conference this very dynamic in siblings (see Chapter Six) in relation to an anorexic patient who killed herself as a result of feeling unable to compete with a revered sibling. The sibling dynamics detailed are mirrored by the tragic case of Karen Carpenter, the famous pop singer, who also killed herself seemingly in the face of feeling disenfranchised by her revered brother Richard.

My mother's rather benign exclusion of me in her dyadic relationship with her murder novels prompted me to adopt the familiar forensic defence of "identification with the aggressor"—if you can't beat them, join them. I needed to belong to this world that my mother was so passionately connected to and from which I felt so excluded. So, perhaps not unsurprisingly, I have lived a life rooted in murder taking place and pursuing an understanding of its enactment, just like my mother. By extension, you should, I hope, begin to see that Thomas Watt Hamilton's mother's own early life of exclusion resulted in her subsequently excluding her son (which gave him the experience of loss that had hitherto been her own). She projectively identified (unconsciously passed) her unresolved issues on to him and a powerful collusion/enmeshment then took place between the experiences of mother and son, exacerbated by the absence of a mediating third. This all resulted in his subsequent projection of loss into his substitute adopted family of the larger group, that is, the community of Dunblane.

In relation to this analysis and chapter, it is crucial that you the reader wear your 3D glasses to triangulate. That is, in the face of very powerful innate and external pressures to eliminate the third (the triangular, three-way, inclusive of difference thinking), you resist this powerful and ubiquitous pull to murder off the third, and keep your truly reflective functioning in place. 3D offers the perspective about what is in front of you in relation to its background. By contrast, it is the two-way dyadic—right and wrong; good and evil; "You are for us or against us"—rhetoric that is so murderous of the third/difference/male and of all it represents. You will be tested in your capacity to hold two different scenarios in mind at the same time, the first being the trans-generational family history of Hamilton (that is, what happened to him) alongside the second, which is the events that unfolded in his relationship with his community (that is, what happened to them), and you will see that one mirrors the other quite remarkably. Over the years, I have experienced this dynamic whereby the clinical group experiences and enacts the individual patient's psychopathology and, in extending this concept more broadly, in this particular case, his group was the small, quiet, respectable Presbyterian community of Dunblane.

In the absence of a third (ordinarily the father) there is an increase in the potential for enmeshment to take place between mother and child, particularly if the mother's needs have not been met in her own life, thus affecting her capacity to allow for the difference between herself and her child. Mother's inability to allow for the difference of her child, and her inability to triangulate healthily in herself, is exacerbated by the absence of an external third, which could compensate for any absence of this capacity in her. Estela Welldon says:

> I suggest that a perverse mother experiences her baby as part of herself, never to let it go or develop its own gender identity, let alone individuate. She derives a great sense of elation in making her baby respond to her own inappropriate needs ... which is a process that spans at least three generations.

> (Welldon, 1988, p. 83)

This chapter presents my research into the causes of the Dunblane Massacre where Thomas Watt Hamilton walked into the gym of Dunblane Primary School and shot dead sixteen children, their teacher, and then himself. I will demonstrate that his trans-generational story is one of exclusion and loss, with desperate measures being taken to be included and to fit in. His family even went to the extent of per- versely altering the natural order, whereby authority on the vertical axis (parental) was eliminated and replaced by a peer relationship (sibling) on the horizontal axis. This was the re-configuration that took place in his family shortly after his birth, whereby his mother elected to become his sister and by extension his grandparents became his parents. We may also note that these parents/grandparents were actually Thomas' great uncle and great aunt. He therefore grew up believing his mother to be his sister and it is certainly no surprise to me, given its familiarity, that he went on to live his life as a suspected paedophile within the community with all of the confusions around adult/child, vertical/ horizontal relationships. Moreover, it would appear that a complete inability to triangulate healthily in his family resulted in the experiences of his mother and her story being played out in an identical form in his life, in that this enmeshed relationship lacked a mediating third person. It is a story of a life of unresolved trauma from one generation being played out in the next, particularly in relation to loss and shame.

I start his trans-generational history (Appendix 1) with his biological grandmother's loss (Rachel Hamilton) through the unexpected death of her husband (John Laird) after four years of marriage. This was followed by the shame and humiliation of exclusion from the normal expectations and mores of society by shortly afterwards conceiving a child out of wedlock in 1931 by another man, William Rankin (Appendix 2). We can hazard a guess that this conception, which took place six months following the loss of her husband, helped her fill the vacuum created by her loss. The child that was born was Thomas Watt Hamilton's mother Agnes. Given the stigma associated with the bastard child Agnes, she was given up for adoption (Appendix 3) thereby sustaining a loss herself of her biological mother and father. Agnes was adopted by her maternal uncle and his wife, who became her "mother and father". With hindsight, in relation to subsequent events and the passing on of unresolved conflicts from her own life, we could reasonably surmise that she grew up being unable to triangulate healthily and reconcile herself to her own past. This affected her capacity to allow for the difference of the child she then gave birth to, namely Thomas Watt Hamilton (Appendix 4), who also experienced being born without a father following his birth, exactly mirroring his mother's early experience. Thomas Watt Hamilton then displaced all of the trans-generational dynamics of loss into his relationship with the wider "family" he created in the group, that is, his community, as a direct result of feeling intolerable shame and alienation (rejection).

Professor James Gilligan has identified the link between shame and violence: "[T]he purpose of violence is to diminish the intensity of shame and replace it as far as possible with its opposite, pride, thus preventing the individual feeling overwhelmed by the feeling of shame" (Gilligan, 1999, p. 111).

Thomas Watt Hamilton was destined to repeat his mother's story, unless there was a thoughtful active intervention (a third) and there wasn't. This will lead us to consider what interventions could have been made in relation to Thomas Watt Hamilton and perhaps more importantly what interventions are required in society today that could prevent such violence and mass murder from continuing. I am very aware that in order to address such issues we face enormous resistance.

Indeed are we not all subject to wilful blindness, which is why I have stressed the importance in the face of resistance of keeping your 3D glasses on, given our minds' tendency to filter out information that contradicts our worldview or threatens our cherished way of life. We might say our dyadic enmeshment within ourselves creates an unwillingness to confront information that challenges the accepted order and, in this case, that resonates with the stigma directed towards giving birth out of wedlock.

Six days before Thomas Watt Hamilton exploded into a murderous raging spree, he wrote a letter (Appendix 5) to parental figures of authority in society (the Queen, a local MP, a local councillor, and headmasters of local schools, including Dunblane Primary school) and I want to draw your attention to his final sentence where he writes (added emphasis): "I turn to you as a last resort and am appealing *for some kind of intervention* in the hope that I may be able to regain my self esteem in society"; his letter received no response. It powerfully suggests that he recognised that he needed an intervention—indeed he had required one all of his life. Events unfolded in such a way that he was to re-visit upon the community of Dunblane the feelings of loss, (out)rage, and attack upon the "innocence of infancy" that was his own and had hitherto been his mother's. This attack upon the innocence of infancy appears to lie at the core of all such incidents, and I noted with much interest that this was a phrase often used to describe the atrocity in Norway of July 2011. The cycle repeated itself, and now I feel that there is a desperate need for a meaningful intervention by society in relation to the part it plays in unwittingly promoting violence (particularly by men) and I will offer my own thoughts and recommendations in my concluding comments, in the hope that in the long term we may be able to reduce and even eliminate the likelihood that such events will reoccur and also as a true testament to the memory of those who died.

Our trans-generational picture starts in 1931 when Thomas Watt Hamilton's mother, Agnes, was born illegitimately to Rachel Hamilton (a widow of six months when she conceived) and her lover William Rankin.

The stigma (shame/humiliation) associated with a child born out of wedlock at the time represented a local scandal, with the associated anxiety of not belonging. Agnes was given up for adoption at birth to her mother's brother and sister-in-law—James and Catherine (see Appendix 1). Catherine was referred to by neighbours in the press reports following the Dunblane incident as the "mother from hell". In 1936, Agnes was formally adopted by James and Catherine at the age of five and I am more than struck by the coincidence that five was the predominant age of the children killed by Thomas Watt Hamilton. Her adoptive parents were childless, and Agnes was brought up by them an only child until Thomas Watt Hamilton was born. It is worth noting that the avuncular can have an important triangulating function in family life. This triangulating function was eliminated, in response to shame, by the pretence that uncles and aunts were parents (mother and father).

So Agnes had two families. The first rooted in loss, shame, and exclusion/rejection, where she had little sense of belonging and also experienced the loss of being given up, losing her father and mother at birth, and the second, her adopted family. She was formally adopted, which I assume gave her the experience of inclusion in a family and community and a sense of belonging. We are left to ponder the type of relationship that existed between Rachel (the natural mother) and Catherine (her adopted mother) who was Rachel's sister-in-law. Certainly, Agnes' natural father William, and her adoptive father James were peripheral and non-existent figures in her life. There are numerous accounts in press reports that Catherine concocted detailed stories for the local community about her "pregnancy" in order to disguise the shame-laden true origins of her adopted daughter.

Agnes grew up and married Thomas Watt when she was nineteen and at twenty-one gave birth to our subject also called Thomas Watt in 1952, later, after adoption, to be named Thomas Watt Hamilton. She was able to achieve what her adoptive mother Catherine couldn't, which was to conceive and give birth to a child.

Very shortly after Thomas Hamilton's birth, an affair his father had been having came to light, which resulted in him leaving his wife and child and cutting his son out of his life completely. The absence of contact was permanent and thereby constituted a real elimination/ exclusion (and we can only speculate what his father might have been unconsciously passing on to his son from his own history (Appendix 6a and 6b—statements photographed from the Cullen Enquiry 1996). This abandonment by the father left Agnes destitute and, once again, ashamed, replicating her early experience of an absent father and resulting in her not fitting into the accepted norm of society. Her son, Thomas, then went on to have the same experience. In her early life Agnes had lost her father and her mother and became adopted by a new father and mother. In her subsequent marriage, following the birth of Thomas, she again experienced a significant loss, of her husband. Likewise, Thomas in his early life also lost his father, and by being subsequently taken in by Agnes' adoptive parents, gained new parents. In so doing he lost his biological mother, who elected to become his sister. He was formally adopted at the age of four by James and Catherine, the adoptive parents of his own mother (Appendix 7). The arrangement that was made meant that Thomas would lose his mother, in the same way that Agnes had lost her mother. Agnes "became" his sister, while Catherine and James "became" Thomas' parents. It is reported that Catherine again went to great lengths to describe, locally, details about her "pregnancy" with Thomas to promulgate the idea that she was his natural mother. Thomas was born to Agnes but could not be acknowledged to be alive, until, to lift the burden of shame, he was reborn to Catherine. This has resonance with his circumstances and actions at the time of the shooting in that his suicide perhaps repeated this death-and-rebirth fantasy only this time under his control (in contrast to the previous occasion in infancy when he was the passive victim), and that this also occurred within the affective field of shame within his community. Quite what lay at the root of this arrangement we can only speculate. Perhaps to save face Agnes simply gave up her motherhood in exchange for a home for herself and Thomas, enabling the deceit that Catherine and James could be regarded as actual parents. At a much more unconscious level, Agnes was now able to displace her own experience of having lost a mother and father and being adopted by Catherine and James, on to her own son Thomas. She may also have lacked the maturity to handle parenting, choosing instead to continue to have her own unmet dependent needs attended to by her adopted parents.

In any event, when we look back over the two generations, what we see is children losing their mothers and mothers losing their children at an early age, with adoption occurring subsequently at five and four respectively. This results from the fathers, the third in the relationship, being either eliminated or eliminating themselves in the context of pejorative pressures from society in not fitting in by feeling excluded.

This was then to be powerfully re-enacted (repeated) by Thomas Watt Hamilton at Dunblane. As a result of the same experience, the father figure he saw himself being, as a Scout and Boys' Club leader, became progressively excluded and eliminated through pressures from the community (even though he was unaware that he was provoking his own exclusion). Ultimately and gravely, this resulted in parents losing their five-year-old children. It is worth repeating here that Agnes's illegitimate father William Rankin may have been used by her mother, Rachel, to overcome the loss of her husband (you will recall that she was widowed just a few months before conceiving) and that her unresolved loss was then displaced into Agnes who in turn would displace her own loss into her son Thomas, and he in turn into the parents of Dunblane. This repeating cycle of projection required an intervention, and draws our attention to the absence of a continuing/ reflective function in the mind (the third, that takes account of history), thereby perpetuating the dyadic dynamic of victim becoming perpetrator.

Throughout his life Thomas Watt Hamilton failed to fit into his community (he quintessentially represented the misfit), which resulted in a revenge attack to make the community experience the very same feelings that were his own trans-generationally. To put it simply, his loss became theirs, in the same way that his mother's loss had been passed on to him.

It needs to be stressed that I am in no way attributing any blame to the specific community of Dunblane, but emphasising how Thomas' own story was unfolding quite unconsciously within the larger group of the community, to a disastrous end, and that the community were unwittingly caught up in playing a part in his unfolding internal world and trauma, whereby an intervention was crucial yet profoundly lacking. Similarly, in clinical situations we can often get caught up, individually and in clinical teams, in our patient's story (acting into the countertransference) so that we can lose our capacity for reflective functioning (embracing the third) to intervene, that is, interpret in the transference. It is only through healthy triangulation in all clinical work that real progress can be made.

I will now describe what happened to Thomas Watt Hamilton. He was brought up in a family relating to a sister, not consciously knowing that she was his mother. Quite how Agnes maintained this deceit is impossible to know, although it is reported that she continued to relate to him as a sister long after Thomas was informed she was his mother, when he was twenty-two years old. What mustn't be underestimated is that the dynamics of this arrangement must have had a profound effect on his personality. I believe it is a given that he did not know what he knew, until told, that is, that his sister was his birth mother; that in his relationship with her there would have been an intuitive sense that things were not as they seemed, even though it could not be proved. A form of wilful blindness was seemingly maintained, and while he may have harboured powerful suspicions alongside attendant confusion that the boundaries of their sibling relationship were somewhat blurred and inappropriate, nothing could be proved, neither by him nor, perhaps, by the local community. The community, we might say, were looking in on this family, feeling uncomfortable and suspicious that something was not quite right, but couldn't prove it. Moreover, given the twenty-one year age difference between Agnes and Thomas, there must have been some real curiosity. This mix of knowing and not knowing describes the very same experience that Thomas Watt Hamilton was to give his own community over the exact same period of twenty-one years (from the age of twenty-two up to his death at forty-three) with his running of Boys' Clubs—discomfort and suspicion and a feeling of things not being quite right, but an inability to prove anything. The number of letters of complaints and enquiries into his Boys' Clubs was staggering and addressed at the highest level, and yet nothing could be proved.

Following on from being a Venture Scout at the age of twenty-one, Thomas Watt Hamilton was appointed assistant Scout leader of the Fourth/Sixth Stirling Troop, and a few months later became the Scout leader of the Twenty-fourth Stirlingshire Troop, resulting in him achieving the position of "parent" (*loco parentis*) to boys in the Scouting Movement. Moreover, when I visited one of his childhood homes in Stirling, I was not surprised to see that his home faced the village hall that housed the First Stirlingshire Scout Group (where he had hitherto been an active member of the Venture Scouts).

So at twenty-one he became a "parent", at the same age that his mother was when she became a parent to him.

I want now to return to the phenomena of critical dates (hitherto highlighted in earlier chapters) and a rather unknown publication by Averil Earnshaw called *Time will Tell* (1995). Earnshaw writes:

> We are all living in two sorts of time: clock time and family time. Clock time is consciously—agreed—upon time. Family time is the time which rules our internal world. Not attending to family time has far greater repercussions … we need to connect ourselves in ages with our parents and link with our children (trans-generational). Failing this, we find ourselves involving other people in our personal drama … I have found that most people find these ideas quite overwhelming.

> (Earnshaw, 1995, p. 13)

I am often asked in clinical work when thinking about a patient in an attempt to understand his psychopathology and offending, "That's all very well, Peter, but why have plenty of other people who have been, say, adopted not ended up as killers?" My response to this perfectly sensible question is carried in the following scenario borrowed from Earnshaw: "If six men walk through the jungle and mosquitoes bite all six, why is it that one gets malaria and the others do not?" (1995, p. 25). Vulnerability is the answer here and armed with awareness of family time and the repetitions that take place across generations, we can consider where we are at vulnerable times in our lives when we might get bitten. Only when we appreciate where we are in family time do we begin to have the choice of moving meaningfully in our own lifetime.

My own clinical and personal experience confirms Averil Earnshaw's research that repetitions of family events occur across the generations. These events can be precisely predictable in time, in relation to events experienced by parents with children and manifested by mental, emotional, and/or physical disturbances at the particular time, particularly marked when a new born arrives in the family.

The effect of lack of awareness of the phenomenon of family time is a blurring of identity (enmeshment) between parents and children and the result is confusion as to who is who. I am very aware that Earnshaw's thinking and research can be passed off as either coincidence and/or idiosyncratic and at best a good parlour game by looking at repeating patterns of events in family histories. I do, however, want to stress how important it is not to relate to her thinking in a dyadic, at face value, way and to relate more to any meaning it may offer by reflecting upon the facts. In any history taking (exemplified in Hamilton's case) looking at any potential critical date phenomena has illuminated areas of family malfunction/perversity/trauma/conflict. With Thomas Watt Hamilton, the critical dates draw our attention to an enmeshment and identification with his mother with the inevitability that past events would be repeated, given the absence of an intervening father/third/ reflective presence. In the absence of a thoughtful reflective third either within the object itself (by being unable to process his own experience, increasing the likelihood that it will be passed on/projected onto the next generation), and/or an external third to compensate for the deficits in reflection in the object, the likelihood that aspects of the object's experience will be passed on (repeated) is extremely high.

"There is properly no history: only biography" (Emerson, 1983, p. 240).

If a man or woman is in a position of power (with guns in this case) his or her "time bomb" erupting from a personal inner world can alter the lives of many people. I am setting out that while Earnshaw's research informs us that this was the case with Adolf Hitler, who was responsible for the death of countless millions, and J. Robert Oppenheimer, whose critical dates were played out in 1945 causing the deaths of 120,000 people in Hiroshima and Nagasaki (Oppenheimer was the director of the Los Alamos centre, where the bombs were made), it was also the case with Thomas Watt Hamilton (Earnshaw, 1995, pp. 122–124). In the spirit of triangulation, and with reference to the foregoing, I repeat that I would want to include the possibility that Averil Earnshaw's research and my own use of it could, for some, be considered to be coincidental repetition, and accept that her ideas will perhaps meet with scepticism on the one hand and complete negation on the other. If the critical date feature is removed, what we are nonetheless left with are repeating experiences across generations. Earnshaw underpins her observations with the following:

> DNA [deoxyribonucleic] is present in the nuclei of all the cells in our bodies, and it is defined as the repository of inherited characteristics. (Doubtless the characteristics referred to are physical ones) ... DNA is not immutable; the apparent stability of DNA is in fact an illusion. Its structure is altered by severe changes in the

internal physical conditions of our bodies (such as are caused by fevers or lengthy exposure to cold), and it is repaired by DNA-repairing enzymes. We know that intense emotional states, too, are accompanied by biochemical changes, so I wonder about the physical transmission of "time-tagged" DNA-damaged, repaired, but scarred DNA.

DNA carries messages to our tissues, from within us. For example, there are no messages from outside to our teeth, about when to erupt, and when to stop growing out of our gums. We are pre-set from within by our internal "clocks".

Why then, could not our DNA have been inherited, scarred from our parents' events, and precipitate a disturbance "on time", when we reach the ages of our parents' disturbances? Particularly, this could account for our eruptions at the ages of our parents, of major events which happened before we ourselves were born.

This could be the basis of mutations. Evolution could be thought of negatively, as well as positively. For example, we can inherit negative and positive parental life events.

(Earnshaw, 1995, pp. 26–27)

As a postscript, I have no doubt that this is a primary factor in the horrific incident in Norway of 2011, given that a very brief search of available information on the perpetrator Anders Breivik reveals that he committed his offence ("time bomb") at the age of thirty-two. I understand that his mother was thirty-two when she gave birth to him and that shortly after his father separated from the family, leaving him to develop what has appeared in reports to be described as a perverse and enmeshed relationship with his mother (see Postscript).

So returning to Thomas Watt Hamilton, after becoming a "parent" (to the Scouts) at twenty-one, as Agnes had in giving birth to him at that age, he very soon lost his parentage, aged twenty-two. Concerns had been raised about his capacity to be a "parent" given the perception that he lacked the qualities necessary and suspicions about his moral intentions towards boys, so his Scout warrant was withdrawn. Agnes was also twenty-two when she lost her parentage of Thomas to Catherine and James.

We might say that Thomas was confusing the boundaries between a parental role and relationship with his boys, which had been his own experience as a brother to a sister who was in fact his mother. This is redolent with paedophilic traits, whereby the child becomes adult and the adult becomes child, such that confusion reigns between self and other and all boundaries of appropriate child/adult relationships are blurred, for example, mother becoming sister. In Chapter Six, I detailed my work in Broadmoor with a paedophilic offender, from the perspective that he is fundamentally seeking a sense of belonging that is perversely provided by young children. He had, not unlike Thomas Watt Hamilton, had the experience of being given up for adoption in his early life. Is it not uncommon that adopted children can crave belonging as a result of powerful feelings of rejection?

Thomas Watt Hamilton, at the age of twenty-two, encountered a time-linked event in losing his own identity as "parent" in the Scouts. In addition, at this time/age he was also informed about the true nature of his relationship with his sister and his parents, that in fact they were his mother and adoptive grandparents respectively. We can reasonably guess the impact that this knowledge had and its effect.

The sudden realisation of an "unknown known" being a "known known" must have provoked feelings of huge betrayal, deceit, loss of a sense of identity, rage, and shame. The community that hitherto had been his family was never going to be the same again and given that his feelings in relation to such an experience were seemingly suppressed, this process provided the likelihood that the feelings would subsequently be re-enacted in the community of Dunblane, in the same way that previous generations had displaced and projected their traumas/conflicts on to him.

So the exact mirroring by Thomas and his birth mother of becoming a parent at twenty-one and then losing that role a year later at twenty-two leads me to the following.

His mother, Agnes, was forty-three in 1974 when Thomas, aged twenty-two, had experienced not only the traumatic loss of his Scouting warrant (mirroring his mother's loss at twenty-two as a parent) but additionally suffered the shattering realisation that his sister was in fact his birth mother.

Thomas Watt Hamilton was also forty-three when he walked into the gym at Dunblane Primary School, and vented his murderous rage by revisiting upon the community his own trans-generational losses and annihilation of innocence (Appendix 8).

What is indisputable is the grave impact that losing his Scouting warrant had upon him in 1974 (aged twenty-two). He fought for the following twenty-one years, not only to contest the decision, but also to address the ongoing challenges to his Boys' Clubs, which he felt were all linked to this original decision. This incident was sufficient in itself, linked as it is in time with his mother's loss at twenty-two. Additionally, I also wish to highlight that, both in the public enquiry and elsewhere, virtually no significance has been attributed to Thomas being told about the true relationship in his family, that his sister was in fact his mother, and its effect on him. I want to stress its importance, and by doing so draw attention to other independent reports, in particular the statement from James Hamilton, his adoptive father, to the Cullen Enquiry, where he said that in 1974 Thomas was informed by Catherine, his adoptive mother, that she was not only his adoptive grandmother but also that his sister was in fact his natural birth mother. So that together with losing his Scouting warrant, this horror of the attack upon his innocence and sense of identity additionally compounded his feelings of loss, anger, betrayal, rejection, and exclusion (Appendix 8).

He was re-enacting this scenario in involving his community in his story in a way that they had no way of knowing, mirroring his own experience. His natural grandmother had lost her husband, and daughter Agnes. His mother Agnes had lost her child, and he had lost his children (from Scouts and Boys' Clubs), and the community were then to lose theirs. A common thread in all of this is the absence/exclusion of a healthy triangulating third, conventionally and stereotypically represented by the father.

When he reached the age of forty-three he committed his crime at Dunblane Primary School, giving the community the experience of losing their children which was the unfolding trans-generational story in his family. Moreover, from the age of twenty-two, for the next twenty-one years, Thomas Watt Hamilton gave the community the very experience he had had for the first twenty-one years of his life of unknown knowns. He represented a parent in the community in holding responsibility for children. There was considerable suspicion that things were not right and that his parenting was inappropriate, although it was always difficult to establish any proof. Then the time came when the truth revealed itself and real loss, rage, and despair (which he had experienced at the age of twenty-two, when his mother was forty-three) became re-enacted when he reached that critical date of forty-three. In the end, what began originally as an attack by society in its moral inflexibility and incapacity to tolerate difference (child born out of wedlock, etc.), thereby excluding that difference, led to the disastrous revenge attack and re-enactment by attacking the society for not accommodating *his* difference and the type of parenting he was perversely offering.

He enacted a murderous rage against those that he felt had disowned him (ultimately his father, mother, and then, through displacement, society). This was promoted by his unconscious provocation of the community by behaving in a way that led to and exacerbated his own exclusion (he couldn't help himself), all rooted in his trans-generational family history of feeling disowned and excluded.

"We are all in this together" is a well-worn and often meaningless phrase but it really applies here. We can turn a blind eye and maintain wilful blindness or choose to find a way of facilitating a meaningful intervention at the highest level in ensuring that we truly take account of difference, which is essentially the place men represent in the mother and child dyad and the third in all relationships. Too often this difference is experienced as a threat to the status quo. Men (the third) in addition to when they exclude themselves can too often represent the equivalent of difference and dangerousness and be excluded, which can blind us to the mature, generative third/male, whose difference needs to be embraced and not undermined/ridiculed, emasculated, and excluded. It is the latter intervention of this third that was so disastrously missing in Thomas Watt Hamilton's life, not only in his family environment but also, by extension, in the community.

I came across one example of an attempt at an intervention in Thomas Watt Hamilton's activities when a parent who was extremely concerned about the ex-Scoutmaster's "parenting" of his Boys' Clubs said:

> I contacted a reporter for the *Sunday Mail* [Scottish tabloid] and suggested Thomas Watt Hamilton may be worthy of investigation (after removing my children and having seen what they do at the club, together with discussing the issue with him in my home). They carried out an in depth investigation. The paper, however, said they could not run with the story as they had been told not to do so by their lawyers.

(*Sunday Mail*, 1996)

(The story was published after the killings.) He added:

> This struck me as typical brick wall which you seemed to run into when dealing with this man … and seemed that nothing could be done about him.

(*Sunday Mail*, 1996)

Moreover, another statement made to the inquiry by one of Thomas Watt Hamilton's closest acquaintances indicates the unease that he clearly aroused, which perhaps in hindsight should have been reported (Appendix 9).

To put these events in to contemporary context, I would suggest that there is an urgent need to support and not emasculate the healthy third/male and all it represents, as otherwise we are in danger of fuelling an already raging fire.

To return to Thomas Watt Hamilton: after losing his Scouting warrant and seeking unsuccessfully through appeal to re-establish himself in the Scouting Movement, he sought to create a rival movement by setting up his own Boys' Clubs. This paralleled a feeling of being disowned by his own original family and being adopted by another. As stated, at twenty-two he lost his Scout warrant as a parent to a legitimate family (like Agnes at twenty-two). To compensate for his feelings of shame, loss, and anger at losing his warrant as parent (which he complained affected him all his life) he started up a new family (of Boys' Clubs) and "adopted" children (as he had been) while progressively raising significant concerns about the appropriateness of his parenting (I repeat, a displacement of his own experience). From the age of twenty-two, he began setting up freelance Boys' Clubs throughout the central belt around Stirling. In all, he set up and singularly ran in the region of fifteen Boys' Clubs until his death (Appendix 10). This can be construed as a manic attempt to establish credibility in the community as an adoptive parent rivalling the original family, the Scouts, who had disowned him. So not unlike being given up as a Watt and taking on the adoptive name of Hamilton (while retaining the name Watt, as his middle name, associated with his original family), he used the name Rovers, taken from the Scouts, when he named his first Boys' Club the Dunblane Rovers Group. His explanation of his objectives was that he wanted to give the boys something to do and keep them off the streets, and that the boys needed discipline and exercise. He blamed parents for what was lacking in their lives (a denial of his own feelings towards his parents, which required projection to get the feelings contained) and for allowing their children to get overweight. Interestingly, I noted from my research in the national archives that aged eleven (the predominant age of the boys at his clubs) he attended his general practitioner for a bad back and posture and was, himself, told to exercise.

The following is lifted from the Cullen Enquiry into the killings and provides a feel of Hamilton's activities and behaviour.

At the same time Thomas Hamilton appeared to show an unusual interest in individual boys after only one appearance at the club and to put pressure on them to obtain parental permission to attend one of his summer camps. He appeared to helpers to have favourites. He was also very eager to collect boys from their homes and was keen to find out more about their family background than was acceptable to their parents after a short acquaintance. Parents were particularly concerned about Thomas Hamilton's insistence that for gymnastics the boys wore black (and ill-fitting) swimming trunks which he provided and that they changed into them in the gym rather than in the changing rooms. He argued that they often arrived in unsuitable clothing and hence this "uniform" was needed ....

Another matter which was of concern to parents was his practice of taking photographs of the boys posing in their black trunks while taking deep breaths, without the knowledge or permission of their parents. For this purpose he used not only a still camera but also a video camera which he acquired about 1989 and possessed for about five years. He argued that it was quite normal for photographs to be taken for training and advertising purposes and said that parents could obtain copies from him. On a number of occasions he offered parents a videotape so that they could see what kind of activities he ran. These only served to increase their concern. Their overriding impression was that there was something unnatural. The boys did not seem to be enjoying themselves but appeared silent and even frightened. There was also an over-concentration on parts of the boys' bodies, especially the naked upper parts along with long lingering shots of the area between the waist and the knees. When confronted with complaints about this Thomas Hamilton argued that it was necessary to identify what muscles were being used so that wrong movements could be corrected. When challenged about videotapes being made and photographs taken without parental knowledge or consent he responded that parental consent was not necessary but that parents could have access to any photographs which he had taken. Individual parents through contact with each other discovered that their anxieties were shared. At home Thomas

> Hamilton kept a large collection of photographs of boys, many of them wearing black swimming trunks. These were in albums or attached to the walls of his rooms.
>
> (Cullen Enquiry, 1996, 4.12, 4.13)

In relation to the last reference to displaying photographs on his walls in his home, this was something he did not hide from anybody; indeed they could apparently be seen from the street and the odd visitor/neighbour often saw them, noting that it was a perhaps a little odd. Our minds, I would suggest, are automatically drawn to the indication in this of dangerousness to the boys regarding any paedophilic traits, which is of course a natural preoccupation for us to have. What is less available to our minds is the potential pride (albeit perverse) of displaying his "sons" in this "family way" by a "father". Is it not after all conventional practice for families to display photos of their loved ones on the walls of their home?

The enquiry contains an enormous amount of material relating to Thomas' Boys' Clubs and the suspicions about his behaviour, which could never be substantiated. He felt progressively that the original accusations from the Scouts were being used by the community and the police to undermine his attempts to develop and maintain Boys' Clubs. He went to great lengths to address the unease he provoked and was not a man to be underestimated with his clever use of challenging letters and explanations. At one time he appealed successfully against the termination of the let of a hall at Dunblane High School by obtaining the support of thirty letters from parents, together with a petition of seventy signatories in his favour. The letter ended: "[W]e are all proud to have Mr Hamilton in charge of our boys: he has a most activated, excellent quality of leadership and integrity and absolutely devoted to his lads: above all he cares" (Cullen Enquiry, 1996, 4.18).

Local opinion was divided; some parents had a gut feeling (including George Robertson MP, whose son went to one of the clubs), although it was difficult to often identify what was wrong. Over the years, there was extensive contact with the police, even though he was never charged with any offences. Thomas Watt Hamilton progressively felt that there was a conspiracy between the Scouts/police/regional council which, in symmetrical form, could represent the three important women: in Rachel his natural grandmother; Catherine his adoptive grandmother/great aunt; and Agnes his mother.

The clubs filled most of his life; for example in May 1994 he was running clubs on Mondays in Falkirk, Tuesdays in Bannockburn, Wednesdays in Dunblane, and Thursdays in Alloa, together with the summer camps he organised, often as the only adult (he claimed to have undertaken some fifty-five camps).

Strikingly, it was a feature that while away on camp the boys were denied contact with their parents, and on one particular camp on Inchmoan Island there was no telephone. This again echoes his own history, being cut off from contact with his own parents. Moreover, this also has resonance with him cutting the telephone wires outside Dunblane Primary School before entering it.

His exasperation grew in attempts to rebut the suspicions, slander, and innuendo, even though his behaviour was encouraging such a reaction. In other words, he was seemingly at a loss to see the part that he was playing in his own downfall. While he had first obtained a gun licence in 1977 aged twenty-five, it would appear that he had not legally purchased any ammunition from 1987 up until 1995. I will not document his firearms use here, other than to say that towards the end of his life his guns and ammunition appeared to have replaced the loss of his boys at his clubs to the extent that he was once observed talking to his guns as if they were his babies.

By September 1995 there had been a substantial decline in his clubs and at the same time he sent a large number of circular letters to parents in Dunblane in order to deal, he said, with the false and misleading gossip about him that had been circulated by Scout officials. The letter stated that it was rumoured he had been put out of the Scouts or asked to leave in sinister circumstances, whereas it was he, he claimed, who had left the Scouts (an example of his denial). On 26 January 1996, two months before the killings, Thomas Hamilton sent a letter to a councillor and copied it to all local schools, stating that "at Dunblane primary school teachers have contaminated all the older boys with this poison ... that I am a pervert ... that has led to losses of attendance at my club, my public standing and capacity to earn a living" (Cullen Enquiry, 1996, 5.26). He went on to say that it had all reached epidemic proportions and had resulted "in a death blow to my difficult work with children as well as my standing in the community" (Cullen Enquiry, 1996, 5.26). I would suggest that much of this resonated with his own story whereby responsible adults "contaminate" children with falsehoods. By March, he felt his reputation was in ruins. He could no longer walk down the street without feeling ridiculed, and was close to bankruptcy: he had debts totalling £8,694 and was living off credit cards and an income of £75 per week provided by income support and housing allowance.

I have often used the analogy of a combination lock to explain the exact sequence of events that are required for a murderous act to be unleashed, not unlike the exact sequence of numbers for the lock to snap open. For Thomas Watt Hamilton at this time, all four of the five numbers were in place from the trans-generational transferences of traumas, to the feelings of exclusion, ridicule, and not belonging, to the loss of parenting alongside the huge debts he now faced. It just required the arrival of the critical date of forty-three years of age before the inevitable decline into total symmetry with his past completed the combination so that the lock snapped open.

Robin Kowalski, a psychologist at Clemson University in South Carolina, USA has co-written a comprehensive study on fifteen school shootings from 1995 to 2001 (Leary, Kowalski, Smith, & Phillips, 2003). A common factor identified was an acute rejection episode, which usually takes place shortly before the killer acts, with teasing and bullying also present (i.e., ridicule) and that underlying psychological problems featured. Moreover, she cites features about perpetrators planning their attacks some time in advance. This study was undertaken at about the same time that the US Secret Service (at the National Threat Assessment Centre), in collaboration with the Department of Education, conducted a major study of forty-one school attacks from 1974 to 2000 under the Safe School Initiative Programme. This concluded that most attacks were conducted by "loners" with a grievance and were perpetrated out of revenge. All of these features mirror our subject's experience and I am particularly emphasising the underlying dynamics to Thomas Watt Hamilton's susceptibility to rejection and ridicule and that his psychological problems were inextricably linked to his complex family history. Many people share a few of the same numbers on their lock (loneliness, rejection, bullying, etc.) but so long as their own history prevents the combination of numbers from being completed, the lock will not snap open.

After the incident it was discovered that Thomas Watt Hamilton had been enquiring about the layout of Dunblane Primary School premises for some time, in that he had been asking the boys at his clubs for details of the inside of the school and its timetable. Six days before the incident he made his plea for an intervention—by letter—as I mentioned earlier (Appendix 5). The day before the incident Thomas Watt

Hamilton visited Agnes, his sister/mother, spending some four hours with her, taking a bath, eating, and chatting as normal and, after going back home, telephoning her as he always did to inform her that he had returned safely. This is one of the best examples of dissociation I have come across (Appendix 11). He also spoke to a former Boys' Club member the night before when he said he was lonely, and it was not good to be alone. He had, however, reached his nadir and not unlike the loss, betrayal, and horror he had experienced twenty-one years earlier, when his mother was forty-three, he was about to give the same experience (at the same age of forty-three) to his community group and mother for their disowning of him. Moreover, he'd spent the twenty-one years from the age of twenty-two to forty-three giving his community the same experience he had had, in the first twenty-one years of his life, of suspicion, inappropriate parenting, and confusion around vertical/horizontal dynamics. His mother Agnes had had the experience of being mothered by a woman who was the sister (in-law) to her natural mother and Thomas Watt Hamilton had the experience of being mothered by a woman who was also a sister (in her own law) to his natural mother. The shattering experience of loss around parenting (his own in being a "parent" together with the truth about his own parenting) was to be revisited upon the parents of Dunblane.

I know from clinical experience that he was not in control of his provocation of his community nor in their disowning him (this is unconscious re-enactment). Moreover, Agnes gave him the experience of a parent and sibling confusion, as Agnes herself had experienced. Repetitions of loss had occurred whereby the cycle would continue unless an active, meaningful, and thoughtful intervention was made to ensure that real understanding and empathy could be achieved in the face of powerful forces to enact revenge.

Thomas Watt Hamilton's murderousness had been unleashed as a result of feeling disowned, and effectively killed off, first by a father and then a mother, followed by the wider family group in society (authority), which all emanated from his grandparental generation whose experience was similarly rooted in a deep feeling of not belonging (rejection) with attendant loss and shame. In my research, an interesting comment was made by a member of the community at the time about the aftermath of the incident: he said that the community did not really feel that it had someone to represent them as a figurehead/voice/authority (father), unlike similar atrocities like the 9/11 incident, where the

Mayor of New York and the President were felt and perceived to hold the parental position. This absence is a deeply significant observation, given the foregoing understanding of the situation I have suggested, as if the circle was now complete, with the community feeling an absence of a containing parent to help them with their loss.

Before concluding I want to refer to the song "Knockin' on Heaven's Door" (Appendix 12), the lyrics of which were originally penned by Bob Dylan, and which was chosen by the Dunblane community to represent the loss it had sustained, to generate support for a change in gun law, and generate funds for charity. This was taken up by Ted Christopher, a Scottish musician, who adopted new lyrics to the original tune, and renamed it "Throw These Guns Away".

This song reached number one in the charts and was played world-wide. This adoption of new lyrics replaced the original, in a mirror adoption of Thomas Watt Hamilton's life. I think you will agree that the original lyrics (original family relationship) are really quite profound and catch not only something of the relationship between Thomas Watt Hamilton and his mother, but have poignant references to Scouting with the use of the word "badge" in the opening line. This reinforces the power of unconscious functioning, which all too often is missing in the thinking that takes place after such horrendous incidents. My real fear is that this wilful blindness of not taking account of history will continue, not only in relation to the abhorrent slaughter in Norway of 2011, but also when other mass killings occur, as they will. In the aftermath of tragedy there is a tendency to lose perspective on the role of the unconscious, of history, and reduce our thinking to the two dimensions of good *vs.* evil, victim *vs.* perpetrator, and see understanding only as condoning. Tragedies will reoccur until we as a society are able to reach for true meaning, as opposed to conclusions based on prejudice and dyadic functioning, which replicates the perpetrator's psychopathology.

Conclusion

Towards the end of facilitating a clinical group presentation/discussion I will often explore how the group might consider triangulating the knowledge it has gained following the intra-psychic and inter-psychic process it has undertaken and applying it to the interpersonal. In other words, that is, how to translate knowledge and understanding into practical change and improvement.

In relation to our subject the question arises, armed with the knowledge and understanding regarding the underlying historical factors provoking such murderousness, how does society deal with individuals in their midst like Thomas Watt Hamilton? Moreover, and of crucial importance, we need to establish what needs to be done to try to prevent such events from reoccurring.

The first thing I want to emphasise is that all unexplained violence, murder, and particularly mass killings worldwide of the type similar to Dunblane, needs to include a full understanding and meaningful reflection of the trans-generational history of the perpetrator in an attempt to answer the question of "why". This will offer the only opportunity we have to establish the fundamental truth. My experience informs me that this way of looking at the crime should be applied to all such cases.

If Thomas Watt Hamilton was a time bomb waiting to explode at a particular moment, directly linked to his trans-generational history, then this suggests that he was susceptible to increased vulnerability to acting-out, with implications regarding his capacity to exercise free will. This reminds me of a unique legal case in Tennessee, USA, in 2009, where Professor William Bernet, a forensic psychiatrist, successfully argued in court that the accused Bradley Waldroup (a man charged with the brutal murder of his wife and her friend in 2006) had the toxic combination of the MAO-A gene, colloquially referred to as the warrior gene, together with an abusive and traumatising early environment. With these two factors together, Bernet suggested that Waldroup had a vastly increased vulnerability to rage. Bernet was successful in convincing the jury of the crucial importance of Waldroup's early experience and resulted in a capital punishment being reduced to a thirty-two year prison sentence on the grounds of diminished responsibility. The implications of this case are potentially considerable for crime and punishment in that for the first time the impact that the perpetrator's history and environment had upon the propensity to commit crime was legally recognised. By extension, this case also reinforces the importance of triangulating the inherited characteristics together with the environmental history to fully understand subsequent events. Should somebody possess the MAO-A gene without experiencing a malevolent environment then the numbers on our combination lock are not in place for it to snap open.

While this court judgement is a refreshing step forward it is, sadly, after the forensic event has happened, with the corollary of bereaved victims and enormous costs to the penal and welfare system, which will all continue unless society focuses on prevention.

We have been powerfully reminded in the UK with the recent mass killings by Derrick Bird in Cumbria that unresolved family conflicts lie at the heart of such murderousness. The clear parallels worldwide with similar incidents to Dunblane are that perpetrators feel fundamentally excluded and marginalised by lacking a sense of belonging, and that they have been acutely susceptible to re-enacting trans-generational trauma/conflict, particularly in areas where the mediation by a loving and supportive father (or an equivalent) has been absent in the context of an enmeshed and dyadic primary relationship often with a perverse mother.

This has deep resonance with the conclusions of a recent report called "Dad and me", undertaken by Martin Glynn (2011) and commissioned by the charity Addaction—who work with young people who have drug and alcohol problems. The report states that those who have not known their father can suffer from dangerous subconscious anger. Glynn suggests that this type of anger goes unnoticed and unchecked, and is not detectable, and if triggered or released the outcome is detrimental to friends and family, who have to pick up the pieces once the bomb has exploded. The report interviewed children and young people from across the UK and it laid bare a common sense of abandonment, lack of guidance, and a dearth of fatherly love, which has led in some cases to mental health problems. The authors describe what is happening (given that there are currently 3.1 million children in single-parent families) as an epidemic of "father hunger" that should be treated as a public health issue. I would like to robustly assert that the demonising of one-parent families is clearly prejudicial given that many single parents of either gender are able to provide a nurturing and containing environment by compensating for the absence of an actual "third" given their internal, triangulating, resources. However, it would also be morally perverse, representing a collapse of healthy triangulation, if we did not take account of the fact that, on some occasions, there are adverse effects upon children in such circumstances where the father/mother has either chosen to relinquish all contact or finds resistance to being included, and the internal resources of the sole carer are unable to triangulate in a compensatory way. Simon Antrobus, the charity's chief executive (who chaired an enquiry into gangs by Iain Duncan Smith's think-tank, the Centre for Social Justice) was quoted in *The Times* newspaper (28 October 2011) saying:

> Working with young people now can ensure that they are much more responsible parents in the future. It is highly likely that a young man who has real challenges in his life because of an absent father is going to replicate that …. [E]arly intervention with fathers of the future is absolutely critical.

(Antrobus, 2011, p. 29)

While a level of sophistication and considerable experience is required in unpicking the dynamic factors after the forensic event, we need to apply the maxim that prevention is better than cure, bearing in mind that it is enormously difficult to act upon a hunch/intuition/unease about somebody when the law hasn't yet been contravened. Thomas Watt Hamilton had no real awareness of how his own life, conflicts, and traumas, and the lack of a thoughtful and supportive male presence or equivalent (one which could mediate the dyadic enmeshment with his mother and her life) would lead to such catastrophic consequences. The severe marginalisation through rejection/exclusion in families and then society is a particularly malevolent form of scapegoating and suggests that we have not yet found a healthy way of functioning without creating exclusion.

We see it after all in examples worldwide when interventions are made to address perverse relationships between a dictator ("parent") and his people ("children"). Indeed, the current wave of unrest in the Middle East started from feelings of humiliation, emasculation, and powerlessness—in the fruit seller Mohamed Bouazizi in Tunisia—in relation to a local council official and law enforcer, which provoked his resultant murderous rage, enacted in suicidal form, by setting fire to himself. This was a clear example of a lack of triangulation by the "authority", which led to countless deaths, and which still continues.

As a society we urgently need to address what is going on under our own noses and in our own backyard, otherwise the proliferation of violence to compensate for this vulnerability, emasculation, powerlessness, and exclusion will continue to be communicated through violence.

H. G. Wells once said that human history becomes a race between education and catastrophe (1920, p. 55). Given that prevention is better than cure, my recommendations would be the following, based on a prediction that in 100 years' time historians will look back and view our current system of core education as dangerously dyadic and wilfully blind. In doing so I augment the thrust of thinking contained in *The Social Animal*, by David Brooks (2011), about ensuring that key human relationships are supported by government, and that this should be the bedrock of their policy making.

Given that it is sadly inevitable that as a society we will continue to experience individuals committing criminal acts as a corollary to fundamentally feeling uncontained, excluded, and emasculated (originating from the experience in their first tier of socialisation, the family) there is a vital role to be played by the next tier of socialisation, namely education, which will of course have significant cost implications. The alternative is the huge, ongoing, and ultimately unsustainable cost to the health service and penal system, let alone the victims, by maintaining the status quo. I believe we need to educate the next generation of mothers and fathers, starting at the earliest phase of schooling and continuing it right through to upper sixth form and on to university, about *relationships*. Where we have always had an emphasis upon the "3 Rs" (Reading, Writing, and Arithmetic), this needs to be joined by a fourth "R" with equal if not greater importance, standing for something like the Art and Science of Relationships (insight), which would intrinsically include the vital importance of developing the capacity to reflect. I am sure that opponents will draw my attention to the components currently on the curriculum of Personal, Social, Health and Citizenship lessons, even though they do not in any way attend to this vitally important area in any depth. Currently such classes only take up a mere five per cent of the school week; they are also at the greatest risk of being eliminated. I am suggesting a complete sea change and elevating relationship lessons as core to the educational needs of our future parents, alongside any necessary academic priorities, otherwise, not unlike the X-ray scanning machines at airports that cannot detect the murderous mind of the traveller, we will continue to exercise a wilful blindness to what is really important in our lives and in our relationships with one another. Inoculating future parents with insight is, I believe, the key.

I have recently written to an advisor to the education secretary Michael Gove on this matter, given that I seek to take the government at its word in relation to mass killings (following the Cumbrian slaughter) that lessons will be learnt. While I note that free parenting lessons will be offered to 50,000 couples with children under five (covering areas such as communication, managing conflict, discipline, and creating routine and boundaries) on a £5 million government trial in various parts of Middlesbrough, Derbyshire, and Camden, my suggestion is to approach the parenting issue starting with the child—the next generation of parents.

Given that all violence can be said to represent uncontained emotion, any measure that helps to raise emotional awareness (intelligence) is crucial. I suggest that this will provide the greatest prophylactic for society, provided that governments can assign the highest status to its position in the curriculum, so that our emotional functioning is considered alongside and triangulated with the rational/intellectual/academic. Moreover, are we not all anxious about finding a way to counteract the progressive and increasing engagement with the two-dimensional screen existences of video gaming, surfing, and social networking? Professor Baroness Greenfield explores the effect upon identity of this unprecedented impact of information technology. This two-dimensional (dyadic) literal world is devoid of metaphor and she cites a recent report on 1,400 US college students that showed a decline in empathy over the past thirty years, with a particularly sharp drop in the past decade (Greenfield, 2011). This is akin to humanity becoming computerised—indicative of an absence of feeling and reflective thinking.

This dyadic way of relating can be extrapolated to include the way we relate to one another as nations. Historically, each country has largely acted in its own self-interest, and the question remains as to whether we will be able to move from this dyadic way of relating to the world into a triadic, inclusive of others, position for the common global interests of us all. Whether it is in families, in society, or between countries, we need to help one another in the way we relate, to keep our minds open to the ubiquitous propensity to exclude all that pertains to difference (inherent in all splitting processes like racism, etc.), represented developmentally by the father in the mother and child dyad. Moreover, are we not all culpable in the way that we can exclude ourselves and others as collaborative third parties in any given relation as we go about our everyday lives?; whether that is by not sufficiently taking account of our emotional lives in the relationship between our own selves and our thinking or interpersonally by eliminating the consequences of our actions (aggressive) or inaction (passive aggressive) in our relationship to others. This is perhaps stereotypically represented by being a wilfully blind neighbour in all neighbour relations, be it in local, national, and international settings. I am saying that we all have a responsibility as potential collaborative thirds to augment any formal structures in place and/or proposed (like those in education that I have recommended), to intervene where it may not only be of practical help but, more crucially, enhance the ordinary business of relating towards developing a sense of belonging for all concerned.

There is also a strong case for including in the training of all criminal justice professionals, including police officers, an educational component that includes the identification of vulnerability and need in the potential perpetrator, in the same way that any parent might where a misdemeanour or a behavioural problem occurs with her child. If someone like Thomas Watt Hamilton comes into the field of vision of a criminal justice professional she not only, and quite rightly, focuses upon his potential dangerousness as a perpetrator, but is also equipped to flag up to other services that there exist underlying indicators of need. It is perhaps my own journey that informs this suggestion. Thomas Watt Hamilton certainly came to the notice of police, but only as a concern as a potential perpetrator and not a potential victim. The police in their role of the protective male (father/parent) in society should be able to exercise their authority in a truly triadic and represent a combined parental figure of the masculine (authority/rule of law), married to the feminine (care giver/nurturer/observer of need). This whole emphasis on the male/father and the third reflective position is crucial in developing a society relatively liberated from violent acting-out, largely, although not exclusively, by males, who are not evil but in some way wounded and in pain.

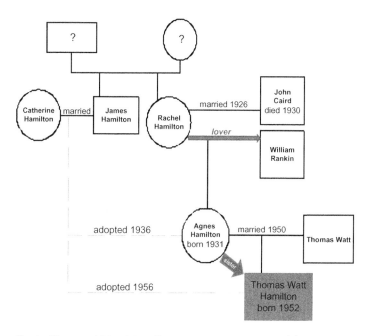

Appendix 1. Thomas Watt Hamilton's trans-generational history.

Extract of an entry in a REGISTER OF BIRTHS
Registration of Births, Deaths and Marriages (Scotland) Act 1965

193 / .   BIRTHS in the DISTRICT of HAMILTON   in the COUNTY of LANARK

No.	Name and Surname.	When and Where Born.	Sex.	Name, Surname, and Rank or Profession of Father. Name, and Maiden Surname of Mother. Date and Place of Marriage.	Signature and Qualification of Informant, and Residence, if out of the House in which the Birth occurred.	When and Where Registered, and Signature of Registrar.
1098	Agnes Graham Hamilton Junior	193/. October Sixteenth 4h 30m a.m. Registered ... HAMILTON	F	William Rankin Graham (Ronalds Servant) Rachel Hamilton Graham M.S. John Currie	Rachel Graham mother ... William Rankin Junior ...	193/. November ... At HAMILTON ... Registrar.

Died 16th May 1930

Given under the Seal of the General Register Office, New Register House, Edinburgh on 3 March 2011

The above particulars incorporate any subsequent corrections or amendments to the original entry made with the authority of the Registrar General

This extract is valid only if it has been authenticated by the seal of the General Register Office. If the particulars in the relevant entry in the statutory register have been reproduced by photography, xerography or in other convenient process the seal must have been impressed after the reproduction has been made. The General Register Office will authenticate only those reproductions which have been produced by that office

Appendix 2. Agnes Hamilton's birth certificate.

Extract of an entry in the ADOPTED CHILDREN REGISTER

Adoption Act 1958, S 22

4287

No. of entry	Name and surname of adopted child	Date of birth, where Adoption Order directs entry of date of birth	Sex	Name and surname, occupation and address of adopter or adopters	Date of Adoption Order and description of Court by which made	Date of registration and signature of Registrar General
225	Agnes Graham Hamilton	1931, October sixteenth	F	James Hamilton, Electric Welder, and Catherine Newlands or Hamilton his wife, 41 Maxwell Street, Glasgow	5th February 1936, Sheriff Court of Lanarkshire at Glasgow	1936, February 7, *Registrar-General.*

The above particulars are extracted from the Adopted Children Register kept in the General Register Office.

Given under the Seal of the General Register Office, New Register House, Edinburgh on 4 March 2011

Appendix 3. Agnes Hamilton's entry into adopted children register.

Extract of an entry in a REGISTER OF BIRTHS
Registration of Births, Deaths and Marriages (Scotland) Act 1965

19 52. BIRTHS in the DISTRICT of COLLEGE in the BURGH of GLASGOW

Given under the Seal of the General Register Office, New Register House, Edinburgh on 3 March 2011

The above particulars incorporate any subsequent corrections or amendments to the original entry made with the authority of the Registrar General

This extract is valid only if it has been authenticated by the seal of the General Register Office. If the particulars in the relevant entry in the statutory register have been reproduced by photographic, xerographic or by other convenient process the seal must have been impressed after the reproduction has been made. The General Register Office will authenticate only those reproductions which have been produced by that office.

Warning

It is an offence under section 53(3) of the Registration of Births, Deaths and Marriages (Scotland) Act 1965 for any person to pass as genuine any copy or reproduction of this extract which has not been made by the General Register Office and authenticated by the Seal of that office

Any person who falsifies or forges any of the particulars on this extract or knowingly uses, gives or sends as genuine any false or forged extract is liable to prosecution under section 53(3) of the said Act

This extract is evidence of an event recorded in a register. It is NOT evidence of the identity of the person presenting it

Appendix 4. Thomas Watt Hamilton's birth certificate.

7 March 1996

Your Majesty,

I understand you are Patron of the Scout Association and in that capacity I would like to make you aware of a longstanding complaint against the Scout Association.

Over 20 years ago, as a young man of about 20 years of age, after my time as a Venture Scout, I was asked to become a Scout Leader, which I did with enthusiasm and in a fair and competent manner. I was at that time, however, somewhat disillusioned with the general management which existed in this District at that time. After a period of a year, I was offered a better position by District Commissioner, J. Don, within the Association in Mr Don's nearby district of Hillfoots which I accepted. However, my transfer was refused by Scottish Scout Headquarters without any explanation. D. C. Don approached my previous D.C., Mr R. Deuchars, and as a result of this, reported in confidence to me that Mr R. Deuchars was attempting to have me branded as a pervert. When Mr Don demanded justification of this, Mr Duechars' only response was that I was "friendly" with the boys. Mr Don remarked that a Scout Leader was supposed to be friendly with the boys and as a conclusion Mr Don reported to me that he had nothing on me but he may cause me considerable damage if unchecked.

In what I consider to be a breach of natural justice, Mr R. Deuchars then submitted a confidential report on me in line with the Policy Organisation and rules of the Association. I know that no child has ever made any complaint of a sinister or sexual nature against me but D. C. Deuchars, together with the A. D. C. Mr Samuels and the G. S. L. Mr McKenzie, visited and interviewed every child in my old Group including especially everyone who had been a member and left. Nothing of a sinister nature came to light. However, in a bid to justify his actions, Mr McKenzie reported that Mr Deuchars had sought to create innuendos about me with the statement Why is he so enthusiastic—think about it? Mr J. Don referred to jealousy as the likely cause.

My attempts to approach Scottish Scout Headquarters were ignored and I could get nowhere since I was blocked from all angles. I was unable to get any response as to whether or not I was blacklisted or informed about details of the confidential report by Mr Deuchars. As time passed, numerous and various reports were received that Mr Deuchars was passing information within the District Scout area that I was a pervert which was passed to the public in an underhand manner.

Over the past 20 years of youth work, this has caused me untold damage including Council, Police and Social Work investigations where they had acted as a direct result of information received in absolute confidence from officials of the Scout Association. Any subsequent investigation was instigated on a whim and without proper complaint, cause or justification. For the purpose of the police complaints procedure, the investigative skills of the police are put into reverse. It seems to be a tactic of the police during any investigation, to spread innuendos to as many people as possible and in such a way as to cause maximum damage and then when their investigation comes to nothing, they do nothing about retracting their accusations. This has probably been the most damaging of all on the part of the Police and Council.

I have been involved with the organisation of Boys Sports Clubs for over 20 years and the rumours circulated by officials of the Scout Association have now reached epidemic proportions across Central Region. As well as my personal distress and loss of public standing, this situation has also resulted in loss of my business and ability to earn a living. Indeed, I cannot even walk the streets for fear of embarrassing ridicule.

All of this and more has been caused by the maladministration of the Scout Association and their denial of natural justice and duty of care. To some Scout Officials, it was simply a rouse to oust a rival (deleted) group.

I turn to you as a last resort and am appealing for some kind of intervention in the hope that I may be able to regain my self-esteem in Society.

I am,

Your Obdeient Servant,

Appendix 5. Letter from Thomas Watt Hamilton to the Queen.

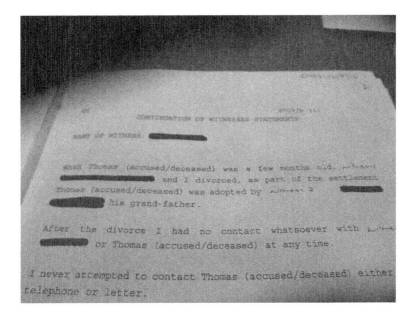

Appendix 6a. Statement from the Cullen Enquiry 1996.

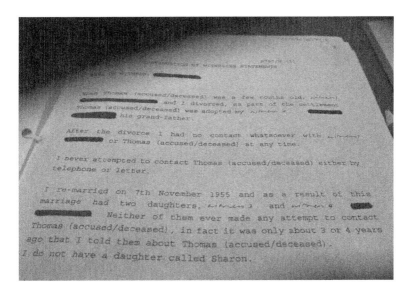

Appendix 6b. Statement from the Cullen Enquiry 1996.

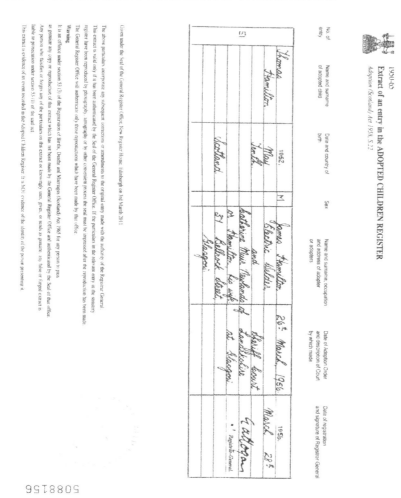

Appendix 7. James Watt Hamilton's entry into adopted children register.

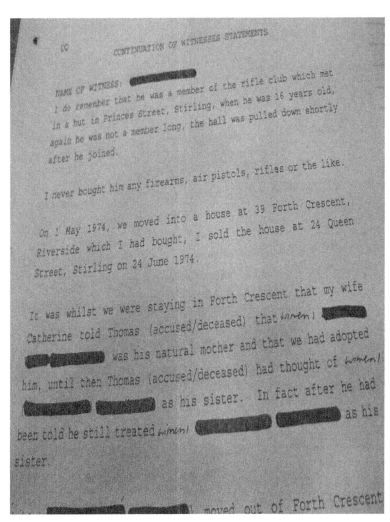

CONTINUATION OF WITNESSES STATEMENTS

NAME OF WITNESS: ███████████

I do remember that he was a member of the rifle club which met in a hut in Princes Street, Stirling, when he was 16 years old, again he was not a member long, the hall was pulled down shortly after he joined.

I never bought him any firearms, air pistols, rifles or the like.

On 1 May 1974, we moved into a house at 39 Forth Crescent, Riverside which I had bought, I sold the house at 24 Queen Street, Stirling on 24 June 1974.

It was whilst we were staying in Forth Crescent that my wife Catherine told Thomas (accused/deceased) that (women) ███████ ████████ was his natural mother and that we had adopted him, until then Thomas (accused/deceased) had thought of (women) ████████ ████████ as his sister. In fact after he had been told he still treated (women) ████████ ████████ as his sister.

████████ ████████ moved out of Forth Crescent

Appendix 8. Statement from James Hamilton (adoptive father) to the Cullen Enquiry.

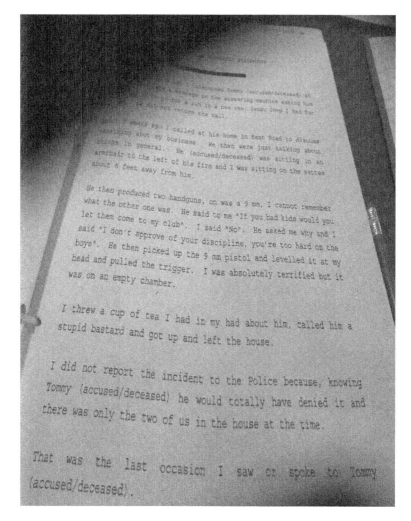

... telephoned Tommy (accused/deceased) at ... a message on the answering machine asking him ... for a run in a new van; Isuzu Jeep I had for ... did not return the call.

... weeks ago I called at his home in Kent Road to discuss ... everything about my business. We then were just talking about ... things in general. He (accused/deceased) was sitting in an armchair to the left of his fire and I was sitting on the settee about 5 feet away from him.

He then produced two handguns, on was a 9 mm, I cannot remember what the other one was. He said to me "If you had kids would you let them come to my club". I said "NO". He asked me why and I said "I don't approve of your discipline, you're too hard on the boys". He then picked up the 9 mm pistol and levelled it at my head and pulled the trigger. I was absolutely terrified but it was on an empty chamber.

I threw a cup of tea I had in my had about him, called him a stupid bastard and got up and left the house.

I did not report the incident to the Police because, knowing Tommy (accused/deceased) he would totally have denied it and there was only the two of us in the house at the time.

That was the last occasion I saw or spoke to Tommy (accused/deceased).

Appendix 9. Statement from close acquaintance of Thomas Watt Hamilton to the Cullen Enquiry.

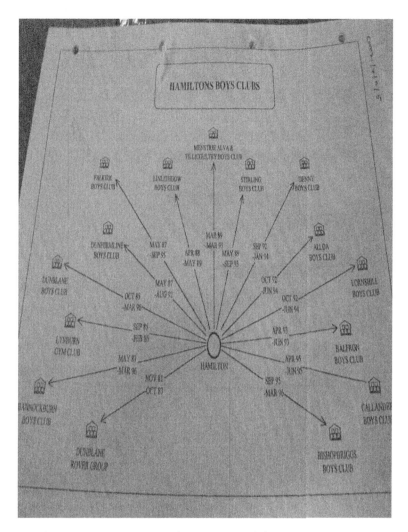

Appendix 10. James Watt Hamilton's Boys' Clubs.

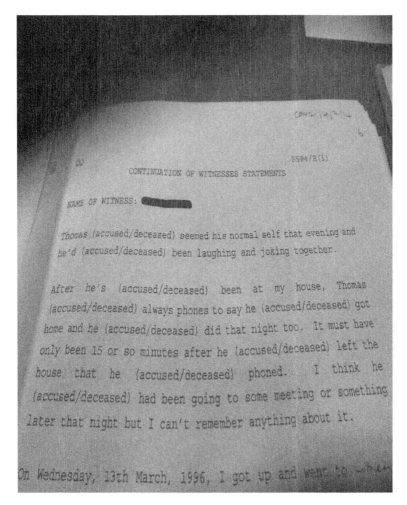

Appendix 11. Witness statement from Agnes Hamilton to the Cullen Enquiry.

Knockin' On Heaven's Door

Mama, take this badge off of me
I can't use it anymore.
It's gettin' dark, too dark for me to see
I feel like I'm knockin' on heaven's door.

Knock, knock, knockin' on heaven's door
Knock, knock, knockin' on heaven's door
Knock, knock, knockin' on heaven's door
Knock, knock, knockin' on heaven's door

Mama, put my guns in the ground
I can't shoot them anymore.
That long black cloud is comin' down
I feel like I'm knockin' on heaven's door.

Knock, knock, knockin' on heaven's door
Knock, knock, knockin' on heaven's door
Knock, knock, knockin' on heaven's door
Knock, knock, knockin' on heaven's door

Written by Bob Dylan

Appendix 12. Lyrics to "Knockin' On Heaven's Door".

POSTSCRIPT

Anders Breivik

The trial of Anders Behring Breivik (ABB) in Oslo, for his mass killing of seventy-seven people in July 2011, which represented the worst case of murder in Norway since the Second World War, is struggling with the question as to whether he can be considered responsible for his actions.

I have had the opportunity to read the initial psychiatric report "Anders Breivik Psychiatric Report 2011-11-29" (ABPR Report), by Torgeir Husby and Synne Sorheim, which established that ABB was psychotic, and I have also scanned his "manifesto" called *2083: A European Declaration of Independence* (2083.EDI, 2011). The ABPR report concluded that he met the ICD-10 (International Classification of Diseases) diagnosis of Paranoid Schizophrenia. If the court accepted this assessment, it would mean that ABB would be referred to a hospital for treatment instead of being sent to prison.

This diagnosis received widespread criticism (including within the psychiatric profession) amid intense public debate in Norway and so the court made an unprecedented decision to commission a second opinion by Terje Toerrissen and Agnar Aspaas, who concluded that he was not psychotic but demonstrated signs of narcissistic and antisocial personality disorders (grandiose thoughts and lack of remorse/empathy).

197

If the court favours this view, he could be sent to prison. (I have not been given the opportunity to read this second report.)

This second opinion is ABB's preferred option in that in his view it would maintain his credibility (he has said that to be labelled insane would be a fate worse than death) although Norwegian society finds it painful to accept that one of their own could have sanely and deliberately carried out such a murderous act. Paradoxically, if he were to be considered psychotic and referred to hospital this would also deeply concern many in Norwegian society (even if the simplest response is that he must be mad) in that this raises the perception and anxiety that ABB would avoid answering for his crimes.

This whole debate hinges upon an either/or dynamic and appears to resist the consideration of *and*: either prison or hospital, either punishment or care, either sane or insane, either nationalism or multi-culturalism (he sees himself as a pawn in the ideological struggle that is going on in Europe (ABPR 2.4.1)), either liberalism or conservatism, either rational or emotional, either masculine or feminine, and either mum or dad ("I do not approve of the super-liberal matriarchal upbringing, as it completely lacked discipline and has contributed to feminize me to a certain degree" (2083.EDI, 2011)). I believe that this splitting process (either/or) lies at the heart of the Norwegian dilemma and has profound parallels with the perpetrator at Dunblane, Thomas Watt Hamilton (TWH).

It would in my view be naïve to take ABB's views and 1,500-page manifesto at face value and consider whether he has a valid point or not (that Norway is being taken over by Muslims). His communications need to be considered as a total projection of his conflicted internal world, as if he desperately needs to defend himself against the abject fear of being taken over (he is Norway and Norway is him) by a foreign and malign influence, and he is attempting to lead the fight against his own internal terror, by projecting it. The question that arises is: What is this internal dynamic that he needs so desperately to externalise?

His crime could be seen to represent a revenge attack upon the Norwegian community, by way of giving back to Norway the very experience that hitherto had been his own (they are as one as I have said). His own experience of being "killed off" in his family of origin was by his father, who left him shortly after he was born (betrayed him) and was at best a peripheral presence throughout his life up until his late teens and early twenties (the age group of his victims) when all contact ceased. This early experience of loss resulted in his formative years being subject to an environment dominated by what he considered to be a matriarchy, which he came to despise (mother and older sister), with the absence of a father as a potential mediating third.

It is particularly significant, as I have stated elsewhere in my book, that with the concrete absence of a father, a greater responsibility falls upon the mother to provide the paternal function from her own resources, which if absent exacerbates the original loss. In addition, one also has to consider the destruction of any representation of a third (reflection/authority/order, etc) by ABB in relation to his mother. This third is so crucial in health with all of the connotations of reflection and difference to ensure that the one and two (ordinarily the mother and child) in the dyad do not become enmeshed. In his case, there are numerous examples to indicate that it is this third that represents the missing link.

Not unlike TWH, who saw himself as a father figure in his community (in compensation for the lost father) in his running of Boys' Clubs, etc., ABB identified (in compensation for his lost father) with being a father figure for Norway (in the Knights Templar organisation), only to repeat a similar atrocity by betraying his position as father and killing off "his children" (in identification with father). This betrayal lies at the heart of ABB's rhetoric about the multi-culturalists in Norway allowing such an influx of perceived malevolent forces, taking over its identity; this is exactly the same way that he deeply feels has been the case in his own life.

The Knights Templar are an organisation ABB started/joined in 2002, which coincided with the time when contact with his own father finally ceased. In looking back at other pivotal moments of transition (in addition to his parents' divorce, etc.), I noted that at fifteen his mother became ill and required surgery, his sister left the home, they moved house, and his father divorced his third wife—and so perhaps it was not surprising that he was caught in a form of acting-out by spray-painting graffiti. It appears that his real deterioration took place in 2006 when he became financially bankrupt with all of his business ventures failing and he was unable to pay the rent on his apartment resulting in him moving back home with his mother.

Moreover, in exactly the same way that I identified critical date phenomena in relation to TWH I have also found that it is a primary factor with ABB. That is, he was thirty-two years and five months old when he committed his atrocity, and given the dyadic (perverse and enmeshed?) relationship he had with his mother (exacerbated by an abandoning father) I was not surprised to learn that his mother was exactly the same age when she gave birth to him. There are, in addition, other powerful similarities with TWH, namely that ABB's parents separated and divorced soon after his birth and that as a single mother she struggled in her relationship with him. This is exemplified by her request for respite when he was in his infancy, aged two/three, followed by a referral to the State Centre for Child and Youth Psychiatry where serious concerns were raised about the possibility of prodromal characteristics for psychopathology in him (ABPR, 2011, 2.7.2). A court case subsequently ensued whereby his father (then living in France with his new wife) sought to take over his care, given the major difficulties Breivik and his mother were experiencing, only to withdraw the gesture soon after, when he felt that he might have to put up a fight. This is reminiscent of the clinical case I describe in Chapter Eight where the patient's rage with his own father (who also lost out in a court battle for care) at approximately the same age as ABB, had a powerful effect upon his own identity. He subsequently saw himself as the supreme father of all he surveys, and this culminated in the killing of a mother and her two young children.

ABB's mother's need for respite (perhaps a task ordinarily provided by a partner) was commented on by the care services who assessed her, reporting: "[W]e will discuss with mother if she is interested in a support person or weekend leave for ABB to get other adult contacts than just herself" and "[i]t is also important that the parents find a practical solution regarding the possibility of ABB to have contact with his father" (ABPR, 2011, 2.7.2). I was reminded of this dynamic when Husby and Sorheim commented: "Neither intellectually nor emotionally would we be able to carry out one to one talks. It was a very demanding situation to be in conversation with him and it was necessary to switch the focus from actor to observer to be able to carry it out with quality over time" (ABPR, 2011, 5.0). This illuminates beautifully the importance of the third/father as it was experienced in the transference with ABB by the clinicians. Their countertransference feelings informed them that the burden of engaging with him alone would prevent them from being able to engage with any real quality, and so they felt the need to triangulate the experience into a threesome.

There are additional parallels with TWH alongside the loss of father soon after birth and the critical dates highlighted. Both suffered financial bankruptcy, which undermined their sense of potency in the world. Both had no previous convictions. Neither had a history of drug use or alcohol abuse (aside from the ECA stack—a stimulant combination of ephedrine, caffeine, and aspirin, which ABB took to enhance his performance on the day of the attack). Both were considered a little odd and not a part of the mainstream, giving the impression that they struggled with achieving a sense of belonging. Both became increasingly withdrawn within their own circles and communities. Finally, each met with his mother the night before the attack and we can only speculate as to their mothers' subsequent experiences following the respective atrocities. One wonders whether their mothers felt that they had been completely cut out of something of enormous significance, which could not be shared. This all has the potential of another powerful mirroring back by their sons of feeling cut out by the father and/or by the reflective part (the third) of their mother's mind (represented by the father), which was of enormous significance.

I would like to add that in my experience of the assessment, treatment, and supervision in the field of homicide it is highly likely that during his visit to his mother the night before the attack he would have subliminally referred to his plans, as if revealing, whilst concealing, his intentions. At such moments an acute antennae is required to pick up the message, which all too often is missed.

This absence of a father for ABB, particularly in his formative years, up until the age of six, is, I believe, crucial, in understanding his psychopathology and offence. He claims his attack was upon "individuals who are betraying Norway" (ABPR, 2011, 5.7). I interpret this as a projection of his experience of a father who abnegated his responsibility (betrayed him) leaving him vulnerable to the total invasion by mother and sister, that is, the feminisation he refers to, and I repeat: "I do not approve of the super-liberal matriarchal upbringing, as it completely lacked discipline and has contributed to feminize me to a certain degree" (2083.EDI, 2011, p. 1,387).

If the repetition compulsion (of ABB's psychopathology) continues into the courtroom and further re-enactments occur then the outcome will be that either one or other of the parental representations (prison or hospital) will be chosen as opposed to a healthy combination of both— the creative parental couple in support of development. He appears desperate for a prison sentence (terrified to be aligned again with all that he associates with mother, namely madness and a loss of identity and a loss of a sense of self) and seeks to be identified with his father in the same way that TWH was desperate for the intervention (connection) with the third (father). The accused (ABB) missed close contact with his father (ABPR, 2011, 2.6.10). He also sought to impress his father that one day he could manage, and that he would assert himself (ABPR, 2011, 2.6.10). ABB was bitter about his father since he did not spend enough time with him (ABPR, 2011, 2.6.10).

I have absolutely no doubt that ABB requires the administration of both punishment and treatment and not either/or. I do not assert this out of revenge but in meeting the fundamental needs of the offender patient. I comment elsewhere in my book about the crucial importance that punishment can play for the offender in mediating feelings of guilt, let alone satisfying the feeling of a sense of justice for the victims and society. It is not an uncommon reaction to the events unfolding in Norway to hear the comment "Where is the justice?" (punishment), meaning metaphorically where is the father or, more importantly, who he represents in terms of the law, boundaries, authority/order, and discipline.

It is in many respects an admirable characteristic to respond as Norway has by extending incredible accommodation to such a per-petrator. A corollary to this is that he is being afforded a public plat-form to voice his views. Over time, the picking apart of his thinking in public has the potential to systematically ridicule and humiliate him. This may have deep resonance with his early trauma of exclusion and marginalisation by his father.

In my reading of the reports I noted the references and allusions to the battle between the parents, whether this is represented in the battle between punishment and care, prison and hospital, or sanity and insanity. Another impression given is that he is being over-accommodated in the same way that his mother over-accommodated him most of his life and particularly from 2006 onwards when she shopped, cooked, cleaned, and attended to all his needs, while experiencing his progres-sively angry, withdrawn, and bizarre behaviours. For instance, she could not sneeze in the house, in that he was deeply concerned about being infected by her (ABPR, 2011, 4.1). On 13 April 2011 (three months prior to the attack) ABB made a phone call to his GP complaining that he had been infected (surely this was a communication about feeling emotionally/psychologically infected) by his mother and needed to wear a face mask in the house (ABPR, 2011, 2.11). It indicates that there may have been an absence in the mother's mind (representing the absent third/father) that prevented reflection and any meaningful intervention at such a time, particularly when he began to acquire a range of guns. This ensured that their perverse dyadic relationship remained stuck. ABB claimed that his own radicalisation was influenced by the fact that he grew up with his mother and sister (ABPR, 2011, 5.4), adding: "[M]y mother managed to infect me anyway" (ABPR, 2011, 5.6), "She is the only one who can make me emotionally unstable. She is my Achilles' heel" (ABPR, 2011, 5.13).

It appears that at some level (not unlike TWH) ABB knew the roots of his own problem:

> The subject (ABB) considers his own private and personal experience of paramount importance to social issues and decisions. As an example of this, one mentioned the subject's understanding of how the court case regarding the care take over when he was small justified the need for introduction of patriarchy and restrictions on women's involvement outside the home.
>
> (ABPR, 2011, 5.11)

Moreover, he makes the statement: "I despise Marxism for my own parents' divorce and for the matriarchy" (ABPR, 2011, 5.11).

This was a deeply held injury for ABB in that he also stated: "90% (of women) are emotionally unstable. That's why we (his organization) support an amendment to the law so that the fathers automatically get custody" (ABPR, 2011, 5.11).

I remain concerned that little credibility will be given to this core area of absence in ABB's life (of a third/father) and the catastrophic effect this had upon his psychic development. His rage at betrayal and abandonment became projected into his environment/community towards those who externally represented his experience of betrayal (leaving the country/himself to be invaded and taken over by the invasion of difference represented by mother/feminisation). His forlorn hope may have been that through this desperate and atrocious act he might manufacture and create a response in the state, representing the lost father, to contain, discipline, and offer a less liberal and more conservative presence as a mediation to his enmeshed and invaded relationship with mother, which of course may ultimately fail if he is deemed psychotic and sent to hospital.

The ABPR is littered, as is his manifesto, with constant references to England, Norway, and France. All three of course are direct associations to his father, in that ABB was born in England, spending the first few months of his life there with his father who was working there as a diplomat for the Norwegian government, before his father separated from him and moved to France.

In essence his terror has been enacted upon his community in exactly the same way that occurred in Dunblane, which represented a murderous rage with a father (state) who failed in his responsibility to prevent an invasion of foreign forces from taking over (feminising him). I return to, and repeat, a comment I made at the beginning about the experience that Norwegians are struggling with at present that strikes at the core of ABB's psychopathology. There is an apparent symmetry in the feelings of the Norwegian public towards ABB *and* ABB's pain at being abandoned by his father. Both feel confounded by the question of how one of their own can sanely and deliberately carry out such a murderous act? For ABB, Norway in its admirable liberalism resonated too closely with his own history (and the absence of the representation of conservatism) and they became as one. He sought to become a father to himself and the father for the nation he believed to be lacking such a figure. I am saying that without considering these underlying unconscious factors then inaccurate conclusions will be reached with the likelihood that very little will be learnt, and that the needs of his victims and, by extension, all of us, will suffer, in our pursuit of understanding such atrocities.

In my view, the humane response would be to confine him within the prison system (and the new Halden Fengsel high-security prison in Norway is far removed from its punitive equivalent at ADX Florence in Colorado) *and* at the same time to treat him psychotherapeutically. This bridges the either/or split, and supports the view that there is merit in both sides of the argument (prison or hospital, masculine or feminine), underlining the important premise that neither has a monopoly on morality or solutions to such problems, and that both have a vital contribution to make. This would offer him his first experience of a metaphorical healthy parental couple (in the guise of a single parent triangulating the paternal function, if a mother, and the maternal function, if the single parent is a father), the primary task being to help him to reconcile himself to his past and his offending, which despite the common misconception about treatment, is an enormously difficult and painful task that most offender patients would prefer to avoid. It needs to be stressed that suicidal ideation is likely to emerge should he ever begin to reconcile himself to his history and internal conflicts.

Inherent within the foregoing is the view that not unlike TWH he suffers with a co-morbidity of an underlying psychosis with a personality disorder. That is, he is motivated by powerfully repressed unconscious factors relating to his past, which became unleashed in a planned way when the externally perceived circumstances in his life/country approximated to this internal configuration and became the same (as one). He, therefore, feels totally justified in his attack in that it relates to his own internal world and experiences that are completely symmetrised with the world externally. ABB lives with terror and gave his community a very brief albeit horrifying snapshot of his internal experience.

REFERENCES

2083: A European Declaration of Independence (2011). Unitednations.ispnw. org/archives/breivik-manifesto-2011.pdf (last accessed 15.6.12).

Albelin, E. L. (1980). Triangulation: The evolution of the early triangulation model. In: R. F. Lax, S. Bach & J. A. Burland (Eds.), *Rapprochement: Critical Subphase of Separation Individuation* (pp. 151–169). New Jersey: Jason Aronson Inc.

Anders Breivik Psychiatric Report 2011-11-29 (ABPR). https//: sites. google.com/site/breivikreport/anders-breivik-psychiatric-report-of-2011 (last accessed 15.6.12).

Antrobus, S. (2011). Absent fathers are blamed for crime addiction. *The Times*, 28 October, p. 34.

Aylward, P., & Wooster, G. (2004). Perverse triangulation. *Forensische Psychiatrie und Psychotherapie [Forensic Psychiatry and Psychotherapy]*, 63–74.

Aylward, P., & Wooster, G. (2008). Murder: Persecuted by jealousy. In: R. Doctor (Ed.), *Murder, A Psychotherapeutic Investigation* (pp. 35–49). London: Karnac.

Balier, C. (1993). Pedophilie et violence. L'eclairage apporte par une approche criminologique. [Paedophilia and violence: Highlighting a criminological approach.] *Revue francaise de psychoanalyse*, 2: 572–589.

Baron-Cohen, S. (2011). *Zero Degree of Empathy: A New Theory of Human Cruelty*. London: Penguin Books.

207

Bion, W. R. (1950). The imaginary twin. In: *Second Thoughts* (pp. 3–22). London: Heinemann, 1967 [reprinted London: Karnac, 1984].

Bion, W. R. (1959). Attacks on linking. *International Journal of Psycho-analysis*, 43: 306–10.

Bird, S. (2006). Bright pupil and budding actor who took on role of a serial killer. *The Times*, 17 March, p. 4.

Bourne, S. (1992). *Psychological Aspects of Stillbirth and Neonatal Death: An Annotated Bibliography*. London: Tavistock Publications Ltd.

Bourne, S. & Lewis, E. (1984). Pregnancy after stillbirth and neonatal death. *The Lancet, 2*: 31–33.

Bourne, S., & Lewis, E. (1992). *Psychological Aspects of Still Birth and Neonatal Death: An Annotated Bibliography*. London: Tavistock Clinic.

Brooks, D. (2011). *The Social Animal*. New York: Random House.

Brunori, L. (1998). Siblings. *Group Analysis, 31(3)*: 307–314.

Buckroyd, J., & Rother, S. (Eds.) (2008). *Psychological Responses to Eating Disorders and Obesity: Recent and Innovative Work*. Chichester: John Wiley & Sons Ltd.

Chesterton, G. K. (1922). *Illustrated London News*, 29 April.

Corstophine, E. (2008). Addressing emotions in the eating disorders: Schema mode work. In: J. Buckroyd & S. Rother (Eds.), *Psychological Responses to Eating Disorders and Obesity: Recent and Innovative Work* (pp. 85–99). Chichester: John Wiley & Sons Ltd.

Cox, M. (1987). *Mutative Metaphors in Psychotherapy: The Aeolian Mode*. London: Tavistock Publications Ltd.

Cutler, I. (2006). Obituary. Ivor Cutler: Anti-intellectual poet, artist and performer who delighted and irritated for 50 years. *The Times*, 7 March, p. 66.

Davar, E. (2001). The loss of the transitional object: Some thoughts about transitional and pre-transitional phenomena. *Psychodynamic Counselling, 7(1)*: 5–26.

De Masi, F. (2007). The paedophile and his inner world: Theoretical and clinical considerations on the analysis of a patient. *International Journal of Psychoanalysis, 88(1)*: 147–165.

Drapeau, M., Kether, A. C., & Brunet, L. (2004). When the goals of therapists and patients clash: A study of paedophilia in treatment. *Journal of Offender Rehabilitation, 38(3)*: 69–80.

Drapeau, M., Körner, A., Brunet, L., Granger, L., Caspar, F., Despland, J. N., & de Roten, Y. (2003). A psychodynamic look at pedophile sex offenders in treatment. *Archives of Psychiatry and Psychotherapy, 5(3)*: 31–42.

Earnshaw, A. (1995). *Time Will Tell*. Sydney: A & K Enterprises.

Emerson, R. W. (1983). The American scholar. In: *Essays and Lectures* (p. 402). New York: Library of America.

Engel, G. (1975). The death of a twin: Mourning and anniversary reactions. Fragments of 10 years of self-analysis. *International Journal of Psychoanalysis, 56(1)*: 23–40.

Frean, A. (2006). Mentally ill face new detention powers. *The Times*, 24 March, p. 34.

Freud, A. (1993). *The Ego and The Mechanisms of Defence*. London: Karnac.

Freud, S. (1900). The interpretation of dreams, *S. E.* 4 and 5. London: Hogarth.

Freud, S. (1908). Creative writers and day-dreaming. In: J. Strachey (Ed. & Trans.), *The Standard Edition of the Complete Psychological Works of Sigmund Freud, Vol 9. (1906–1908)* (pp. 141–153). London: Hogarth & Institute of Psychoanalysis, 1953–1974.

Freud, S. (1911). Psycho-analytic notes on an autobiographical account of a case of paranoia (dementia paranoides). *S. E., 12*: 1–82. London: Hogarth Press & Institute of Psycho-Analysis, 1958.

Freud, S. (1911a). Formulations on the two principles of mental functioning. *S. E., 12*: 213–226. London: Hogarth Press & Institute of Psycho-Analysis, 1958.

Freud, S. (1914). Remembering, repeating and working-through. *S. E., 12*: 145–156. London: Hogarth Press & Institute of Psycho-Analysis, 1958.

Freud, S. (1915). The unconscious. *S. E., 14*: 159–215. London: Hogarth Press & Institute of Psycho-Analysis, 1957.

Freud, S. (1916). Some character-types met within the course of psychoanalytic work: Criminals from a sense of guilt. *S. E., 14*: 309–333. London: Hogarth Press & Institute of Psycho-Analysis, 1957.

Freud, S. (1919). The uncanny. *S. E., 17*: 217–256. London: Hogarth Press & Institute of Psycho-Analysis, 1955.

Freud, S. (1920g). Beyond the pleasure principle. *S. E., 18*: 1–64. London: Hogarth Press & Institute of Psycho-Analysis, 1955.

Freud, S. (1924). Neurosis and psychosis. *S. E., 19*: 147–154. London: Hogarth Press & Institute of Psycho-Analysis, 1961.

Freud, S. (1933). New introductory lectures in psycho-analysis. *S. E., 22*: 1–267. London: Hogarth Press & Institute of Psycho-Analysis, 1964.

Gilligan, J. (1999). *Violence: Reflections on our Deadliest Epidemic*. London: Jessica Kingsley Publishers.

Glasser, M. (1979). Some aspects of the role of aggression in the perversions. In: I. Rosen (Ed.), *Sexual Deviation* (pp. 278–306). Oxford: OUP.

Gledhill, R. (2006). *The Times*, 8 March, p. 3.

Glynn, M. (2011). *Dad and Me: Research into the Problems Caused by Absent Fathers*. London: Addaction.

Greenfield, S. (2011). www.newscientist.com/article/ mg21128236.400-susan-greenfield-living-online-is-changing-our-brains. html [last accessed 13 January 2012].

Grinberg, L. (1992). *Guilt and Depression*. London: Karnac.

Hastings, M. (2006). It is better to halt mass murder than to clean it up afterwards. *The Guardian*, 13 March, p. 32.

Home Affairs Committee (1999–2000). Managing Dangerous People with Severe Personality Disorder, First Report. HC.

Howlett, M. (2006). *The Times*, 24 March, p. 34.

Human Rights Act (1998). www.direct.gov.uk/en/ governmentcitizensandrights/yourrightsandresponsibilities/ dg_4002951 [last accessed 24 January 2012].

Jacobs, M. (1999). *The Presenting Past* (2nd edn). Buckingham: Open University Press.

Jordan, J. F. (1990). Inner space and the interior of the maternal body: Unfolding in the psychoanalytic process. *International Review of Psycho-Analysis*, 17: 433–444.

Joseph, J. (2004). Blood really is thicker than water. *The Times*, 15 December, p. 23.

Kalsched, D. (1996). *The Inner World of Trauma: Archetypal Defences of the Personal Spirit*. London: Routledge.

Klein, M. (1946). Notes on some schizoid mechanisms. In: *Envy and Gratitude and Other Works 1946–63.* London: Hogarth Press, 1975.

Klein, M. (1963). On the sense of loneliness. In: *Envy and Gratitude and Other Works 1946–63* (pp. 300–313). London: Hogarth Press, 1975.

Leary, M. R., Kowalski, R. M., Smith, L., & Phillips, S. (2003). Teasing, rejection, and violence: Case studies of the school shootings. *Aggressive Behavior*, 29: 202–214.

Linehan, M. (1993). *Cognitive Behavioural Treatment of Borderline Personality Disorders*. New York: Guildford Press.

Lloyd-Owen, D. (2003). Perverse females: Their unique psycho-pathology. *British Journal of Psychotherapy, 19(3)*: 285–296.

Lord Cullen (1996). *The Public Inquiry into the Shootings at Dunblane Primary School on 13 March 1996: The Government Response*. London: HMSO.

Malan, D. (1997). *Anorexia, Murder and Suicide*. London: Hodder Arnold.

Matte Blanco, I. (1975). *The Unconscious as Infinite Sets*. London: Karnac.

Matte Blanco, I. (1988). *Thinking, Feeling and Being*. London: Routledge, 1999.

McDougall, J. (1972). Primal scene and sexual perversion. *International Journal of Psycho-analysis*, 53: 371–384.

Menzies Lyth, I. (1959). The functioning of social systems as a defence against anxiety. In: *Containing Anxiety in Institutions, Selected Essays* (pp. 43–85). London: Free Association Books, 1988.

Mitchell, J. (2000). *Mad Men and Medusas.* London: Penguin Books.

Money-Kryle, R. (1971). The aim of psycho-analysis. *International Journal of Psycho-analysis, 52*: 103–106.

Morgan, D. (2004). Mad or bad? A critique of proposals for managing dangerously disordered people. *Journal of Community and Applied Social Psychology, 14*: 104–114.

Rayner, E. (1995). *Unconscious Logic: An Introduction to Matte Blanco's Bi-logic and its Uses.* London: Routledge.

Rayner, E., & Wooster, G. (1990). Bi-logic in psychoanalysis and other disciplines: An introduction. *International Review of Psycho-Analysis, 17*: 425–431.

Reeves, V. (2004). *Who Do You Think You Are?*, BBC, 14th December.

Rosenfeld, H. (1984). *Psychotic States: A Psychoanalytical Approach.* London: Maresfield Library.

Rosenfeld, H. (1987). *Impasse and Interpretation.* London: Karnac.

Sarkar, S. (2005). The other 23 hours: Special problems of psychotherapy in a "special hospital". *Psychoanalytic Psychotherapy, 19*: 4–16.

Segal, H. (1978). On symbolism. *International Journal of Psycho-Analysis, 59*: 303–314.

Segal, H. (1986). Notes on symbol formation. In: *The Work of Hanna Segal, Delusion and Artistic Creativity and Other Psycho-analysis Essays* (pp. 49–68). London: Free Association Books, Maresfield Library.

Shakespeare, W. (2005). The Tempest. In: S. Wells, G. Taylor & J. Jowett (Eds.), *Collected Works of William Shakespeare* (pp. 299–371). Oxford: Oxford University Press.

Sophocles (2008). *Antigone, Oedipus the King, Electra.* E. Hall (Ed.). H. D. F. Kitto (Trans.). Oxford: Oxford University Press.

Sugden, J. (2011). Absent fathers are blamed for crime and addiction. *The Times*, 28 October, p. 29.

The Bible (1952). Revised standard version. Glasgow: William Collins Sons.

The Concise Oxford English Dictionary (2002). Tenth edition. Revised. Oxford: Oxford University Press.

Welldon, E. (1988). *Mother, Madonna, Whore.* London: Free Association Books.

Welldon, E. (2011). *Playing with Dynamite.* London: Karnac.

Wells, H. G. (1920). *Outline of History.* Native American Books Distributor [3rd edn 2008].

Winnicott, D. W. (1947). Hate in the countertransference. In: *Through Paediatrics to Psychoanalysis, Collected Papers* (pp. 194–203). London: Karnac, 1984.

Winnicott, D. W. (1951). Transitional objects and transitional phenomena. In: *Through Paediatrics to Psychoanalysis, Collected Papers* (pp. 229–242). London: Karnac, 1984.

Woodhouse, J. (2006). Baptist Padre. *The Times*, 8 March.

Wooster, G. (1983). Resistance in groups as developmental difficulty in tri-angulation. *Group Analysis, 16(1)*: 30–41.

Wooster, G. (1998). The resolution of envy through jealousy. *Group Analysis, 31(3)*: 327–340.

Wooster, G. & Buckroyd, P. (2006). *Psychoanalytic Ideas about Shakespeare. Grief, Loss & Creativity: Wither the Phoenix.* London: Karnac.

Young, J. E., Klosko, J. S., & Weishaar, M. E. (2003). *Schema Therapy: A Practitioner's Guide.* New York: Guildford Press.

Zigmond, T., & Howlett, M. (2006). Mentally ill face new detention powers. *The Times*, 20 March, p. 34.

Zilbach, J. (1987). I in the I of the Beholder: Towards a separate line of women's development. S. R. Slavson Lecture, 44th Group Psycho-therapy. New Orleans, LA: American Group Psychotherapy Association.

INDEX

213

Printed in Great Britain
by Amazon

82066302R00139